OXFORD ENGLISH MONOGRAPHS

General Editors

Coleridge and
The Friend
(1809–1810)

DEIRDRE COLEMAN

CLARENDON PRESS · OXFORD
1988

Oxford University Press, Walton Street, Oxford OX2 6DP
Oxford New York Toronto
Delhi Bombay Calcutta Madras Karachi
Petaling Jaya Singapore Hong Kong Tokyo
Nairobi Dar es Salaam Cape Town
Melbourne Auckland
and associated companies in
Berlin Ibadan

Oxford is a trade mark of Oxford University Press

Published in the United States
by Oxford University Press, New York

British Library Cataloguing in Publication Data
Coleman, Deirdre
Coleridge and "The Friend" (1809–1810).—
(Oxford English monographs).
1. Poetry in English. Coleridge, Samuel
Taylor, 1772–1834. Publications. Newspapers.
Coleridge, Samuel Taylor, 1772–1834.
Friend, The
I. Title
072'.786
ISBN 0–19–812957–2

Library of Congress Cataloging in Publication Data
Coleman, Deirdre.
Coleridge and the friend (1809–1810)/Deirdre Coleman.
p. cm.—(Oxford English monographs)
Bibliography: p.   Includes index.
1. Coleridge, Samuel Taylor. 1772–1834. Friend. 2. English newspapers—England—Lake
District—History—19th century. 3. Lake District (England)—Intellectual life—19th century.
I. Title.   II. Series.
PR4480.F73C65 1988   824'.7—dc 19   87–34930
ISBN 0–19–812957–2

Set by Cambrian Typesetters
Printed in Great Britain
at the University Printing House, Oxford
by David Stanford
Printer to the University

For my Parents

Acknowledgements

THIS book was initially supported by a Melbourne University Travelling Scholarship. Generous funding was also given by the Australian Federation of University Women, the Australian Academy of the Humanities, and the Violet Vaughan Morgan Trust, Oxford. For making my long postgraduate stay in England such a pleasant one I thank the President and Fellows of Corpus Christi College, Oxford.

I am indebted to the library staff of the Bodleian and of Corpus Christi College, especially to the college librarian, David Cooper, for his good-humoured tolerance of a very untidy library-user. Malcolm Thomas of Friends' House Library, London, was very helpful in sorting through boxes of papers, as was Jeff Cowton in the Wordsworth Library, Grasmere. For permission to quote from manuscript material I would like to thank the Trustees of Dove Cottage.

For academic guidance I am grateful to George Russell, who first got me going, to my supervisor Jonathan Wordsworth, who gave me many opportunities to work in Grasmere, and to Marilyn Butler, always so generous and encouraging.

Many friends cheered me along the way: Paula Boddington, Clive Burgess, Thomas and Gifford Charles-Edwards, Nicholas Cronk, Kara Hattersley-Smith, Harriet Jump, Pat Rae, and Mike and Mary Whitby. Philip Hardie and Susan Griffith kindly did the proof-reading, and for typing the original thesis and much else besides my heart-felt thanks go to Carol Willock. The University of Wollongong made the final stages of work easy and pleasurable by providing me with a research grant, superb facilities, and the happiest of English Departments. Finally, I thank Kay McKinnon for doing such a fine job of putting the work on disc, and Robin Eaden for compiling the index.

Deirdre Coleman   *University of Adelaide*

Contents

Abbreviations

A Brief Account	William Penn, *A Brief Account of the Rise and Progress of the People called Quakers* (London, 1694).
Allsop	[Thomas Allsop], *Letters, Conversations and Recollections of Samuel Taylor Coleridge* (2 vols.; London, 1836).
AR	S. T. Coleridge, *Aids to Reflection*, ed. Derwent Coleridge (London, 1854).
BL	S. T. Coleridge, *Biographia Literaria*, ed. James Engell and W. Jackson Bate (2 vols.; London and Princeton, 1983).
CL	*Collected Letters of Samuel Taylor Coleridge*, ed. E. L. Griggs (6 vols.; Oxford, 1956–71).
CN	*The Notebooks of Samuel Taylor Coleridge*, ed. Kathleen Coburn (London, 1957–).
Curry	*New Letters of Robert Southey*, ed. Kenneth Curry (2 vols.; New York and London, 1965).
EOT	S. T. Coleridge, *Essays on His Times in 'The Morning Post' and 'The Courier'*, ed. David V. Erdman (3 vols.; London and Princeton, 1978).
ER	*The Edinburgh Review* (Edinburgh, 1802–1929).
Friend of Slaves	E. L. Griggs, *Thomas Clarkson: The Friend of Slaves* (London, 1936).
Groundwork	Kant's *Groundwork of the Metaphysic of Morals*, trans. H. J. Paton (London, 1976).
History	Thomas Clarkson, *The History of the Rise, Progress, and Accomplishment of the Abolition of the African Slave Trade by the British Parliament* (2 vols.; London, 1808).
Howe	*The Complete Works of William Hazlitt*, ed. P. P. Howe (21 vols.; London, 1930–4).
IS	*Inquiring Spirit: A New Presentation of Coleridge from his Published and Unpublished Prose Writings*, ed. Kathleen Coburn (rev. edn., Toronto, 1979).

Lawes	Richard Hooker, *Lawes of Ecclesiasticall Politie* in *The Folger Library Edition of the Works of Richard Hooker*, ed. W. Speed Hill, (vols. i– , Cambridge, Mass., 1977–).
Lects. 1795	S. T. Coleridge, *Lectures 1795: On Politics and Religion*, ed. Lewis Patton and Peter Mann (London and Princeton, 1971).
LLP	*Letters from the Lake Poets, Samuel Taylor Coleridge, William Wordsworth, Robert Southey to Daniel Stuart, 1800–1838* [ed. Mary Stuart and E. H. Coleridge] (London, 1889).
LMNA	Edmund Burke, *Letter to a Member of the National Assembly* in *Works*, ed. Charles William, Earl Fitzwilliam, and Sir Richard Bourke (8 vols.; London, 1852).
LS	S. T. Coleridge, *Lay Sermons* [being *The Statesman's Manual* and *A Lay Sermon*], ed. R. J. White (London and Princeton, 1972).
LSF	Library of the Society of Friends, Friends' House, London.
Marginalia	S. T. Coleridge, *Marginalia*, ed. G. Whalley (2 vols. published; London and Princeton, 1980–).
Marrs	*The Letters of Charles and Mary Anne Lamb*, ed. Edwin W. Marrs, jun. (3 vols.; Ithaca, NY, 1975–8).
MR	*The Monthly Review, or Literary Journal*, enlarged (London, 1790–1825).
MY	*Letters of William and Dorothy Wordsworth: The Middle Years, 1806–11*, ed. Ernest de Selincourt, rev. Mary Moorman and Alan G. Hill (2 vols.; Oxford, 1969–70).
PMLA	*Publications of the Modern Language Association of America.*
Portraiture	Thomas Clarkson, *A Portraiture of Quakerism as Taken from a View of the Moral Education, Discipline, Peculiar Customs, Religious Principles, Political and Civil Economy, and Character, of the Society of Friends* (3 vols.; London, 1806).

PR   Cobbett's *Political Register* (London, 1802–18).

PW   *The Complete Poetical Works of Samuel Taylor Coleridge*,
                 ed. E. H. Coleridge (2 vols.; Oxford, 1912).

Reflections   *Edmund Burke,* Reflections on the Revolution in
                 France and on the Proceedings in Certain Societies
                 in London Relative to that Event, ed. C. C.
                 O'Brien (Harmondsworth, 1969).

Reiss   *Kant's Political Writings*, ed. Hans Reiss and trans.
                 H. B. Nisbet (London, 1970).

SC   J. J. Rousseau, *The Social Contract*, trans. G. D. H.
                 Cole (Everyman's Library, 1959).

S. Life   *The Life and Correspondence of Robert Southey*, ed. C. C.
                 Southey (6 vols.; London, 1849–50).

TF   S. T. Coleridge, *The Friend*, ed. Barbara E. Rooke
                 (2 vols.; London and Princeton, 1969).

TT   *Specimens of the Table Talk of the late Samuel Taylor
                 Coleridge*, ed. H. N. Coleridge (2 vols.; London,
                 1835). Cited by date.

Warter   *Selections from the Letters of Robert Southey*, ed. J. W.
                 Warter (4 vols.; London, 1856).

Watchman   S. T. Coleridge, *The Watchman*, ed. Lewis Patton
                 (London and Princeton, 1970).

WLL   Wordsworth Library Letters.

WL MS A   Wordsworth Library, Grasmere: Alphabetical
                 Sequence.

All references to *The Prelude* are to the 1805 version, published in *The
Prelude, 1799, 1805, 1850*, ed. Jonathan Wordsworth, M. H. Abrams,
and Stephen Gill (Norton Critical Edition, New York, 1979). Other
references to Wordsworth's poems are to *The Poetical Works of William
Wordsworth* (Oxford, 1940–9), and to the Cornell Wordsworth Series:

   The Borderers, ed. Robert Osborn (Ithaca, NY, 1982).
   Poems, in Two Volumes (abbrev. *P2V*), ed. Jared Curtis (Ithaca, NY,
   1983).

Editorial Symbols in Letters and Notebooks

<word>	A later insertion by Coleridge
[?word]	An uncertain reading
[?word/wood]	Possible alternative readings
[word]	A word editorially supplied
[. . .]	An illegible word
[?]	Space left blank

The true sorrow of humanity consists in this;—not that the mind of man fails; but that the course and demands of action and of life so rarely correspond with the dignity and intensity of human desires.

Wordsworth, *The Convention of Cintra* (1809)

Introduction

THE FRIEND was issued from the Lake District as a newspaper between 1809 and 1810. Apart from a brilliant stylistic review by John Foster in 1811,[1] the work went virtually unnoticed, leading Coleridge to speak of it in later life as a well-kept 'secret' entrusted to the public (Allsop, i. 233). *The Friend* is still something of a secret, particularly in its earliest, newspaper form. Barbara Rooke, the journal's most recent editor, takes the revised 1818 version as her main text, relegating the chaotic 1809–10 *Friend*, with some of its numbers ending in mid-sentence, to an appendix. Despite this foregrounding of the 1818 *Friend*, Rooke does not dismiss the early *Friend* as a failure. On the contrary, she presents an attractive picture of the work, describing it uncritically in Coleridge's own promotional terms as a journal written to 'found true PRINCIPLES' and to awaken 'the nobler Germ in human nature' (*TF*, vol. i, pp. xxxvii, xlii). She also suggests that Coleridge's frame of mind was relatively tranquil at this time, that there was a harmonious atmosphere at the Wordsworths' house, Allan Bank, where *The Friend* was composed, and that Coleridge proved to be 'far from unastute' in his business management of the periodical (*TF*, vol. i, p. xlviii).

This book puts forward a different view. Taking the 1809–10 *Friend* as my text, I present the work as one of mismanagement and failed goals, an exercise not so much in principles as in muddy thinking and anxious equivocation. That Coleridge ever launched the journal was something of a miracle. It was clear to all that he underestimated the task ahead of him, and it was generally agreed that his temperament was completely unsuited to the intricate business of launching a newspaper. Dorothy Wordsworth spoke of how

---

[1] *Eclectic Review*, 7 (1811), 912–31; repr. in *Coleridge: The Critical Heritage*, ed. J. R. de J. Jackson (London, 1970), 92–110.

easily he was overturned, 'made ill by the most trifling vexations or fatigue' (*MY* i. 293), an opinion seconded by her sister-in-law, Sara Hutchinson. Writing of the 'Alps upon Alps of Hindrances, and Uncertainties' which soon beset Coleridge at every turn (*CL* iii. 178), she confided: 'He has had a vast of plague—more than suits one of his temper & habits—indeed few would have ventured to engage in it if they could have had an idea of the obstacles—and he least of any man I know is calculated to overcome them.'[2] There was also the problem of his addiction to opium and spirits. Only a month before the first number appeared, Coleridge was sunk in a prolonged opium-induced stupor. Charles Lloyd, with whom he was staying, described his house guest as 'so miserable in mind & body that he pays no attention to the most urgent of his own affairs . . . The Friend is now as far from being arranged as it was 6 months ago—In fact he attends to nothing but *dreamy* reading & still more *dreamy* feelings.'[3]

To the Wordsworths, it seemed '*impossible* utterly impossible' that Coleridge should ever begin, for they feared at times for his life. On the eve of *The Friend*'s appearance, Wordsworth entreated Thomas Poole to come north 'in order that something may be arranged respecting [Coleridge's] children, in case of his death' (*MY* i. 352). The prelude to this request was stark and uncompromising:

I give it to you as my deliberate opinion, formed upon proofs which have been strengthening for years, that he neither will nor can execute any thing of important benefit either to himself his family or mankind. Neither his talents nor his genius mighty as they are nor his vast information will avail him anything; they are all frustrated by a derangement in his intellectual and moral constitution—In fact he has no voluntary power of mind whatsoever, nor is he capable of acting under any *constraint* of duty or moral obligation.

(*MY* i. 352.)

---

[2] *The Letters of Sara Hutchinson from 1800 to 1835*, ed. Kathleen Coburn (London, 1954), 17.

[3] E. V. Lucas, *Charles Lamb and the Lloyds* (London, 1898), 232–4. For the link in Coleridge between a dreamy and a miserable state of mind, see Dorothy Wordsworth, *MY* i. 110.

When Number 1 actually appeared, Wordworth's response was nothing more than the perfunctory, 'I am sorry for it—as I have not the least hope that it can proceed' (*MY* i. 354), an opinion held with equal emphasis by Robert Southey.[4]

Coleridge was to prove both his friends wrong, for against all odds, *The Friend* ran to twenty-seven numbers, sustained over a period of nine months. It was some time, however, before he managed to say anything of importance. The problem lay in an anxiety-ridden inability to carry out his stated intentions, a failing which provoked William Hazlitt to caricature the journal as nothing but an 'enormous title-page, the longest and most tiresome Prospectus that ever was written' (Howe, vii. 115). It is part of the purpose of this book to explain why Coleridge found it so difficult to write *The Friend*. To say that the chief obstacle lay within—in his 'diseased' will, and his tendency to rely too heavily upon others—is to say nothing more than what we already know so well, both from Coleridge himself and from everyone who knew him. But what has not been so generally recognized about this period is the significance of his dependence upon two people in particular, Sara Hutchinson and Thomas Clarkson. Both were central to the production of *The Friend*, and there is little doubt that each, in the end, had reason to regret the roles they had played. Sara was Coleridge's amanuensis: without her there, taking the words down from his mouth,[5] the periodical would never have come into existence. But Coleridge's strong passion for her generated unbearable tensions in the period after his return from Malta, and in the spring of 1810 Sara left Allan Bank, her departure marking the end of *The Friend* and the beginning of Coleridge's final split with the Wordsworth circle. Clarkson's role was as practical as Sara's, but less romantic. It was his job to underpin *The Friend* financially by finding subscribers, and his

---

[4] 'The *Friend* will never go on. It is impossible that he should carry it on to 20 Numbers. I regard every number as a dead loss, and worse than all I fear he will totally degrade himself before he has done.' (Curry, i. 511.)

[5] Of Coleridge's methods of composing his weekly numbers, Dorothy wrote, 'He has written a whole Friend more than once in two days. They are never re-transcribed, and he generally has dictated to Miss Hutchinson, who takes the words down from his mouth' (*MY* i. 391).

immense influence in Quaker circles led to more Friendly supporters than was comfortable for a writer whose chief ambition in 1809 was to win the patronage and approval of the orthodox and conservative. Issues relating to Coleridge's Quaker readership are most clearly focused in an examination of Number 1, a piece of writing so obscure as to be almost wholly unintelligible without some knowledge of the circumstances surrounding its production.

The problem of writing for a mixed audience of Dissenters and Tories was exacerbated by the fact that Coleridge had done no political writing under his own name since *The Watchman* (1796). That he should now appear, not as a critic of Government, but as its 'advocate' and 'upholder',[6] caused him great uneasiness, and the diversity of his readership meant that he was forever stretched to find common ground whenever he dared approach the 'delicate subjects of Religion and Politics' (*TF* ii. 13). So acute was his nervousness about these topics that he dedicated Number 2, not to his promised exposition of 'the views, which a British Subject in the present state of his Country ought to entertain of its actual and existing Constitution of Government' (*TF* ii. 13–14), but to a lengthy and highly defensive refutation of the charges of deism, immorality, and Jacobinism laid against him by the *Antijacobin* ten years earlier. The unearthing of these old and for the most part, forgotten calumnies appalled and mystified the Wordsworths; and the spectacle of Coleridge, now separated from his wife, boasting of the homesickness he had felt as a husband and father ten years ago in Germany, seemed foolish beyond belief (*MY* i. 355–6). Others were similarly dismayed,[7] and one old friend, George Caldwell, was so irritated by Coleridge's coy allusions to the dangerous terrains of politics and religion that he felt obliged to remind him he was living and writing in 1809, not in the 1790s:

I have no fears on those subjects connected with Politics & Religion . . . Surely the reign of terrorism is over; and a man may express his sentiments fearlessly on such points, if he does it with

[6] These were both early titles for *The Friend* (see *CN* iii. 3366, 3390, 3393, 3400).
[7] See Curry, i. 511.

decency and means honestly, though they should not exactly tally
with the standard of faith at Fulham or St James.

(WL MS A/Caldwell/1.)

The pressures generated by Coleridge's uneasiness with the
past, and by the tricky undertaking of retaining his old
supporters whilst making his début as a Government apologist,
can be traced in numerous addresses to his subscribers, and
in those numbers of the journal where he attempts to lay down
his new political creed. Roughly speaking, these are Numbers
7–11, comprising Essays IV, VI, and VII: 'On the Principles
of Political Philosophy', 'On the Grounds of Government as
laid exclusively in the Pure Reason; or a Statement and
Critique of the Third System of Political Philosophy, viz. the
Theory of Rousseau and the French Economists', and 'On the
Errors of Party Spirit: or Extremes Meet'. Hooker, Burke, and
Kant (the latter particularly in respect of his critique of
Rousseau)[8] play a large part in Coleridge's emergence in these
essays as an upholder of custom and tradition, rather than
universal rules drawn from Reason and natural law. His
conservative political theory includes a new toleration of
political expediency, heard most clearly in his nationalistic
rhetoric as it counters not only pacifism, but the moralistic,
individualistic, 'principled' approach to politics generally
adopted by Dissenters. The claims of expediency were
troubling, however, because it is one of Coleridge's major
purposes in *The Friend* to demonstrate the importance of
principle in the public sphere, and to deny that there is any
irreconcilable conflict between religion and politics; the values
appropriate to private, individual life are presented by him as
central to the world of public affairs, and only Christians are
entitled to the name of true patriots. This interdependence of
Christianity and patriotism had long been an assumption of
Coleridge's political writing,[9] but whereas the Christianity he
espoused in the 1790s taught its disciples 'never to use the arm
of flesh, to be perfectly non-resistant' (*CL* i. 282), the
Christianity of 1809 forms an uneasy alliance with a warring

---

[8] Rooke gives very little indication of Coleridge's debt to Kant in *The Friend*.

[9] See the essay 'Modern Patriotism' (*The Watchman*, 98–100), which infuriated
Coleridge's atheist friend John Thelwall (*CL* iii. 212–15).

nationalism. The conflicting claims of religion and politics result in a rather uncomfortable division of purpose in his writing, a division reflected in his argument that we must recognize certain 'moral differences' between the duties attaching to individual and to national life. The practical implications of this creed are revealed in Number 24, 'On the Law of Nations', where he allegorizes Britain's attack on neutral Denmark in 1807. Here, as elsewhere, it can be argued that while it is his aim to demonstrate the supreme importance of religious values in the political realm, Coleridge in fact fails to achieve a balance in *The Friend* between the claims of moral justice and a fervent nationalism.

Number 11 marks the end of Coleridge's political theory and the beginning of a quite different, more miscellaneous journal. With many of his subscribers complaining of the difficulty and obscurity of *The Friend* he vowed 'to render [his] manner more attractive and [his] matter more generally interesting' (*TF* ii. 151), but it is clear from his increasingly vituperative attacks on periodical readers' expectations that he was now writing against the grain and fast losing enthusiasm. Wordsworth came to his aid with some poetry and the first of his *Essays upon Epitaphs*, and he also wrote a lengthy reply to an enthusiastic letter from a young admirer, John Wilson. Other numbers were filled out with translations from a seven-volume German travel book,[10] 'Specimens of Rabbinical Wisdom', also taken from a German source,[11] old letters of Coleridge's written from Germany in 1798 and 1799, epitaphs translated from an Italian poet, Gabriello Chiabrera, and finally, a hopelessly dull life of Sir Alexander Ball, under whom Coleridge had served in Malta, and who died during the writing of *The Friend*. These sections of *The Friend* demonstrate the readerly constraints under which Coleridge felt himself to be labouring, but they are peripheral to his political and moral objectives in 1809 and thus lie outside the scope of this book.

[10] J. L. von Hess, *Durchflüge durch Deutschland, die Niederlände und Frankreich* (Hamburg, 1793–1800). Hess is the source for the essay on Luther in Number 8 and the Gothic tale of Maria Schöning in Number 13. For an examination of Coleridge's plagiarism and transformation of the Schöning tale, see my article 'A Horrid Tale in *The Friend*', *The Wordsworth Circle*, 12 (Autumn 1981), 262–9.

[11] J. J. Engel, *Schriften*, i (Berlin, 1801), and *TF* i. 370.

1

Some Unresolved Conflicts

WHEN *The Friend* came to a temporary halt after the first two numbers, Coleridge wrote to one of his Quaker subscribers, Thomas Woodruffe Smith, to thank him for his approbation of 'the Principle' on which he had based his periodical. This principle was his opposition to the prudential and utilitarian ethics of 'Hume, Paley and their Imitators':

Believe me, nothing but a deep and habitual conviction of it's[1] Truth absolutely, and of it's particular Importance in the present generation could have roused me from that dream of great internal activity, and outward inefficience, into which ill-health and a wounded spirit had gradually lulled me. Intensely studious by Habit, and languidly affected by motives of Interest or Reputation, I found in my Books and my own meditations a sort of high-walled Garden, which excluded the very sound of the World without. But the Voice within could not be thrust out—the sense of Duty unperformed, and the pain of Self-dissatisfaction, aided and enforced by the sad and anxious looks of Southey, and Wordsworth, and some few others most beloved by me and most worthy of my regard and affection.   (*CL* iii. 216.)

The profound and troubled interconnection at the time between Coleridge's intellectual and emotional life can be clearly heard in the twofold emphasis of this passage, moving as it does from an assertion of the great contemporary importance of *The Friend* to an admission of the personal obstacles which made the performance of this public task so difficult. This interconnection of public and private life informed Coleridge's first conception of *The Friend*, and is central to our understanding of his work in the troubled years after Malta.

Coleridge's earliest thinking about *The Friend* can be traced to a project called 'Comforts and Consolations', mentioned

---

[1] Coleridge often denotes the possessive in this way.

amongst a number of planned works in a notebook entry of
November 1803 (*CN* i. 1646). This entry also includes a
memorandum about a work on 'My Life & Thoughts',
generally believed to refer to the *Biographia Literaria*.[2] That *The
Friend* and the *Biographia* should be linked together in their
earliest origins is not surprising, for both are intellectual
biographies, offshoots of a general decision taken by Coleridge
at that time:

Seem to have made up my mind to write my metaphysical works, as
my Life, & *in* my Life—intermixed with all the other events/ or
history of the mind & fortunes of S. T. Coleridge.   (*CN* i. 1515.)

In keeping with the spirit of this decision, Coleridge's
notebook memoranda for 'Comforts and Consolations' are
given over to recording his thoughts and feelings, and
transcriptions from his voluminous reading.[3] Five years later,
self-observation is presented in *The Friend*'s Prospectus as the
inspiration of the new project. It was, Coleridge writes, his
habit of recording 'all the Flux and Reflux of [his] Mind
within itself' which first encouraged him to undertake the
periodical. Miscellaneous as these notices were, they all
tended 'to one common End': '*what we are and what we are born to
become*' (*TF* ii. 17).

   Patterns of thought and behaviour, familiar to us from
recent and excellent studies of Coleridge in the 1790s,[4] will re-
emerge in these middle years to remind us of the fact that, for
all the inner contradictions, there is an extraordinary consistency in Coleridge's life and thought. But the Coleridge we see
in 1806 to 1810 is also the friend whom the Wordsworths
could hardly recognize upon his return from Malta, a man
'utterly changed' by his two years abroad. Heavily addicted to

---

   [2] See *TF*, vol. i, pp. xxxv–xxxvi, and *CN* i. 1646 n.
   [3] From 1803 onward we see the work taking shape as a catch-all of private
meditations, ranging from reflections on narrowness of heart, the metaphysics of
sleep, dreams, and violent weeping, the virtues connected with love of nature, and
thoughts on childhood (*CN* ii. 2011, 2018, 2026, 3072); see also *CN* ii. 2458, 2541,
2638, 2648.
   [4] Kelvin Everest in *Coleridge's Secret Ministry: The Context of the Conversation Poems,
1795–1798* (Brighton, 1979), Carl Woodring in *Politics in English Romantic Poetry*
(Cambridge, Mass., 1970), and essays by E. P. Thompson and David Erdman in
Power and Consciousness, ed. Conor Cruise O'Brien and W. D. Vanech (London, 1969).

opium, suffering acutely in mind and body, he had withdrawn so far into the 'high-walled Garden' that there were times when his friends despaired of reclaiming him for active life. The Wordsworths' commitment to Coleridge never wavered during these years, although their hopes for him flickered as he moved with alarming frequency in and out of engagement with life, sometimes sunk in stupefying illness and depression, sometimes springing back to life and spinning ambitious and impracticable plans.

The Friend was one such plan, and any understanding of how the work came into existence must take account of Coleridge's relationship with Sara Hutchinson. Coleridge made many things of Sara. Most important of all, she was his conscience, the external embodiment of 'the Voice within'; as such it was her task to rouse him to the work and restore him to a much needed sense of connection with the world. But this idealized conception of Sara, in so far as it sprang from a need to believe in the moral impeccability of his feelings, had to vie so strenuously with his sexual passion that the relationship which was supposed to bring his whole being into harmony became a deep source of confusion, guilt, and instability. The failure of Coleridge's idealistic language of love anticipates the struggle of his political idealism to transcend pressures inimical to its moral integrity and forcefulness.

The uneasiness of Coleridge's relationship with Sara, and with the wider circle at Allan Bank, increased his awkwardness and self-consciousness as an author. The lack of confidence his close friends displayed affected *The Friend* directly by provoking him to vindicate the value and integrity of his inner life. To the Quaker, Smith, he claimed that his motive for writing *The Friend* lay in the hope that a few of his readers might learn to fix their attention on the concept of 'being' rather than 'doing', on what men '*are* instead of *merely* what they *do*' (*CL* iii. 216), a Kantian doctrine which was both an oblique challenge to his friends and a much needed form of self-defence. Kant's emphasis on the quality of intentions rather than of actions was extremely important to Coleridge in this period; and Kant's concept of the moral law, as it was developed in the *Groundwork of the Metaphysic of Morals* (1785), can be seen at every point of *The Friend*'s moral and political argument. On one level, the sublime concept of acting, not out of inclination or self-interest but solely for duty's sake, accorded well with Coleridge's half-mystical reverence for man's spiritual and moral potential; on a political level, however, the very sublimity of Kant's categorical imperative lent authority to Coleridge's cautious distinction between the duties owed by an individual to his conscience, and the duties owed to his country.

Coleridge's anxiety at the potential conflict between the two spheres of religion and politics gains a new significance when we consider the number of Dissenters amongst his subscribers, many of whom were old friends from *The Watchman* period. Much has been said of the literary *Angst* generated in the early nineteenth century by the new impersonal conditions of writing for the public at large, but we see a very different set of constraints at work in the case of a journal. Unlike a one-off production, such as a poem or essay, a journal is necessarily open to reader influence, for it seeks to create an audience which will stay faithful over time. But it is a matter for speculation as to how far Coleridge was aware of the very special conditions governing periodical publication. He was highly susceptible to the pressure of audience, the desire to please and to avoid controversy often leading him to tell his listeners what he imagined they wanted to hear. Yet he also held to a strictly authoritarian view of the intellectual superiority of the writer over his readers, and as *The Friend* began to fail, bitterly inveighed against the intellectual laziness of his subscribers. Although fascinated by the reading process, and forever conscious of the actual men and women who financially supported his journal, he seems to have failed to realize (or perhaps refused to admit to himself) that *The Friend* was not simply a vehicle for his own views, but that it belonged in several important ways to his subscribers.

It was on the subject of politics that he ran the greatest risk of alienating his more liberal readers, for his conservatism was such that he would not venture any criticism of the Government. Unlike Wordsworth, he was 'decidedly against reform'

(*MY* i. 359),[5] and *The Friend* makes no reference whatsoever to the nation's social and economic problems, topics which had recently been taken up by Southey with extraordinary power in his *Letters from England* (1807). Southey's attack on the manufacturing system, complete with horrific descriptions of the pitiable living conditions of Birmingham's industrial workers, infuriated Coleridge, who complained bitterly that his friend had deprived him 'of at least a 100 Subscribers' in that city (*CL* iii. 165). Nettled by Southey's claim that the wealth of the country did not circulate equally and healthfully, but collected in fatal aneurisms 'which starve and palsy the extremities',[6] Coleridge replaced the metaphor of aneurism with a less invidious one from the natural world, and then went on to celebrate the national debt as a cause of great national unity and health (*TF* ii. 159–60). With his approval of all aspects of the Government's war policy, and his determination to ignore controversial subjects, it is not surprising that his old friend Peter Crompton wrote to warn him that some believed he was writing solely to please those in power and 'to get a good berth' for himself (WL MS A/Crompton/1).

In style and content, *The Friend* appears to mark a break with *The Watchman*, for whereas the earlier periodical was predominantly a work of political journalism, *The Friend* advertised itself as an apolitical and ambitious work of moral and political philosophy. But despite Coleridge's projection of himself as a second Burke, 'an Authority equally respected by both of the opposite parties' (*TF* ii. 21), and his repeated insistence that he would avoid controversial topics for the sake of national unanimity, *The Friend* is not disinterested, and was never intended to be. Southey predicted that it would prove 'a tremendous battery' if successful (Warter, ii. 114), and it is clear from Coleridge's letters that he intended to swim with the party in power and not in 'the muddy yet shallow stream' of the Whigs (*CL* iii. 195). Like the *Quarterly Review* whose first

[5] Wordsworth believed that without reform 'the destruction of the liberties of the Country is inevitable' (*MY* i. 345).

[6] Letter XXXVIII, 'The Manufacturing System', *Letters from England*, ed. J. Simmons (Gloucester, 1984), 210.

issue appeared in February 1809, *The Friend* formed part of a
Tory reaction against those who questioned the need to
continue the war, a doubt aired in what Southey described as
the 'base and cowardly politics' of the *Edinburgh Review*
(Warter, ii. 107).[7] Coleridge shared Southey's contempt for
the doubters, and in an article written soon after the last
number of *The Friend*, attacked the very stance of independence
and impartiality which he had officially adopted for his own
journal. The Whigs and Edinburgh Reviewers who stationed
themselves on an 'Isthmus' of neutrality and moderation, far
removed from the strife, were contemptible for looking down
upon 'the agitation of the vessel of state, and the conflict of
hostile factions' with 'a sort of tranquil delight arising from a
consciousness of security' (*EOT* ii. 102–3).

Fearing the present 'stupor of Despondence' (*TF* ii. 85), it
was Coleridge's hope to rekindle the nation's 'animal spirits'
and give 'a sort of muscular strength to the public mind' (*TF*
ii. 305). Exhausted by the long years of war, the country's
enthusiasm for the fight had evaporated, and whatever energy
remained was dissipated by party faction. The years 1807 to
1809 were 'unrelenting and fearful' ones for the country,[8] a
time when patriotism was a light 'in danger of being blown
out' rather than a fire which needed to be fanned 'by the
winds of party spirit' (*TF* ii. 328). The rising of the Spaniards
against the French in 1808 had, for a brief moment, united all
parties and given a fillip to the nation's flagging energies, but
the signing shortly afterwards of the Convention of Cintra,
removing French troops from the war zone, only strengthened
the Opposition's case against continuing the Peninsular War.
Thus, with a large section of the nation clamouring for peace
and for a withdrawal of troops from the Continent, the
lacklustre and unpopular Portland ministry found itself
working in 'a new atmosphere of criticism'.[9] Coleridge's
conviction that such criticism was dangerous at times of crisis

---

[7] Disgust with the politics of the *Edinburgh Review* came to a head in Oct. 1808,
with the publication of a review of Don Pedro Cevallos's *On the French Usurpation of
Spain* (*ER* xiii. 215–34).

[8] K. G. Feiling, *The Second Tory Party 1714–1832* (London, 1938), 256.

[9] Ibid. 257.

led to his emphasis in *The Friend* upon the urgent need for national consensus, but the air of independence and impartiality which accompanied his rejection of party wrangling and division fitted conveniently with his partisanship: his support for the status quo and the Tory government.

If the rejection of sectarianism and party politics was not quite what it seemed, the same could be said of a number of Coleridge's stances in *The Friend*. In general, the pattern of his behaviour is to adopt official postures which bear little relation to what he actually feels; his occasional disgust with his country, freely admitted in his letters, is, for instance, nowhere to be seen in his periodical. This posturing was an old habit of which he was well aware. In a letter of 1800 he confessed that, whilst overwhelmed by 'the present melancholy state of Humanity', he had yet made up his mind 'to a sort of heroism in believing the progressiveness of all nature'. In the same letter he admitted to the weakness of knowing what he ought to do, yet doing the opposite. In this particular instance, he found himself caught in a dilemma between private and public worlds, between lofty disengagement from passing events and an irresistible involvement with life. Believing that 'a man's private & personal connections & interests ought to be uppermost in his daily & hourly Thoughts, & that the dedication of much hope & fear to subjects which are perhaps disproportionate to our faculties & powers, is a disease' he none the less admits that the disease has had him in its clutches for so long, that he knows not how to get rid of it, 'or even to wish to get rid of it': 'Life were so flat a thing without Enthusiasm—that if for a moment it leave me, I have a sort of stomach-sensation attached to all my Thoughts, like those which succeed to the pleasurable operation of a dose of Opium' (*CL* i. 558).[10]

The adoption of an official, positive line, the guilty sense that he ought to be standing back to take a wider perspective, and the irresistible surrender to enthusiasm—all these recur nine years later when he is writing *The Friend*. Shifting

---

[10] Erdman quotes this letter in his perceptive essay 'Coleridge as Editorial Writer', in *Power and Consciousness*, ed. O'Brien and Vanech, p. 187. This essay forms the basis of his introduction to *Essays on His Times* (Princeton, NJ, 1978).

uneasily in his view of what he is trying to do in his periodical, he at one time strikes his official pose as the philosopher in retirement, secure from the warping influences of the metropolis (*TF* ii. 6); at another he reveals his true design by anxiously pointing out that rural retirement does not entail the isolation it once did (*TF* ii. 28). Desirous of the elevated status of philosopher, he is none the less reluctant to disqualify himself as a well-informed and up-to-date commentator on current affairs. This impossible desire to be simultaneously a philosopher and publicist is reflected in the conspicuous unsuitability of *The Friend*'s newspaper format to its weighty pseudo-philosophical subject matter.

The Coleridge we see in 1809, uneasily caught between two roles, is the same Coleridge who could not decide in the 1790s whether he should become a journalist or a religious minister. The Wedgwood annuity saved him from the dilemma of having to choose, but it also meant that he was left oscillating between two careers, attempting to reconcile the seemingly incompatible claims of the religious and political life. The conflict, which I shall argue is still there in 1809, has been captured by Hazlitt in his remarkable essay recalling January 1798 when he trudged ten miles through the mud to Shrewsbury to hear Coleridge preach. When he arrived, the organ was playing the hundredth psalm, and when it was done, Coleridge rose and spoke the following words: 'And he went up into the mountain to pray, HIMSELF, ALONE.' Hazlitt continues,

As he gave out his text, his voice 'rose like a steam of rich distilled perfumes', and when he came to the two last words, which he pronounced loud, deep, and distinct, it seemed to me, who was then young, as if the sounds had echoed from the bottom of the human heart, and as if that prayer might have floated in solemn silence through the universe. The idea of St. John came into my mind, 'of one crying in the wilderness, who had his loins girt about, and whose food was locusts and wild honey'. The preacher then launched into his subject, like an eagle dallying with the wind. The sermon was upon peace and war; upon church and state—not their alliance, but their separation—on the spirit of the world and the spirit of Christianity, not as the same, but as opposed to one another. He talked of those who had 'inscribed the cross of Christ on banners dripping with human gore'. (Howe, xvii. 108.)

Looking back over a period of nearly twenty years, Hazlitt dramatizes the two aspects of Coleridge's personality and career. On the one hand, we have Coleridge in the image of St John, the visionary and the mystic. In his withdrawal into the desert, in his meekness, humility, and self-denial, St John embodies a certain ideal of Christianity—'the Religion of the meek and lowly Jesus, which forbids to his Disciples all alliance with the powers of this World' (*Lects. 1795*, p. 66). On the other hand, Coleridge is seen as the eagle, imperiously swooping down upon its prey—in this case, the bishops and all within the Church of England who hailed the war against revolutionary France as a holy war carried forth in God's name. Then, as though to heighten the conflict between religious withdrawal and political activism, Hazlitt silently points the irony of Coleridge preaching politics from the pulpit, harnessing his religious authority to the service of politics; for the message which he preaches is that the spirit of religion and of politics are opposed to one another.

Hazlitt's account gives no hint that Coleridge was inhibited by his dual roles, or even that he was aware of the ironies of his position. Neither was the case. Two years earlier, in 1796, when touring the Midlands in search of subscribers for *The Watchman*, Coleridge had shown a lively and humorous awareness of the difficulties to which he was exposed. Preaching in a blue coat and white waistcoat, so that not 'a rag of the woman of Babylon' be seen on him (*BL* i. 179), he once felt obliged to exchange his '*coloured Cloths*' for more sombre and orthodox ones, his reason being that his sermon was of 'so political a tendency' that, had he worn his coloured garb, the minister he was standing in for would have been accused by his congregation of sticking a 'political Lecturer in his pulpit' (*CL* i. 180). Thus, the more outspoken the politics, the more he stood in need of the cover and sanction of religion: 'the *Sacred* may eventually help off the *profane*' he wrote at this time, 'and my *Sermons* spread a sort of sanctity over my *Sedition*' (*CL* i. 179).

Despite the humour and high spirits of the letters written on this *Watchman* tour, the strain of playing two roles at once eventually took its toll. A year after *The Watchman* had come to an end, its last issue proclaiming Coleridge's intention to cease crying 'the state of the political Atmosphere', he wrote to his Unitarian friend John Prior Estlin: 'I am wearied with politics, even to soreness.—I never knew a passion for politics exist for a long time without swallowing up, or absolutely excluding, a passion for Religion.' (*CL* i. 338.) Feeling alienated from the democrats on account of his religious convictions and temperament, the balance of his work tilted away from radical politics to the Christian conservatism which had always been its accompaniment and qualification.[11] The movement is one from politics to principle, from the local and temporary to the general and permanent, from activism to quietism. To his brother George he claimed he had withdrawn himself almost totally 'from the consideration of *immediate* causes, which are infinitely complex & uncertain, to muse on fundamental & general causes—the "causae causarum" ' (*CL* i. 397). But this was telling his elder brother very much what he wanted to hear. Although Coleridge's disgust with the contemporary scene was genuine enough, he never really turned his back on the claims of the world. The vow that he would cease to cry the state of the political atmosphere was an impressive gesture of renunciation but no more, for within a year he was contracted to supply the *Morning Post* with verse and political essays; and in the first three months of 1798, he had published no less than nine political articles.[12]

A similar oscillation between political involvement and religious withdrawal can be seen in 1809, for Coleridge's uneasiness with politics as a realm of contingency, calculation, and expedience, only increased over the years. Full of self-doubt, and conscious of inner weakness, he is more anxious than ever to refer, in all subjects, 'to some grand and comprehensive Truth' (*Lects. 1795*, p. 6). The quest for a single, unchanging principle which would resolve all difficulties was a deep-seated need of his nature, manifesting itself

---

[11] See Editors' Introduction, *Lects. 1795*, pp. lv–lviii.
[12] See *EOT*, vol. i, pp. lix, 7–28.

in his writing as a reaching outwards for some thing, or some person, higher than self:

our nature imperiously asks a *summit*, a *resting place*—it is with the affections in Love, as with the Reason in Religion—we cannot *diffuse* & equalize—we must have a SUPREME—a *One the highest*. All languages express this sentiment.   (*Marginalia*, i. 752.)

But this striving for absolutes or principles, and its accompanying rhetorical expansiveness, coexists with a more cautious rhetoric, and an intense dislike of abstractions. Such caution is particularly evident in his writing on politics, the realm presided over by the Understanding, or 'the faculty of suiting Measures to Circumstances' (*TF* ii. 103).

The tension between these two rhetorics goes under many names in *The Friend*: it is the tension between principle and prudence, between Reason and Understanding, between private and public life. The problem first reveals itself in Coleridge's equivocal commitment to principle, and then ultimately in his failure to spell out what these principles are.[13] The equivocation can be seen in his letters advertising *The Friend*, for it is a curious feature of their argument that, whereas they begin by setting up an opposition between principles and prudence, they end with a bid to rescue prudence from the darkness into which it has been cast. The pattern emerges clearly in a letter to Sir George Beaumont as Coleridge's denunciation of utilitarianism in the form of the 'prudential understanding' gets modified towards the end of the letter by an admission that he listens 'with gladness and an obedient ear to Prudence, while it remains subordinate to, and in harmony with, a loftier and more authoritative Voice— that of PRINCIPLE' (*CL* iii. 147).

Coleridge does not jettison prudence because it is itself a principle of his political thought. In *The Friend* he describes himself as 'a zealous Advocate for deriving the origin of all Government from human *Prudence*, and of deeming that to be just which Experience has proved to be expedient'; thus,

[13] The failure of *The Friend* to spell out its principles was commented upon by Wordsworth (*TF*, vol. i, p. lxvi). The same fault was noted in 1795 by a critic of one of Coleridge's Bristol lectures (*Lects. 1795*, pp. lvii–lviii). .

'every Institution of national origin needs no other Justification than a proof, that under the particular circumstances it is EXPEDIENT'. While unlocking Coleridge's political creed, these statements involve (as he admits himself) an embarrassing avowal, exposing him to the charge of 'inconsistency'— for up until this point he had spoken 'with something like contempt and reprobation' of prudence and expedience (*TF* ii. 103–4).

This book charts a curve of affirmation and reserve as Coleridge moves in and out of adherence to principle or prudence, depending upon his treatment of man as a creature of God or as a citizen of a political state. The movement between a religious or private perspective, and a political or public one, is clearly discernible in *The Friend*, despite Coleridge's repeated emphasis upon the inseparability of the two spheres. His understanding of an incompatibility between the claims of public and private life is clear from his vow early on in *The Friend* that he will not refer to politics 'except as far as they may happen to be involved in some point of private morality' (*TF* ii. 27). His failure to abide by the resolution is manifest later in the periodical where he is obliged to distinguish between writing as a 'Christian Moralist' and writing as a 'Statesman' (*TF* ii. 200).

Uneasy at the tendency of religion and politics to spring apart, Coleridge devised two ways of resolving the problem: either he pretended he was not talking about politics, or he tried to redeem his political writing by harnessing to it a rhetoric of religious fervour and intensity. The latter resulted in a rapturous nationalism which reads very much like an extension of his religious feeling. Recourse to a religious idealization of politics cannot surprise us in an author as 'enthusiastic' as Coleridge,[14] and historical circumstances certainly legitimized it, the war against France being easily represented as a clash between the forces of good and evil. But the elevated and sacramental ambience of his political writing

[14] Writing of the first two numbers of *The Friend*, Charles Lloyd commented that Coleridge's mind was one which 'except in inspired moods, can do nothing' (quoted in E. K. Chambers's *Samuel Taylor Coleridge: A Biographical Study* (Oxford, 1938), 229). For Francis Jeffrey's objection to Coleridge's enthusiasm, see pp. 43, 49–50 below.

has led some critics to overlook areas of tension,[15] especially the difficulties generated by *The Friend*'s commitment to the primacy of national self-survival. The difficulty of reconciling England's security with both individual liberty and international morality is one which dogs the pages of Coleridge's periodical.

Nationalism suffuses *The Friend*. At the level of private morality the dictates of conscience give way to the higher imperatives of public duty. An illiberal aspect of Coleridge's nationalism can be seen in his sneering at the Quakers' pacifism. Their refusal to adapt religious principles to the exigencies of political life, and their tendency to regard the inner Light as the sole authority in all matters, disturbed Coleridge's Kantian belief in a necessary distinction between the realms of Morality (Ethics) and Politics (Ius). At the level of international morality, Coleridge suggests that the strict requirements of virtue must sometimes be overruled by the broader requirements of justice or right. Although he is at pains to point out that nations and individuals are bound by the same spirit of morality, he none the less holds that the circumstances of political action give rise to wholly different duties from those attaching to private life. It was no easy task in 1809 to strike a balance between the journalist's attention to the current political climate and the religious minister's concern for the larger moral issues lying behind political action, but the circumstances were such that Coleridge felt obliged to attempt it: the urgent issue of national survival would not permit him to enter the desert of St John.

Coleridge was not blind to the rights which inhere in the dignity of all men, nor did his acute sense of human weakness exclude a vision of the possible sublimity of our moral nature. This poetic openness to human potential, coexisting with a firmly pragmatic, even Machiavellian, grasp of the realities of political life[16] has its attractions, leading the most recent

---

[15] Some critics tend to endorse Coleridge's rhetoric of unity automatically; see J. R. Barth, *Coleridge and Christian Doctrine* (Cambridge, Mass., 1969), 3, and Russell Kirk, *The Conservative Mind, from Burke to Santayana* (London, 1954), 125.

[16] In 1803 Coleridge urged Southey to read through Machiavelli's historical and political works, adding that he preferred him greatly to Tacitus (*CL* ii. 936).

editor of *Essays on his Times* to speak admiringly of Coleridge as both Jacobin and anti-Jacobin, Radical and Tory (*EOT* vol. i, p. lxv). But the ability to think on both sides of an issue can also be a disability, as Coleridge was well aware, for he saw the fault exemplified in the writings of his revered Burke: 'the principle of becoming all Things to all men if by *any* means he might save *any* . . . thickened the protecting Epidermis of the Tact-nerve of Truth into something too like a Callus' (*CL* iii. 541). Coleridge himself falls into this trap; on more than one occasion in *The Friend* we see him as Hazlitt saw him: a man who, rather than enter one or other of the two camps before him, pitches his tent upon the barren waste without, 'having no abiding place nor city of refuge' (Howe, xi. 38).

References to *Il principe* appear in the notebooks and in *The Friend*, and at one point Coleridge toyed with the idea of analysing contemporary history in the light of Machiavelli's maxims (*CN* ii. 3015).

2

Coleridge and Sara Hutchinson: The Failure of Idealism

Mind, shipwrecked by storms of doubt, now mastless, rudderless, shattered,—pulling in the dead swell of a dark & windless Sea.

Coleridge's *Notebooks*, 1801

FOR the Wordsworths 1806 was a year of anxious waiting for news of Coleridge's safe return to England. Although they had received very few letters from him during the two years of his absence (*MY* i. 72), he was never very far from their thoughts; without him, the family circle seemed incomplete. 'Miss Hutchinson is with us', Dorothy wrote, 'and we should be as comfortable as we could desire to be if Coleridge were but at home in safety' (*MY* i. 2). As long as he was absent, the Wordsworths felt unable to make any important decisions about the future. Although Dove Cottage was no longer big enough for them, they hesitated before accepting the Beaumonts' offer of their house at Coleorton for the coming winter; as Dorothy explained to Lady Beaumont, their plans were 'so far connected with Coleridge that we cannot *decide* upon anything till we hear from him or see him' (*MY* i. 16). It was not until August, when they heard the 'blessed news' of Coleridge's arrival in London, that they were finally able to promise the Beaumonts some 'positive' statement about their journey to Coleorton (*MY* i. 71, 77).

Fearful of the prospect of seeing his wife again, Coleridge tarried in London for three weeks before coming north.[1] Although he had not hidden from the Wordsworths the cause

---

[1] Wordsworth informed Sir George Beaumont that Coleridge was afraid to go home because 'he recoils so much from the thought of domesticating with Mrs. Coleridge, with whom, though on many accounts he much respects her, he is so miserable that he dare not encounter it' (*MY* i. 78–9).

of his misery and procrastination, his letters from London did little to prepare them for the shock of finding him so broken by his experience abroad. In a letter to Catherine Clarkson, Dorothy described their painful reunion in Kendal:

We all went thither to him and never never did I feel such a shock as at first sight of him. We all felt exactly in the same way—as if he were different from what we have expected to see; almost as much as a person of whom we have thought much, and of whom we had formed an image in our own minds, without having any personal knowledge of him . . . He is utterly changed; and yet sometimes, when he was animated in conversation concerning things removed from him, I saw something of his former self. But never when we were alone with him. He then scarcely ever spoke of anything that concerned him, or us, or our common friends nearly, except we forced him to it; and immediately he changed the conversation to Malta, Sir Alexander Ball, the corruptions of government, anything but what we were yearning after. All we could gather from him was that he must part from her or die and leave his children destitute, and that to part he was resolved.   (*MY* i. 86–7.)

Despite this shock, the Wordsworths remained unshaken in their belief that they could help him—provided, of course, that he was prepared to help himself. Domestic tranquillity and, as Dorothy put it, the dedication of himself 'to some grand object connected with permanent effects' (*MY* i. 87), would bring better health and spirits, thus enabling him to fulfil 'the promise of his great endowments, and be a happy man' (*MY* i. 179).

For Coleridge tranquillity had become synonymous with Sara Hutchinson,[2] and with the prospect of living apart from his wife. Five years earlier he had spoken of his life as 'gangrened . . . in it's very vitals—domestic Tranquillity' (*CL* ii. 778), but finding a remedy for this was no more straight-forward in 1806 than it had been in 1801.

In a letter to Lady Beaumont, written the day before Coleridge arrived at Coleorton, Dorothy expressed confidence in their ability to comfort him and keep him from stimulants

---

[2] See George Whalley, *Coleridge and Sara Hutchinson and the Asra Poems* (London, 1955), 109–10; hereafter cited as Whalley.

such as brandy and strong beer: 'if he is not inclined to manage himself, *we* can manage him, and he will take no harm' (*MY* i. 110). Within a year, this confidence had vanished; and what had once been a wish to protect and soothe Coleridge was now transformed into a desire to safeguard their own domestic peace:

we had long experience at Coleorton that it was not in our power to make him happy; and his irresolute conduct since, has almost confirmed our fears that it will never be otherwise; therefore we should be more disposed to hesitation; and fear, of having our domestic quiet disturbed if he should now wish to come to us with the Children. I do not say that we *should not consent*; but it would be with little hope; and we shall never *advise* the measure. (*MY* i. 184.)

An examination of the Wordsworths' reasons for feeling this way, together with an account of Coleridge's state of mind at Coleorton, is central to an understanding of the later period 1808–10, when Coleridge joined the Wordsworth circle for the last time.

Of the many factors at work undermining Coleridge's relationship with the Wordsworths, two were particularly destructive: his addiction to opium and his love for Sara Hutchinson. Instead of loosening both these bonds (as intended), the journey to Malta had brought about the opposite effect: loneliness and despair, the staple of Coleridge's experience abroad, had only intensified his cravings for love, and opium was used to give short-term relief to these, and other, miserable feelings. Thus, with none of his objectives achieved, Coleridge returned to England in a worse condition than that in which he had first set out; he was now heavily addicted to opium, and by no means reconciled to the necessity of renouncing his love for Sara.[3]

It is possible that Dorothy's confident belief that they could 'manage' Coleridge sprang from ignorance of just how deeply he had succumbed to his addiction. Southey has left us a grim account of what it was like to live with Coleridge in the months immediately before he left Keswick for Coleorton:

[3] For Coleridge's attempts at renunciation, see Whalley, pp. 52, 63.

his habits are so murderous of all domestic comfort that I am only surprized Mrs C. is not rejoiced at being rid of him. He besots himself with opium, or with spirits, till his eyes look like a Turks who is half reduced to idiotcy by the practise—he calls up the servants at all hours of the night to prepare food for him—he does in short all things at all times except the proper time—does nothing which he ought to do, and every thing which he ought not.   (Curry, i. 448–9.)

From notebook entries written at Coleorton, it emerges that Coleridge spent his time painfully suspended between a longing to cut the habit altogether, and a fear that such action would result in death: 'I languish away my Life in misery, unutterably wretched from the gnawings of the Disease, and almost equally miserable by the Fear of the Remedy' (*CN* ii. 2990). Furthermore, the 'reprobate Despair' which drove him to snatch at opium was always accompanied by the knowledge that such action delayed the pain only to aggravate it further 'like the pause in the balancing of the Javelin and the muscles, the pause that defers the blow to make it the more forceful' (*CN* ii. 3078). Oppressed by an 'unquenchable Yearning' for release from anguish of body and mind, a yearning which could only be satisfied by further doses of opium or complete renunciation of the drug, Coleridge turned in on himself; and this habit of 'inward Brooding' daily made it 'harder to confess the Thing, I am, to any one—least of all to those, whom I most love & who most love me' (*CN* ii. 3078). Even worse, he found that withdrawal from his friends introduced and fostered a habit 'of negative falsehood, & multiplies the Temptations to positive, Insincerity' (*CN* ii. 3078).

As we have seen, this retreat of Coleridge's was the feature of his post-Malta self which most struck his friends on their first meeting at Kendal. It also formed the subject of Wordsworth's strange, self-regarding lament for his friend:

> There is a change—and I am poor;
> Your Love hath been, nor long ago,
> A Fountain at my fond Heart's door,
> Whose only business was to flow;
> And flow it did; not taking heed
> Of its own bounty, or my need.

What happy moments did I count!
Bless'd was I then all bliss above!
Now, for this consecrated Fount
Of murmuring, sparkling, living love,
What have I? shall I dare to tell?
A comfortless, and hidden WELL.

A Well of love—it may be deep—
I trust it is, and never dry:
What matter? if the Waters sleep
In silence and obscurity.
—Such change, and at the very door
Of my fond Heart, hath made me poor.

('A Complaint', *P2V*. 253)

Painful as Coleridge's withdrawal was to his friends, it was a weapon aimed primarily at himself, for it went entirely against his 'very social' nature (*CN* ii. 2322). Conscious of inner weakness, of what he described as feelings of '*Halfness*', Coleridge yearned to find the '*completer*' of his moral self (*CN* iii. 3325, 3291); in a notebook entry of 1808, he characterized the generous mind as one which 'cannot *think* without a symbol— neither can it *live* without something that is to be at once its Symbol, & its *Other half*' (*CN* iii. 3325). Loving, and being loved in return, had always been felt by Coleridge as a necessity of his nature.[4] In a letter to his wife written from Germany in 1799, he had spoken prophetically of the dependence of his well-being upon love and friendship: 'I am deeply convinced that if I were to remain a few years among objects for whom I had no affection, I should wholly lose the powers of Intellect—Love is the vital air of my Genius' (*CL* i. 471). And during the years leading up to the time of *The Friend*, it was a frequent exercise of his notebooks to establish the dependence of his intellectual life upon states of bodily or mental feeling (*CN* ii. 2638).[5]

[4] It was also seen as a prerequisite for the discovery of truth; during his years of political activism, Coleridge had written that the 'searcher after Truth must love and be beloved' (*Lects. 1795*, p. 46).

[5] The interdependence of mind and body can be seen in numerous notebook entries: 'To lie in ease yet dull anxiety for hours, afraid to think a thought, lest some thought of Anguish should shoot a pain athwart my body, afraid even to turn my body, lest the very bodily motion should introduce a train of painful Thoughts' (*CN* ii. 3149).

Whatever hopes Coleridge had of arousing himself from the miserable stupor induced by opium were closely bound up at this time with his feelings for Sara Hutchinson; with Sara's help, Coleridge believed he could re-establish some meaningful connection with the world around him. The comfort of being near her at Coleorton was, however, to be poisoned for him by the presence of the Wordsworths, and this conflict over Sara was still unresolved two years later when Coleridge moved into Allan Bank in 1808.[6]

In an early and important article, Thomas M. Raysor argued that whilst wintering with Coleridge at Coleorton in 1806–7 the Wordsworths took alarm at his feelings for Sara Hutchinson.[7] The hint that something went seriously wrong at Coleorton, and that this 'something disastrous' had to do with Coleridge and Sara was later reiterated by George Whalley but, like Raysor, he was content to leave the matter there, concluding that we shall never know exactly what this disaster involved.[8]

While no facts as such have come to light, and while it is unlikely that there was ever anything spectacular to reveal, it is clear from Coleridge's notebooks that his love for Sara was sometimes overwhelmed by sexual passion. For the most part, however, critics tend to overlook this aspect of the relationship,[9] a tendency encouraged by Coleridge's own ability to convince himself that no problem existed. But while Coleridge thought he was safe, the Wordsworths appear to have perceived a

---

[6] Rooke seems to me to be quite mistaken when she says that, by the end of 1808, 'the conflict between Coleridge and Wordsworth over Sara Hutchinson seemed settled' (*TF*, vol. i, p. xxxviii).

[7] 'Coleridge and "Asra" ', *Studies in Philology*, 26 (1929), 305–24.

[8] ' "Late Autumn's Amaranth": Coleridge's Late Poems', *Transactions of the Royal Society of Canada*, ser. 4, vol. 2 (1964), 161.

[9] Despite the evidence of these notebooks, Norman Fruman's Coleridge is frigid and impotent, a woman-hater whose passion for Sara was 'wholly distant' (*Coleridge, the Damaged Archangel* (London, 1972), 424–9). A. J. Harding acknowledges Coleridge's sexual feelings for Sara but treats them as unproblematic (*Coleridge and the Idea of Love: Aspects of Relationship in Coleridge's Thought and Writing* (London, 1974), 84, 95–101). A notable exception to the rule is William Empson. Speaking of the way in which Coicridge fretted Sara by incessant demands for attention and reassurance, he writes, 'One could not invent a more decisive moral object-lesson in favour of adultery' (*Coleridge's Verse: A Selection* (London, 1972), 94).

danger, and the notebooks suggest that they attempted to interfere. Of the many grievances voiced by Coleridge against his friends in 1807, one accusation stands out above the rest: that the Wordsworths thought 'foully of that wherein the pride of the Spirit's purity is in shrine' (*CN* ii. 3134). Again, in the same month, he wrote: 'It is not the W's knowledge of my frailties that prevents my *entire* Love of them/ No! it is their Ignorance of the Deep place of my Being—and o! the cruel cruel misconception of that which is purest in me, which alone is indeed pure' (*CN* ii. 3146).

It is not surprising that, as a Christian, Coleridge resented any slur upon the purity of his feelings for Sara. Although separated from his wife at this time, he still regarded himself as married, and it was this Christian perspective which made it so impossible for him to conceive of this extra-marital relationship as anything but chaste. What made the Wordsworths' insinuation even more unacceptable was his idealized and sacramental conception of Sara as a symbol of the divine. She was, for Coleridge, 'the God within me, even as the best & most religious men have called their Conscience the God within them' (*CN* iii. 3996). In 1804, at Syracuse, Sara's face had been 'the guardian Angel' of Coleridge's 'Innocence and Peace of mind' when he had flirted with the opera singer Cecilia Bertozzi; at the bedside of the 'too fascinating Siren', her 'angel countenance' had appeared as a 'heavenly Vision' (*CN* iii. 3404). It was to Sara, too, that he turned, when struggling to keep his opium dose to a minimum: 'O then, for *her* Sake, Coleridge! the sake so dear above all other, & for which all others are chiefly dear' (*CN* iii. 3483; see also *CN* iii. 3468). Most important of all, however, in this post-Malta period, was the galvanizing effect Sara had upon his work. The pre-condition of work consisted, for Coleridge, in a duty 'perfectly felt' as a reality in the external world, and it was precisely this sense of reality which Sara provided. Whereas opium brought with it an ineffectual dreaminess, exacerbating the native tendency of his ideas, wishes, and feelings to be 'to a diseased degree disconnected from *motion* & *action*' (*CL* ii. 782), Sara restored him to a more vivid sense of connection with the world around him. By seeming herself to be the very incarnation of the voice of duty, she dispelled the all too familiar tendency of this voice to deaden inclination; and instead of conflict, Coleridge experienced in her presence an 'Incarnation & Transfiguration of Duty as Inclination'. In the same notebook entry, he spoke of the interdependence of love and work: 'The necessary tendency of true Love to generate a feeling of Duty by increasing the sense of reality, & vice versâ feeling of Duty to generate true Love' (*CN* ii. 3026). To a shadowy self made up of half-hearted resolutions and of undirected desires and aspirations, Sara gave a much needed 'sense of Substance'. In her presence, vivid thoughts acquired forms 'of intensest Reality' (*CN* iii. 3705), a process of self-realization captured in one of Coleridge's favourite puns: outerance.[10] To be utterly deprived of this vital connection would, he believed, leave the self 'only more than a thought, because it would be a Burthen—a haunting of the daemon, Suicide' (*CN* ii. 3148).

But there were other, more pressing reasons for worshipping Sara as a symbol of the divine. During the years 1806 to 1810 the idealization of this love became a necessity of Coleridge's life because he sometimes found himself tormented by sexual desire, and frustrated by Sara's coldness towards his advances. To his notebooks he confided:

If love be the genial Sun of human nature, unkindly has he divided his rays in acting on me and [Sara]—on her poured all his Light and Splendor, & permeated my Being with his invisible Rays of Heat alone/ She shines and is *cold*, as the tropic Firefly—I dark and uncomely would better resemble the Cricket in hot ashes—my Soul at least might be considered as a Cricket eradiating the heat which gradually cinerizing the Heart produced the embery ashes, from among which it chirps, out of its hiding place.—(*CN* iii. 3379.)[11]

At Coleorton he tried to struggle against these sexual feelings, believing that

[10] For this pun, see Coleridge's marginalia on Böhme's *Works (Marginalia,* i. 637 and n.)

[11] Cf. 'Lady, to Death we're doom'd, our crime the same! / Thou, that in me thou kindledst such fierce Heat; / I, that my Heart did of a Sun so sweet / The Rays concenter to so hot a flame. / I, fascinated by an Adder's Eye, / Deaf as an Adder thou to all my Pain; / Thou obstinate in Scorn, in passion I— / I lov'd too much, too much didst thou disdain . . .' (*CN* iii. 3377.)

were the ~~usurper~~ Rebel to sit on the *Throne* of my Being, even tho' it were only that the rightful Lord of my Bosom were sleeping, soon to awake & expel the Usurper, I should feel myself as much fallen & as unworthy of her Love in any <such> tumult of Body indulged toward her, as if I had roamed, <like a Hog> in the rankest ~~Stews~~ Lanes of a ~~prostitute~~ city, battening on the loathsome offals of Harlotry / yea, the guilt would seem greater to me/   (*CN* ii. 2984.)

It is a striking feature of Coleridge's attitude, however, that such vehement defiance of the tyranny of lust coexists with a calmer, more balanced acceptance of sexual desire as an inevitable component of love. In the same entry, and immediately following upon this gesture of defiance, the persistence of desire, at times disruptive in its intensity, finds an explanation and justification in the *depth* of his feeling:

but when Love, like a Volcano beneath a sea always burning, tho' in silence, flames up in his strength at some new accession, o how can the waters but heave & roll in billows!—driven by no wind on the mere Surface, save that which their own tumult creates, but the mass is agitated from the depths, & the waves tower up as if to make room for the stormy Swelling.   (*CN* ii. 2984.)

In his struggle to idealize and unify his various feelings for Sara, Coleridge had little choice but to adopt a positive attitude towards this '*perpetual Burning*', this 'ungratified Priapism of the inward man' (*CN* iii. 3899). If our mixed nature meant that love between a man and a woman was inevitably alloyed with sexual passion, it was a comfort to reflect that it did not follow from this that lust constituted the essence of love. In illustration of this point he argued:

I offer you a cup of cold Sweet-wort instead of fine Ale—and you reject it as Insipid—it wants *Yeast*—Well! then I offer you a goblet of *Yeast*/—Pooh! it is nauseous, beastly/—/—And yet a small portion of that yeast combining with and yet concealing itself, among the sweet wort would have made the sparkling human Beverage? I leave to yourself the application.   (*CN* iii. 3873.)

In another entry, written upon waking from sleep, Coleridge carries this positive attitude towards sex even further, linking concupiscence itself to feelings of virtue and goodness. Sexual desire, at least in the form of 'that dying away or ever-subsisting vibration of it in the Heart & Chest & eyes' is 'the symbolical language of purest Love in our present Embodiment/ for if mind acts on body, the purest Impulse can introduce itself to our consciousness no otherwise than by *speaking to us* in some bodily feeling' (*CN* ii. 2495). Desire of this kind can also lead to self-betterment. In the same entry we read:

I felt strongly how apart from all impurity if I were sleeping with the Beloved these kind and pleasurable feelings would become associated with a Being *out of me*, & thereby in an almost incalculable train of consequences increase my active benevolence < = virtuous Volificence = benevolificence = *goodwilldoingness* >
   O yes, Sara! I did feel how being with you I should be so very much a better man/   (*CN* ii. 2495.)

If love is an activity of the *whole* being, the physical as well as the spiritual,[12] sexual union must have a place in the moral scheme of things. In a marginal note of 1809, written on Sara's copy of *Religio Medici*, Coleridge took issue with Sir Thomas Browne's disgust at the sexual act:

Taken by itself, no doubt, the act is both foolish, & debasing. But what a misery is contained in those words, 'taken by itself'? Are there not thoughts, & affections, & Hopes, & a *Religion* of the Heart,—that lift and sanctify all our bodily Actions where the union of the Bodies is but a language & *conversation* of united Souls?
                                                    (*Marginalia*, i. 754.)

Instead of despising the body's language, it was much more helpful to see this language as an attempt to 'interpret all the movements of the Soul'. Shall the body, he asked, 'not then imitate & symbolize that divinest movement of a FINITE Spirit—the yearning to compleat itself by Union?' (*CL* iii. 305). Unto the pure all things are pure;[13] thus, to a mind true to its elevated self, the physicality of love invited joyous celebration:

---

[12] Love has its essence in 'a divine synthesis of highest reason—and vehementest Impulse . . . vital power of Heat, & Light of Intellect' (*CN* ii. 3092).
[13] Titus 1: 15, quoted by Coleridge in a marginal note on Jakob Böhme's *Works* (*Marginalia*, i. 657).

O many, many are the seeings, hearings, & tactual Impressions of pure Love, that have a Being of their own—& to call them by the names of things unsouled and debased below even their own lowest nature by Associations accidental, and of vicious accidents, is *blasphemy*—   (*CN* iii. 3401.)

That the outward expression of love was felt by Coleridge to be an integral part of his relationship with Sara can be seen in a notebook entry written just before leaving for Coleorton: 'I know, you love me!—My reason knows it, my heart feels it/ yet still let your eyes, your hands tell me/ still say, o often & often say, My beloved! I love you/ indeed I love you/ for why should not my ears, and all my outward Being share in the Joy—the fuller my inner Being is of the sense, the more my outward organs yearn & crave for it/ O bring my whole nature into balance and harmony' (*CN* ii. 2938).

If there is something heroic about Coleridge's acceptance of his sexual feelings, the admission of such feelings was only possible because, by constant self-schooling and an enormous effort of will, he had convinced himself that they formed an essential part of one of the highest orders of moral experience. As long as he felt certain that his feelings for Sara were governed by the correct causal relationship between love and desire—'I desire because I love, & not Imagine that I love because I desire' (*CN* iii. 3284)—his Christian conscience could rest satisfied.[14] But the dynamics of love and desire were, of course, rather less simple and straightforward; and despite his later, somewhat rueful, claim that he had loved Sara in such a way as to 'feel no shame to describe to an Angel' (*CN* iii. 4006), there were aspects of his love which he did feel to be shameful, and which could be expressed only in cipher or in Greek. Of the many instances scattered throughout the notebooks during the period 1807–10, two will suffice.

[14] Similarly, to the hypothetical question, 'Does Lust call forth or occasion Love?', Coleridge answers: 'Just as much as the reek of the Marsh calls up the Sun. The sun calls up the vapor—attenuates, lifts it—it becomes a cloud—and now it is the Veil of the Divinity—the Divinity transpiercing it at once hides & declares his presence—We *see*, we are conscious of, *Light* alone; but it is Light embodied in the earthly nature, which that Light itself awoke & sublimated' (*CL* iii. 305). For a discussion of the relationship between love and lust in Coleridge's thinking, see A. J. Harding, *Coleridge and the Idea of Love*, p. 109.

In the first he is on the defensive: '*I love you* as *a man loves a w[oman]* it is true, but yet I love you' (*CN* iii. 3472 and n.; enciphered words italicized). In the second, expostulation with Sara is followed by an assertion of the oneness and spontaneity of love and desire:

Asra! I am a *man* & not only feel as a *man* but with an *intensity* I had never before no conception of—Yet there is *a something* here, O No! not here! but deeper deeper far, & yet here too, which makes the other but its symbols—even as we *see by the eyes yet know feel nothing of the eyes* while we *are seeing*.'

         (*CN* iii. 3520n.; enciphered words italicized.)

  But it was not just Coleridge's sexual feelings for Sara which strained his relationship with the Wordsworths. There was also his possessiveness, his terrible insistence that Sara love him unequivocally and without reserve. Resenting any influence which he imagined others might have over her, he came to believe that she learned from Wordsworth 'to pity & withdraw herself' from his affections. At Coleorton, in a fit of sexual jealousy he asked: 'is he not beloved, adored by two—& two such Beings—and must I not be beloved *near* him except as a Satellite?' (*CN* ii. 3148). So obsessed did Coleridge become with the idea of Wordsworth's superior attractiveness that he deceived himself into believing that Sara and Wordsworth were lovers.[15] Although he was soon able to recognize this belief as the offspring of a distempered and miserable fancy, he was irrational enough to voice his suspicions a year after leaving Coleorton in a letter to Wordsworth. This letter, written some time in the early summer of 1808, is now lost, but we can reconstruct Coleridge's grievances from two surviving drafts of Wordsworth's reply.[16] Of the charges laid against him by Coleridge concerning his relationship with Sara, Wordsworth did not deign to say more than that these 'most lawless thoughts' and 'wildest fancies' could only have come from a man in a

---

[15] Kathleen Coburn gives a succinct account of the whole episode at Coleorton, and Coleridge's later reflections upon it, in *CN* ii. 2975 n.; see also *CN* ii. 2975, 3148, and *CN* iii. 3328.

[16] *MY* i. 239–45. Further clues as to the contents of this letter can be found in *CN* iii. 3304 and n.

'lamentably insane state of mind' (*MY* i. 240). Wordsworth then passed on to the 'keystone' of their supposed offences against Coleridge: 'viz. our cruelty, a hope in infusing into Sara's mind the notion that your attachment to her has been the curse of all your happiness' (*MY* i. 245). The very opposite was true, Wordsworth claimed; certainly, when speaking to Sara on this subject, Mary and Dorothy did not deny that 'your passion was a source to you of much misery; but they always told her that it was a gross error to appropriate this to herself; they laboured to convincing her of this' (*MY* i. 245).

Such assurances must have been welcome to Coleridge, but he cannot have been satisfied with Wordsworth's account of the reasons which Mary and Dorothy enjoined on Sara, telling her 'that your mind [?must] have had such a determination to some object or other, that she was not therefore the cause, but merely to use your own distinction the innocent occasion of this unhappiness, that in fact as far as *you* were concerned she might congratulate herself; had this passion fixed upon a [?] of a different kind what might you not have suffered?' (*MY* i. 245). While it must have been painful to learn that Mary and Dorothy viewed his desire for an object of love as inevitable and to be regretted, it no doubt hurt much more to learn of their belief that, while it was fortunate for him (given his weakness in this matter), it was bad luck for Sara that his love should have lighted on her. In fact, if Wordsworth's letter reflects the feelings of the Grasmere circle, one can only credit Coleridge's claim that they underrated the very special nature of his bond with Sara. It is possible that Wordsworth never sent the letter (*MY* i. 239, n. 1), but even if this were so, the attitude of mind displayed in its tactlessness and condescension had no doubt been felt by Coleridge in countless other ways. Furthermore, he had understandable grounds for resenting Wordsworth's insensitivity to the frustration and hopelessness of his love for Sara. Six years earlier, during a period of illness and intense personal anguish about his own unhappy marriage, he had urged Wordsworth to overcome his remaining scruples concerning Annette Vallon and 'conclude on marrying' Mary Hutchinson (*CN* iii. 3304 and n.). That marriage had proved to be a 'blessed' one, but the prosperity it brought seemed to

Coleridge to have erased Wordsworth's memory of what it was like to feel shut out from the prospect of happiness. Whereas Wordsworth was once, Coleridge wrote, 'unhappy dissatisfied, full of craving', he was 'now all calm & attached', thanks to 'Love & Friendship'; but this happiness had only brought 'contempt for the moral comforts of others' (*CN* iii. 3991).

The experience of living together at Coleorton was a distressing and chastening one for all concerned, but particularly so for Coleridge. Feeling cast out and forlorn, debarred from any prospect of bettering his miserable condition, he spent a good part of the next eighteen months in London, brooding on past injuries. Some of these were wounds 'too deep & broad for the vis medicatrix of mortal Life to fill wholly up with new flesh'. Even though healed, they 'yet left an unsightly Scar which too often spite of our best wishes lax & of diminished vitality opened anew at other derangements & Indispositions of the moral Health' (*CN* iii. 3309).

Nevertheless, a reconciliation of sorts was achieved,[17] and Coleridge left London for the Lakes, arriving at the Wordsworths' new house, Allan Bank, on the first of September 1808, 'in tolerable health and better spirits' (*MY* i. 270). An amicable separation from his wife had taken place,[18] he felt relatively free of his addiction, and the notebooks suggest that, during the first few weeks at least, Coleridge believed his love for Sara was returned.[19] During this time, he made preparations for *The Friend*, sending out letters advertising his new periodical as an instrument which would enable him to play off his 'whole Head & Heart . . . as from the main pipe of the

---

[17] Catherine Clarkson seems to have played a major role in this. Looking back in 1813 she saw how fragile the reconciliation had been; see *The Correspondence of Henry Crabb Robinson with the Wordsworth Circle (1808–1866)*, ed. Edith J. Morley (2 vols; Oxford, 1927), i. 75.

[18] Mrs Coleridge visited Allan Bank with the children, and on one of these visits stayed more than a week; according to Dorothy, they saw each other 'upon friendly terms' (*MY* i. 280).

[19] On 9 September, he wrote of his gratitude to her, adding triumphantly, 'O well may I be grateful—She loves me—*me*, who—O noble dear generous [Sara]—Herein my Love, which in *degree* cannot be surpassed, is yet in *kind* inferior to yours!' (*CN* iii. 3370). This was not the first time he had felt his love reciprocated; see *CN* i. 1601 and *CN* ii. 2036.

Fountain': it was to be the pipe through which the 'whole reservoir' of his knowledge was to be channelled (*CL* iii. 126, 131). This image of *The Friend* as a pipe was the public equivalent of a more private image associated with Sara Hutchinson: that of a second pipe which gives sound to a silent organ.[20] In 1804, he noted that the huge 'but *dumb!*' organ pipe at Exeter was only made to speak when the organist made 'a second Pipe precisely alike, & placed it by it' (*CN* ii. 1972). Two years later at Coleorton, this cathedral organ provided Coleridge with a poignant image of his creative dependence on Sara:

I have, like the Exeter Cathedral Organ, a pipe of far-sounding Music in its construction, yet is it dumb, a gilded Tube, till the Sister pipe be placed in correspondence/ O *Beloved!*   (*CN* ii. 2998.)

Coleridge's punning reference to his solitary self as an organ's 'gilded Tube', arising as it does out of his longing for union with Sara, springs from a richly suggestive awareness of the link between language and desire. In the same entry, in a discussion of the inadequacy of words to feelings—'of the symbol to the Being'—Coleridge's yearning to transcend linguistic boundaries finds its analogue in the lover's frustrated longing for complete and perfect union with the object of his desire:

Words—what are they but a subtle *matter?* and the meanness of Matter must they have, & the Soul must pine in them, even as the Lover who can press kisses only [on] the garment of one indeed beloved/ O bear witness my Soul! bear witness the permanence of my Being!—even such a feeling must accompany the strictest union, the nearest kiss, that can be—it is still at once the Link & the Wall of Separation/ O what then are Words, but articulated Sighs of a Prisoner heard from his Dungeon! powerful only as they express their utter impotence!   (*CN* ii. 2998.)

Just as the spirit is imprisoned in a web of words, love's soul is imprisoned in sexual desire, so much so that even the most intimate physical union is an inadequate expression of the

---

[20] Harding discusses this pipe image in *Coleridge and the Idea of Love*, p. 83; see also *CN* ii. 2998 n.

lovers' profound yearning for each other; in the two realms of word and body, the wish for transcendence can never be more than a wish. At the same time, however, the entry is a supremely ironic endorsement of language and the sexual act, for no matter how far they both, as external signs, fall short of embodying perfect forms for the spirit, they none the less afford a 'Link' to the ideal.

It was a fitting symbol of the vital connection for Coleridge between love and intelligibility that Sara should become his amanuensis for *The Friend*, but again, as at Coleorton, the obsessive importance he attached to his love seriously unbalanced his relationship with the wider circle. No longer yearning to be part of the whole, he regarded the Wordsworths as competitors for Sara's love and affection, and the poetry he wrote at this time reflects the uneasiness he felt in the Allan Bank household. In one poem he spoke of himself as a 'captive guest/ Some royal prisoner at his conqueror's feast/ An alien's restless mood but half concealing' ('The Visionary Hope', *PW* i. 416).[21] Still suspicious that his private affairs were constantly overlooked by watchful, conspiratorial eyes,[22] he included Sara in his sense of imprisonment:

> Two wedded Hearts, if e'er were such
> Imprison'd in adjoining cells
> Across whose thin partition wall
> The Builder left one narrow rent,
> And there most content in discontent
> A Joy with itself at strife,
> Die into an intenser Life/
>
> (*CN* iii. 3379)

Nor had Coleridge overcome his sexual jealousy of Wordsworth. Not long after his arrival at Allan Bank, a reproach to Sara for her half-hearted commitment to him is inevitably

---

[21] Soon after arriving at Allan Bank, Coleridge mused in his notebooks: 'Assuredly, a Thrush or Blackbird encaged in London is a far less shocking Spectacle, its Encagement a more venial Defect of just Feeling than (which yet one so often sees) a Bird in a gay Cage in the heart of the Country—yea, as if at once to mock both the poor Prisoner, and its kind Mother, Nature, in a cage hung up in a Tree' (*CN* iii. 3359); see also *CN* iii. 3539.

[22] Coleridge had accused the Wordsworths of reading Sara's letters (*MY* i. 244–5).

accompanied by reflections upon her greater devotion to Wordsworth:

You never sate with or near me ten minutes in your life without shewing a restlessness, & a thought of *going*, &c, for at least 5 minutes out of the 10.   (*CN* iii. 3383.)

Something incomprehensible to me in Sara's feelings concerning [. . .] and her <evidently greater pleasure in> gazing on [Wordsworth], supposing a real preference of Love to me,—But how much of her Love is Pity? Humane Dread of inflicting Anguish? Dignified Sense of Consistency & Faith? Perchance, I love enough for both.   (*CN* iii. 3386.)

Other entries capture the desolating intensity and destructiveness of the insistence upon a devotion and love equal to his own:

In the Anger of agony I could almost bid [Sara] look at herself, & into herself, & then ask whether *she* beloved constantly has a right to compare others with me, & love them better because they are more vigorous, or more this thing or the other—Love *more*!—O blasphemy! As if in the Love, I am speaking of, there were any *degrees*—as if more than *one* COULD in this sense be LOVED.   (*CN* iii. 3442.)

And even at those moments when he felt confident of her love, he yet longed 'to make her already loving me love me to that unutterableness, that impatience at the not enoughness of dependence, with which I love her!' (*CN* ii. 3148.)

Cherishing mutual love as 'the best Emblem & Foretaste of Heaven' (*CN* iii. 3284), Coleridge refused to acknowledge (or was unable to see) the danger of demanding too much. If reciprocity was that 'which alone gives a *stability* to love', then it was not (he insisted) 'mere selfishness, that impels all kind natures to desire, that there should be some one human Being, to whom they are *most* dear/ it is because they wish some one being to exist, who shall be the resting-place & summit of their Love! & this in human nature is not *possible*, except the two affections coincide' (*Marginalia*, i. 754).

But to be regarded as Coleridge's 'SUPREME—a *One the highest*' (*Marginalia*, i. 752) must have been an intolerable strain on Sara, for inevitably there were times when she failed to live up to the philosopher's religious and mystical idea of her. One such occasion was at Allan Bank, when Sara shocked and frightened Coleridge by wearing an 'unbecoming Cap'. So shaken was he by her unfamiliar appearance that he could not contain his distress and suffering; nor could he forgive her for falling so far short of his ideal: 'If she believed one 10th part of what is the Fact, she would <not> play these tricks with her angel countenance. It is not, cannot be, other than morally culpable' (*CN* iii. 3404). The failure of the real and symbolical Sara to coalesce at this moment reveals the inherent instability of his worship of her as his God. Small wonder that, shortly after this incident, she appears to have responded to the endearment 'My Angel' with 'Nay, I am no Angel; have no wings, no glory; but flesh & Blood' (*CN* iii. 3406).

At other times, overwhelmed by feelings of his own unworthiness, and seeing (or imagining) all too vividly Wordsworth's superior attractiveness to women, Coleridge clutched at straws, hoping that 'love so intense might demand love—otherwise, who could be secure?' Nor in calmer and more rational moods did he derive much comfort from the certainty that, should Wordsworth behave 'even partly' as Sara's lover, she would inevitably respond with a greater degree of love than that bestowed upon him (*CN* iii. 3148 f. 46, f. 47). In gloomier moods, he felt that her love for him sprang from the knowledge 'that by no one else [is] *or can she expect to be loved so well*' (*CN* iii. 3534 n.; enciphered words italicized).

A very vivid account from Coleridge's daughter of what it was like to be in close contact with him at this period illustrates the way in which the pattern of his feelings— obsessive, jealous, and morbidly sensitive to injury—extended beyond Sara Hutchinson to include all those he loved. Sara Coleridge was only six when she was taken to Allan Bank in 1808, Coleridge's plan being that she should become 'rosier and hardier' during her absence from her mother. It is unlikely that anything of this kind took place, for many years later it still caused Sara some pain to look back upon that time:

I think my dear father was anxious that I should learn to love him and the Wordsworths and their children, and not cling so exclusively to my mother, and all around me at home. He was therefore much annoyed when, on my mother's coming to Allan Bank, I flew to her, and wished not to be separated from her any more. I remember his shewing displeasure to me, and accusing me of want of affection. I could not understand why. The young Wordsworths came in and caressed him. I sate benumbed; for truly nothing does so freeze affection as the breath of jealousy. The sense that you have done very wrong, or at least given great offence, you know not how or why—that you are dunned for some payment of love or feeling which you know not how to produce or to demonstrate on a sudden, chills the heart, and fills it with perplexity and bitterness. My father reproached me, and contrasted my coldness with the childish caresses of the little Wordsworths. I slunk away, and hid myself in the wood behind the house . . .[23]

Coleridge's resentment of Sara's attachment to her mother, his jealous desire that she fasten her affections exclusively on him and, most painful of all, his reproaches and accusations: all these fit the pattern of his love for Sara Hutchinson.

According to Dorothy, everyone, including Coleridge, was relieved when Sara Hutchinson left Allan Bank in spring 1810. She had done what she could to drive him on with the work, and although she had been 'the cause of the continuance of The Friend so long', it was difficult to believe that the periodical, now at a standstill, would have gone on if she had stayed. Coleridge was tired, and seemed grateful that there was nobody now to 'teize' him on with the work (*MY* i. 398).

Dorothy and the rest of the household were glad Sara was gone because Coleridge had 'harassed and agitated her mind continually'. He had wanted, so Dorothy claimed, 'to have her about him as his own, as one devoted to him', and so exhausting were the demands placed upon her that he did her health 'perpetual injury' (*MY* i. 398–400). The notebooks establish the corrosive force of Coleridge's emotional demands, and there can be little doubt that his extremely erratic working habits—sometimes dictating under extreme pressure (*MY* i. 390–1)—undermined Sara's already precarious

---

[23] *Memoir and Letters of Sara Coleridge*, ed. her daughter (2 vols.; London, 1873), i. 18–19.

health.[24] What is revealing, however, is Dorothy's confident conclusion that Coleridge's love for Sara was 'no more than a fanciful dream'; for not only did he seem to have no desire to make her happy, but, 'when she stood in the way of other gratifications it was all over' (*MY* i. 400).

The idealism which Coleridge considered the best part of his love—the schooling of his feelings to coalesce with the *idea* of Sara rather than with the loved object herself—was no doubt responsible for the excesses and oddities of his behaviour. It almost certainly caused the selfishness Dorothy described, for Coleridge was so mastered by a need to love and give of himself that he took no heed (as Wordsworth complained) of the feelings or needs of the object of his devotion. Such, indeed, was his compulsion to love, that it seemed to those at Allan Bank that it was not Sara *qua* Sara that he loved, but the very idea of loving and being loved in return. Whatever the truth of this (and it does not seem improbable given how little we actually learn about Sara from Coleridge) his idealism strained the relationship beyond what it could bear, leaving him in the end with feelings not all that far removed from Dorothy's. In the love poetry written after 1810, we find him constantly puzzling over the problem of whether his love for Sara had been fact or phantom, painful reality or wishful dream fulfilment:

> Uncertain both what it *had* been,
> And if by error lost, or luck;
> And what it was . . .
>
>   ('The Improvisatore', *PW* i. 467)[25]

---

[24] From the spring of 1808 onwards, family letters were full of anxious references to Sara's health. See *MY* i. *passim* and WLL, Monkhouse and Hutchinson.

[25] See also 'Phantom or Fact: A Dialogue in Verse' and 'Love's Apparition and Evanishment' (*PW* i. 484–5, 488–9). I. A. Richards, in 'Coleridge's Other Poems' gives a very perceptive reading of the poem 'Constancy to an Ideal Object' (*Poetries: Their Media and Ends*, ed. Trevor Eaton (The Hague and Paris, 1974), 122–3).

3
False Starts and New Beginnings

> Joanna had a letter from Sara yesterday . . . there are
> two numbers of the 'Friend' written & I suppose you will
> receive [another] one on tuesday. Sara says she has some
> hopes as he has one before hand, & that he is at present
> quite in a writing que, but that he likes to write any thing
> but what he ought, & yet he always pretends he is doing
> his duty. I shall be very sorry if he does not continue this
> work for it will certainly be the ruin of him.

> Mary Monkhouse to Tom Monkhouse, 6 August 1809

THE 'tolerable health and better spirits' which marked
Coleridge's entry into Allan Bank lasted long enough to get
him started in his preparations for *The Friend*. By December he
was sending Prospectuses to friends, boasting of his renewed
vigour, and promising to make up for past inactivity. New
Year's Day seemed an appropriate time to commemorate this
new beginning, and accordingly it was chosen as the
publication date for Number 1. Although no essay had yet
been written, Coleridge wrote to Thomas Poole, 'Begin to
count my Life, as a Friend of your's, from 1 January, 1809'
(*CL* iii. 130); and in a letter to Sir George Beaumont we read,
'Decide on my moral and intellectual character from the
products of the year, 1809' (*CL* iii. 145).

Coleridge was determined that *The Friend* should be distributed
as a weekly newspaper. More specifically, he wanted his
periodical to be modelled upon William Cobbett's *Political
Register*: *The Friend* was, he insisted, to be a sixteen-page octavo
weekly pamphlet, stamped and circulated in exactly the same
way as the *Political Register* (*CL* iii. 196–7).[1]

---

[1] The only difference was that each number of *The Friend* was to cost a shilling,
twopence more than the *Political Register* (*CL* iii. 141–2).

In a sense, nothing could be odder than this decision. Not only was the newspaper trade rather disreputable,[2] but Coleridge coupled his preference for the newspaper format with a firm rejection of news writing. The awkwardness of matching popular form and philosophical content is freely admitted by him in his opening number. *The Friend* is, he wrote, 'embarassed by the very circumstances, that discriminate the plan and purposes of the present weekly paper from those of its periodical brethren, as well as from its more dignified literary relations, which come forth at once and in full growth from their parents' (*TF* ii. 5). As for imitating the *Political Register*, Coleridge detested everything this paper stood for: its partisan politics, written 'under the warp of Heat & Prejudice' (*CL* iii. 142), its calumnies and its demagogic tone.[3] To prospective subscribers, he proudly declared that he had no intention of writing 'for the *Multitude*; but for those, who by Rank, or Fortune, or official Situation, or Talents and Habits of Reflection, are to *influence* the Multitude' (*CL* iii. 143). It is clear from his letters, however, that contempt for Cobbett's populism did not prevent him from viewing the *Political Register* as a powerful rival. An astute observer of public opinion, Coleridge did not underestimate the pervasiveness of Cobbett's influence—the fact that he was read and admired, not just by the working classes, but by all sections of society.[4] On board the ship bound for Malta in 1804, he had written to Stuart, asking him to forward two papers during his absence: *The Courier* and the *Political Register* (*CL* iii. 1135). A year later, he reflected on the 'Sorrow & national Degradation, that 1000 such men as Sir A[lexander] B[all] should *think* COBBETT a national Benefactor' (*CN* ii. 2578). Thus, it was principally Cobbett's influence on

---

[2] The hostility aroused by newspapers in the governing class is discussed by A. Aspinall in *Politics and the Press c. 1780–1850* (London, 1949), 9–12. For a humorous account of Coleridge's own prejudice against newspapers, see *BL* i. 183.

[3] 'He applies to the Passion[s that] are gratified by Curiosity, sharp & often calumnious Personality, the Politics and the Events of the Day, and the names and characters of notorious Contemporaries' (*CL* iii. 141).

[4] The *Edinburgh Review* claimed that Cobbett had 'more influence . . . than all the other journalists put together'. This influence was mainly on the 'middling classes of the community . . . that most important and most independent class of society, which stands just above the lowest' (*ER* x. 386 (July 1807)).

statesmen which prompted Coleridge to adopt his marketing procedures. *The Friend* was to have all the advantages of a stamped newspaper, passing 'into all parts & corners of the Empire without expence or trouble' to its readers (*CL* iii. 173). Although he emphasized that, in terms of its subject matter, *The Friend* was *not* a newspaper, he was none the less adamant that it arrive in the guise of a newspaper, along with the other newspapers of the day (*CL* iii. 165). To Stuart, and to other friends, Coleridge even went so far as to boast that the 'paramount *Object*' of *The Friend* lay in strangling the bad passions awakened by Cobbett's prose (*CL* iii. 141, 143).

Reactions to the newspaper plan varied. Jeffrey thought the idea entirely inappropriate, both in terms of the readers it would attract, and the kinds of expectation which they would inevitably bring with them: 'There is a certain hardness and brilliancy expected in such works—and I am afraid you will be too moral and enthusiastic for the worldlings by whom you must flourish' (WL MS A/Jeffrey/3). Another subscriber wrote to say that he would prefer to patronize 'some finished folio—the ripened harvest of the last Ten years'. A weekly newspaper did not seem suited either to Coleridge's own dignity or to the distinct dignities of coming forward as 'Poet & Philosopher, Moralist & Politician' (WL MS A/ Coulson/1).

Thomas Clarkson's objections sprang from more practical considerations. At an early stage in Coleridge's business arrangements, he advised him 'to drop all weekly publications, & to make them monthly like the Athenaeum', giving as his reason Coleridge's 'vagabond circumstances', his tendency to be 'driven from one settled Plan to another' (WL MS A/ Clarkson/11). By spring 1809 he was writing: 'I wish, with all my Heart, that you had written a Volume annually, and had had nothing to do with the Stamp Office, or with agents to collect money' (WL MS A/Clarkson/12). And there was always, as Thomas Poole and other friends pointed out, the remoteness of Grasmere from any large town, and the extreme irregularity of the post (WL MS A/Poole/2).

After some initial hesitation, Stuart eventually gave his full assent to the newspaper plan.[5] Although with a monthly pamphlet, 'there would be less risk or loss in printing a number on speculation, and . . . the inconvenience of a Newspaper in giving Bonds &c would be avoided', he agreed with Coleridge that 'the Newspaper has this great convenience', 'that one man can put your whole publication into the Post office, & in a minute say,—there;—all your Customers are served, served regularly & infallibly.' (*TF* ii. 480.) Accordingly, towards the end of December, he started to instruct Coleridge in how to begin. For a newspaper, the provisions of the act of Parliament were 'very numerous and must be observed'. The paper had to be stamped, and the printer and publisher were required to give security for advertisements and libels. Knowing Coleridge's tendency to despond, and anxious to reassure him, Stuart wrote encouragingly: 'This will frighten you by the Vastness of the Business; but it may all be done in as short a time as I have been writing.' (*TF* ii. 482.)

In less than a week, however, Stuart's enthusiasm for the newspaper format had cooled; reporting to Coleridge that Thomas Clarkson thought 'it should not be a Newspaper' but a pamphlet, he revealed that, for his own part, he could now no longer decide which plan would be best for Coleridge's purposes (*TF* ii. 485). Coleridge was dismayed by this sudden change of heart, and on 11 February started a letter to Stuart, protesting that *The Friend* 'was & I trust, *is* to be a *Newspaper*' (*CL* iii. 179). Fortunately, his protests were interrupted by a letter from a printer and stationer at Penrith, called John Brown. Coleridge immediately set off across the Kirkstone Pass to interview Brown, and returned with the conviction that he was 'both able & willing to print & publish the Friend' (*CL* iii. 180). Thus, the two-month-old problem of having neither printer nor publisher was solved, and Coleridge was now free to act independently of his London advisers.

Stuart's sudden loss of confidence can be traced to a letter from Southey, warning him of the risks of allowing Coleridge

---

[5] Rooke overstates the case when she claims that 'Stuart first opposed Coleridge's newspaper plan' (*TF* i. xliii); see Coleridge's letter to Stuart, and Griggs's footnote (*CL* iii. 231–2).

to embark on a newspaper plan. As he saw it, the insuperable difficulty lay in

the unlikelihood, or rather the impossibility, of his carrying on any periodical work with regularity. If his habits were regular enough, his health is not, unless he began with a large stock in hand, which certainly he will not do. My advice to him is that he publish a number of half-crown, or five shillings worth, whenever he is ready with it. A 'This day is published' in the newspapers will then be sufficient prospectus, and it will find its way with the other periodicals . . . I have a strong fear—almost a conviction—that, in any other shape, the thing would soon drop.   (*LLP*, 403.)

Southey wrote with conviction because he was shocked by the unseemly haste with which Coleridge had produced *The Friend*'s Prospectus, carrying it 'wet from the pen to the printer, without consulting anybody, or giving himself time for consideration' (Warter, ii. 120). With a weekly deadline every number of *The Friend* would, he believed, be produced in the same hectic, slapdash way.

While Southey was right in his prediction that *The Friend* would be the result of last-minute efforts, he failed to see what was so clear to Dorothy: that Coleridge needed the prompt of a deadline. Commenting on the fact that the Prospectus was hurried out without a single essay ready, she wrote: 'it was the only way for him. I believe he could not have made the beginning unspurred by a necessity which is now created by the promises therein made.' (*MY* i. 282.)[6] Coleridge was an extremely erratic and irregular worker, often doing nothing at all, but capable under pressure of achieving quite astonishing results.[7] By promising his public an essay a week, he was, as Dorothy saw, trying to help himself. Convinced that he lacked

---

[6] John Morgan, an old friend from *Watchman* days, also thought Coleridge's newspaper plan 'admirably calculated' to his 'habits of thinking and acting' (WL MS A/Morgan/2).

[7] Towards the end of *The Friend*'s existence, Dorothy described Coleridge's irregular working habits to Lady Beaumont: 'By the great quantity of labour that he has performed since the commencement of the Friend you will judge that he has upon the whole been very industrious; and you will hardly believe me when I tell you that there have been weeks and weeks when he has not composed a line. The fact is that he either does a great deal or nothing at all . . . He has written a whole Friend more than once in two days.' (*MY* i. 390–1.)

an organizing centre to his personality—an 'essential something' within (*CL* ii. 1102)—he felt the need to depend upon
'something more *apparently* & believedly subject to regular &
certain Laws' than his own will (*CN* ii. 2672). A weekly
deadline would hang weights upon his wayward habits—his
'Want of Perseverance' and 'constitutional Indolence' (*TF*
ii. 16)—and drive him on with the task of writing. It was for
this reason that he spoke of his newspaper plan in the
Prospectus as suited to the nature of his mind, 'both in its
Strength and in its Weakness' (*TF* ii. 17). Thus, when friends
like Southey preached to him, 'no promised time, no promised
quantity, no promised anything' (Warter, ii. 120), they were
in fact denying Coleridge his principal method of getting on
with the work.

The newspaper plan provided Coleridge with other in-
centives too. The weekly essay did not require the same degree
of sustained or systematic thinking as a quarterly, or even
monthly, publication; it also offered Coleridge informal and
frequent access to his readers. There was no need to dress his
opinions in the formal anonymity of the larger periodicals,
and a writer of distinctive personality could quickly establish
a reputation and following for himself. Most important of all
was the open-endedness of the journal format, allowing
Coleridge to gauge his readers' reactions as the weeks passed.
Fearful of rebuff, uncertain of himself and of his readers, he
was reluctant to publish his opinions in the binding and
definitive form of a book; so, rather than make a single,
irreversible appearance in print, he opted for a strategy of
reconnaissance, a series of tentative and cautious manœuvres.
The language of the Prospectus reveals his hidden purposes in
its metaphors of stealth and insinuation. He speaks of
'winning, instead of forcing' his way, and of hoping 'to disarm
the Mind of those Feelings, which preclude Conviction by
Contempt, and, as it were, fling the Door in the Face of
Reasoning by a *Presumption* of its Absurdity' (*TF* ii. 17).
Anxious to defuse hostile criticism, Coleridge sees his weekly
essays as gradual stages in a process of attrition: 'Supposing
Truth on my Side, the Shock of the first Day might be so far
lessened by Reflections of the succeeding Days, as to procure

for my next Week's Essay a less hostile Reception, than it would have met with, had it been only the next Chapter of a present volume.' (*TF* ii. 17.)

Stuart was later to accuse Coleridge of vanity, claiming that his 'desire of instant circulation' arose 'from a feeling unworthy of [him], a desire of producing on the public and receiving on [him]self an instant impression' (*TF* ii. 493). Coleridge strenuously denied that he took any interest in the opinions people entertained of his work (*CL* iii. 232), but there is little doubt that he hoped the difficult process of writing would be eased by encouraging responses from his readers. Five years earlier he had written:

I own myself no self-subsisting Mind—I know, I feel, that I am weak—apt to faint away inwardly, self-deserted & bereft of the confidence in my own powers—and that the approbation & Sympathy of good & intelligent men is my Sea-breeze, without which I should languish from Morn to evening; a very Trade-wind to me, in which my Bark drives on regularly & lightly.

(*CL* ii. 1054–5.)

In the Prospectus too, he admitted that he wanted *The Friend* to be 'in the best Sense of the Word, popular'. It is not clear in what sense he meant 'popular', but he certainly sought approval, and even admiration, from his readers; Southey believed that 'unless a sudden popularity should come upon him, like sunshine, a very few weeks' struggle against inaction will fret and fever him into inability' (*LLP*, pp. 403–4). The prospect of eventually achieving a large circulation may also have been at the back of his mind, for he was fascinated by the speed and power of newspapers; in 1800 he marvelled at the way in which copy written at midnight would 'before 12 hours is over have perhaps 5 or 6,000 Readers!' (*CL* i. 569).

When Coleridge came to write the Prospectus, he cast it in the form of an extract from an intimate letter, a ruse designed to cover over the 'indelicacy' of speaking of himself 'to Strangers and to the Public' (*CL* iii. 151). Authorial sincerity is *The Friend*'s point of pride. There are to be no masks in Coleridge's periodical, no imaginary editors—just an author speaking directly to his readers, as though they were his

dearest friends. This posture of uninhibited fellowship annoyed
Southey. The Prospectus looked to him 'too much like what it
intends to be, talks confidently to the public about what the
public cares not a curse for, and has about it a sort of unmanly
humblefication, which is not sincere, which the very object of
the paper gives the lie to' (Warter, ii. 120). The charge of
humbug was provoked by Coleridge's uncanny ability to be
both humble and arrogant at the same time; for the
Prospectus is an amusing sleight of hand in which personal
weaknesses take on the aspect of virtues. Confessing to a large
number of 'unrealized Schemes' and a mass of 'miscellaneous
Fragments', none of which had been reduced 'to a regular
Form', he attributed this lack of productivity to an 'Over-
activity of Thought', and the being tempted onward 'by an
increasing Sense of the Imperfection of my Knowledge, and
by the Conviction, that, in Order fully to comprehend and
develope any one Subject, it was necessary that I should make
myself Master of some other, which again as regularly
involved a third, and so on, with an ever-widening Horizon'
(*TF* ii. 16). The self-criticism forms part of the self-promotion:
this is why there is no contradiction in the fact that, while
Southey thought the Prospectus a piece of insincere 'humblefication', Francis Jeffrey accused it of 'presumptuousness'.
Coleridge had everything to gain from adopting a humble
posture as an opening gambit: knowing that some of his
closest friends had lost faith in his ability to achieve anything
of importance, and fully aware of his reputation for wasted
talents, he was unwilling to pass up the opportunity of scoring
full points for self-knowledge. At the same time, however, it is
not surprising that he should come out in favour of himself, for
he was anxious to set himself up in a position of authority *vis-
à-vis* his readers;[8] but that he should do this by way of
emphasizing his faults, and then appearing as an apologist for
them, might well be considered as the very height of
presumption.

   Jeffrey's response to the parcel of Prospectuses he received

---

[8] Coleridge confided to Stuart that the letter form of the Prospectus helped him to
establish the grounds of his fitness for writing *The Friend* (*CL* iii. 151).

was refreshingly blunt—exactly what we might expect from a perfect worldling. What he found 'bordering on arrogance' in the Prospectus was the reactionary resolution Coleridge had formed 'of subverting all prevailing opinions and *forcing* us back to the taste and philosophy of the 16th century'. This predilection for elder writers would incur ridicule and contempt, for there could be no doubt, he briskly maintained, 'that Samuel Johnson was a much better reasoner than Hooker [,] and Burke than Jeremy Taylor—it would be strange indeed if it were otherwise' (WL MS A/Jeffrey/4).[9] This antiquarianism was not the only aspect of the plan which Jeffrey disliked. In general, it seemed that Coleridge took himself and his project far too seriously: 'you should try to help being affected . . . I do not like *"year long* absences" "speculative gloom" "moral impulses" and several other phrases in your Prospectus—It certainly has too much solemnity and pretension' (WL MS A/Jeffrey/3).

When Coleridge attempted to defend himself, Jeffrey wrote back reassuring him that he was 'really interested' in *The Friend*'s success; in fact, so great was his interest that he immediately took it upon himself to launch into yet another warning about the pit-falls of swelling the moral trumpet: 'you should not seem so awfully impressed with the importance of your task—nor so perfectly assured that you are right' (WL MS A/Jeffrey 4). Instead of seeking to achieve the impossible, authors ought to rest content with a more realistic view of their trade, resigning themselves to the inevitable limitations of their readers:

If we amuse people—and give exercise to their understandings and some play to their good affections we do quite enough—and more than most writers do—as to reforming the wicked or teaching taste and right opinions to noodles and blockheads—it is a pretty vision but no project of a waking man—I think more soberly of these things—unless indeed you have the sort of mind which can only be roused to exertion by some illusion of enthusiasm . . .

(WL MS A/Jeffrey/4.)

[9] Coleridge's later account of this correspondence with Jeffrey is given in *IS*, pp. 296–7. For the text of Jeffrey's letters to Coleridge, see my article 'Jeffrey and Coleridge: Four Unpublished Letters', *The Wordsworth Circle*, 18 (Winter, 1987), 39–45.

That Jeffrey was absolutely right about the kind of mind he was dealing with was something Coleridge did not deny. In fact, he even went so far as to defend himself by saying that it was impossible 'to succeed in such a work unless at the commencement of it there be a quickening and throb in the pulse of Hope'. What he *did* find cutting was the charge of arrogance. He protested: 'surely to advance as a Teacher, and in the very act to declare yourself inferior to those whom you propose to teach, is incongruous; and must disgust a pure mind by it's evident hypocrisy' (*CL* iii. 150). This was not to be his last word on the subject. Provoked by Jeffrey's criticisms, he dedicated the second half of Number 2 of *The Friend* to an extended discussion of the grounds on which an author can be accused of literary arrogance (*TF* ii. 32–6).

Would to Heaven that the Verdict to be passed on my Labours depended on those who least needed them! The Water Lily in the midst of Waters lifts up its' broad Leaves, and expands its' Petals at the first pattering of the Shower, and rejoices in the Rain with a quicker Sympathy, than the parched Shrub in the sandy Desart.

(*TF* ii. 75.)

As readers of *The Friend* we are sometimes cajoled but more often bullied by Coleridge's projections of an entire range of reader-performance. At one end of the spectrum stands the ideal reader, the reader most like Coleridge himself, upon whom instruction falls in delightful excess. As the image of the water lily implies, the surest indication that one belongs to this class of readers is a keen sense of affinity with the author. Conversely, to stand in a critical relation to the author and his text is to be ranked amongst the lowest and most needy, a parched shrub in the sandy desert.

Coleridge's fascination with the reading process, and his insistence on the active role of the reader in the process of understanding has been well documented in recent commentaries.[10] Much of the thinking on this subject has, however, interpreted Coleridge's emphasis on reader activity as an

[10] One of the best accounts is that given by Paul Hamilton in *Coleridge's Poetics* (Oxford, 1983), 1–2, 15, 20–4, 80, 112–21.

aspect of his liberalism and modernism, without really examining the kinds of activity to which he invites us as readers.[11] The contrasting images of the water lily and the desert shrub are a case in point. Here, by directing attention to the dynamics of the reading process, Coleridge helps us to become more self-conscious readers, but the effect of this new self-consciousness is hardly liberating, for it places the critical reader at the bottom of an hierarchical structure, where even the highest form of response (that of the water lily) is nevertheless a response of the sustained to the sustainer.

If the act of setting up as an author necessarily involved one in assuming the role of sustainer and instructor, then the reader must conduct himself accordingly as the recipient of knowledge. The reversal of these roles, where the reader finds himself appealed to by the author as an infallible judge, was one of the vices of the age, for if the reader really possessed those excellencies, 'to what purpose is he a Reader, unless, perhaps, to remind himself of his own superiority?' (*TF* ii. 86.) Coleridge's insistence on the gap between author and reader (usually presented through the analogy of doctor and patient), and his much vaunted refusal to pander to the reader's vanity, formed an inevitable part of the seriousness with which he viewed his task of inculcating right and true principles for his generation. If such an insistence on authorial superiority exposed him to the charge of arrogance, then he appealed to the inherent absurdity of proceeding with his task in any humbler fashion:

To a sincere and sensible mind, it cannot but be disgusting to find an Author writing on Subjects, to the investigation of which he professes to have devoted the greater portion of his Life, and yet appealing to all his Readers promiscuously, as his full and competent judges, and thus soliciting their favour by a mock modesty, which either convicts him of gross hypocrisy or the most absurd presumption. For what can be conceived at once more absurd and presumptuous, than for a man to write and publish Books for the instruction of those who are wiser than himself, more learned and more judicious! Humility like all other virtues, must exist in Harmony with Truth.   (*TF* ii. 278.)

---

[11] See Timothy Corrigan, *Coleridge, Language and Criticism* (Athens, 1982), 9–35.

Thus, it is not the author who asserts his rightful authority who is guilty of arrogance, but he who addresses his reader as a superior, for 'with whomsoever we play the Deceiver and Flatterer, him at the bottom we despise' (*TF* ii. 87). Similarly, the best kind of reader does not seek to be flattered, but is 'desirous to derive pleasure from the consciousness of being instructed or ameliorated' (*TF* ii. 277). Here we see Coleridge cleverly transforming his authorial condescension into the highest kind of compliment, but what he cannot ecape, in the end, is the fear that readers actually resent enlightenment from above. The very process of instruction is fraught with perils, for 'to attempt to make a Man wiser is of necessity to remind him of his ignorance' (*TF* ii. 282).

Throughout *The Friend* we find Coleridge complaining of the 'general unfitness and aversion of Men to the process of Thought' (*TF* ii. 52). This laziness is 'the mother evil' of all that he proposes to war against, 'the Queen Bee in the Hive of our errors and misfortunes, both private and national' (*TF* ii. 152). To rectify this evil, Coleridge's reader must bring to *The Friend* his own voluntary activity of thought, that 'most difficult and laborious Effort' whereby he reproduces in his own mind those states of consciousness to which the author has referred him (*TF* ii. 277); furthermore, believing that the only knowledge worth possessing is that which the reader arrives at by himself, Coleridge's plan is to kindle the reader's torch, then leave him to himself 'to chuse the particular Objects, which he might wish to examine by it's light' (*TF* ii. 276). This emphasis upon the active role of reading must be seen, however, within the strictly hierarchical model of author–reader relationship adopted by Coleridge; for once we combine the much repeated demand for reader activity with an equally emphatic insistence upon the large gap between an author and his reader, an illiberal dynamic begins to emerge, where an author can only ever be in the right and his reader in the wrong. By calling upon active readers, Coleridge could not have hit upon a more ingenious way of bolstering his own authority whilst simultaneously lightening the burdens of authorship, for readers who are active in the construction of a text must also share responsibility for errors, misunderstandings, and other failures of the communicative process. So high, in fact, were the demands Coleridge placed upon his readers, that, at one point in *The Friend*, he suggests that the success or failure of his periodical lies entirely in their power. If this appeared to be an abdication of authorial responsibility, or an 'unwarrantable assumption of superiority', he urged in his self-defence 'that if it had been my duty to believe, that the main obstacle to the success of my undertaking existed not in the minds of others, but in my own insufficiency and inferiority, I ought not to have undertaken it at all' (*TF* ii. 277–8). It is hardly surprising, then, that as complaints of obscurity multiplied, Coleridge placed the blame on his readers, arguing that 'unintelligibility is a very unequivocal charge. It certainly may arise from the author . . . but it may likewise, and often does, arise from the Reader, and this from more than one cause. He may have an ideotic understanding, and what is far more common, as well as incomparably more lamentable,—he may have an *ideotic heart!*' (*TF* ii. 275.) In illustration of this point, he cited the case of one of his subscribers who had written to abuse him of ' "learned non*sence* and unintelligible Jar*gin*" ' (*TF* ii. 275). Any attempt to elicit the energies of such an illiterate smacked of the absurd case of the physician who recommended 'exercise with the dumb bells, as the only mode of cure, to a patient paralytic in both arms' (*TF* ii. 152).

Coleridge dramatizes the constraints of authorship in his opening number where, just as he is on the point of deducing free will from a strong internal conviction of Conscience, he diverts our attention to the lack of freedom imposed on him by his readers: 'But I am proceeding farther than I had wished or intended. It will be long, ere I shall dare flatter myself, that I have won the confidence of my Reader sufficiently to require of him that effort of attention, which the regular Establishment of this Truth would require.' (*TF* ii. 8.) His stance of authorial superiority was troubled, then, by doubts as to how far his readers were prepared to give scope to this superiority; and there was always, of course, his own self-doubt as to his fitness for the task ahead of him. In the Prospectus we saw him caught between his desire to be an object both of pity and of admiration:[12] he wanted to set himself up as a moral teacher, and yet feel free to confess frankly to all his personal weaknesses. This dilemma of authorial status is exacerbated in Number 1 by the leading conviction of his periodical: that all men are fundamentally in error, and the worrying reflection which arose out of this premiss, namely, that if this were so, it was a piece of 'presumption' on his part to attempt his readers' amendment. Such, at any rate, had been the response of one of his correspondents, an unnamed advisor who warned him against aiming at 'other or higher object than that of *amusing*, during some ten minutes in every week, a small portion of the reading Public' (*TF* ii. 9).

The projection of self-doubt onto an unnamed correspondent is partly a bid to pre-empt similar advice arising from other quarters; more importantly, it is a way of channelling private anxiety into the public drama of the constraints of reader expectation. For, on his own admission, the objection to his assumed superiority, arising as it does from the subject matter of Number 1, is formidable: by what right does he affect to stand aloof from the crowd, even were it prudent, and with what prudence does he even possess the right? (*TF* ii. 10.)

For the moment, Coleridge attempts to convince himself and his readers that he can escape from his dilemma by arguing that

though all men are in error, they are not all in the same error, nor at the same time; and that each therefore may possibly heal the other (for the possibility of the cure is supposed in the free-agency) even as two or more physicians, all diseased in their general health yet under the immediate action of the disease on different days, may remove or alleviate the complaints of each other.   (*TF* ii. 12–13.)

This image of the mutually self-helping physicians is an optimistic rewriting of the opening paragraph of Richard Hooker's *Of the Lawes of Ecclesiasticall Polity* (1593), a work very much in Coleridge's mind at this time.[13] In this

---

[12] For the link between this paradoxical desire and 'the craving to become an Object of Sympathy', see a late notebook entry, quoted by Kathleen Coburn in *The Self Conscious Imagination* (London, 1974), 13.

[13] See *CN* iii. 3268, 3574, *Marginalia*, ii. 1131 ff. and ch. 6 below.

paragraph, transcribed by Coleridge into his notebooks in September 1809, Hooker reflects gloomily upon the debilitating restraints imposed upon authors by their impatient readers:

'As therefore Physicians are many times forced to leave such methods of curing, as themselves know to be fittest, and being overruled by their Patients' impatiency, are fain to try the best they can: in like sort, considering how the case doth stand with the present age full of Tongue and weak of Brain, behold we yield to the stream there of: that way we are contented to prove which being the worse in itself is notwithstanding now by reason of common Imbecillity the fitter & likelier to be brooked.' (*CN* iii. 3574.)

Judging by the opening number's allegory of the maddening rain, Hooker's pessimistic vision of hierarchy overturned comes closer to Coleridge's real feelings than the pious democracy of erring physicians. In this sobering allegory, an Elder receives a divine instruction to warn his countrymen against rains which bring madness to all who are touched by them. The warning goes unheeded, the Elder retires to a cave at the appointed time, and re-emerges to find all his countrymen insane. His predicament, and the steps he takes to resolve it, conclude the tale:

harrassed, endangered, solitary in a world of forms like his own, without sympathy, without object of Love, he at length espied in some foss or furrow a quantity of the mad'ning water still unevaporated, and uttering the last words of Reason, 'It is in vain to be sane in a world of Madmen', plunged and rolled himself in the liquid poison, and came out as mad and not more wretched than his neighbours and acquaintance. (*TF* ii. 12.)

All possible objections to the practicability of going on with his periodical were, Coleridge tersely conceded, summarized by this allegory; as author, he was either 'the Blind offering to lead the Blind', or he was talking the 'language of Sight to those who do not possess the sense of Seeing' (*TF* ii. 12 n.).

Coleridge's anxious awareness of the constraints of authorship goes hand in hand with his fear of the public at large, that fearful bogey and abstraction which haunts *The Friend*. In 1796, in the Preface to his *Poems on Various Subjects*, Coleridge had dismissed the notion of a public as one of those imaginary aggregates to which we wrongly attribute a personal unity: 'What is the PUBLIC but a term for a number of scattered individuals of whom as many will be interested in these sorrows as have experienced the same or similar?'[14] In 1809, Coleridge still hopes to gather in these sympathetic and scattered individuals, but the notion of an abstract Public, ignorant of right and true principles, has gained sway over his imagination. Intoxicated with the power of the printed word, yet fearful of its power for good or for evil, it now seemed that the predominant state of public opinion was the cause of all great national events (*TF* ii. 107); hence the importance of gaining control of it, as the *Edinburgh* and *Quarterly Reviews* had done, and as Coleridge hoped to do. Unfortunately, self-elected critics stood in the way of gaining power, and the 'want of established Door-keepers in the Auditory of Literature' (*TF* ii. 311) meant that anyone could enter. In the middle of his essay on the establishment of rules for the communication of truth, the dizzying proliferation of the printed word induces an acute sense of authorial vulnerability:

But how will these Rules apply to the most important mode of communication? To that, in which one man may utter his thoughts to myriads of men at the same time, and to myriads of myriads at various times and through successions of generations? How do they apply to Authors, whose foreknowledge assuredly does not inform them who, or how many, or of what description their Readers will be? To Books, which once published, are as likely to fall in the way of the Incompetent as of the Judicious, and will be fortunate indeed if they are not many times looked at through the thick mists of ignorance, or amid the glare of prejudice and passion? (*TF* ii. 47–8.)

These worrying speculations are rather disconcertingly contradicted by a clear-cut case of publishers and authors exerting a choice as to their purchasers and readers. These are the itinerant pedlars of 'base and vulgar delusions' who sell their miraculous tales 'not only in a form which placed them within the reach of the narrowest means, but sold at a price less than their prime cost'. Curiously, while waiving this example as an

---

[14] *Poems on Various Subjects* (London, 1976), p. vii.

exception to the rule, Coleridge bolsters the counter-current of his thought by arguing further that what is true for the mountebank is also true for the specialist writer: 'that if the Author have clearly and rightly established in his own mind the class of Readers, to which he means to address his communications; and if both in this choice, and in the particulars of the manner and matter of his work, he conscientiously observes all the conditions which Reason and Conscience have been shewn to dictate, in relation to those for whom the work was designed; he will, in most instances, have effected his design and realized the desired circumscription' (*TF* ii. 48).

Subscription offered the best means of achieving this circumscription. To 'find dispersedly what [he] could not find collectively', Coleridge opted for a readership of hand-picked readers, many of whom were to be signed up by friends (*CL* iii. 176). The act of subscription itself could be interpreted as an encouraging gesture, a vote of confidence in the author's powers before the appearance of a single number. But there was an obvious sense in which writing for a known audience was worrisome, especially when one considers the diversity of political and religious opinion represented by his readership. Being 'ambitious of the patronage of Bishops', as his friend Thomas Poole teasingly remarked (WL MS A/Poole/1), Coleridge was able to boast many establishment figures and Tory MPs on his list, but there were also some prominent Dissenters, and several of his whig MPs were outspoken critics of Government.[15] In one sense, this diversity was entirely appropriate to the independent stance struck by *The Friend*, but it created certain problems, some of which were better left unspecified. At one point in the text, when speaking of how he had 'counted on a share of favour and protection from the soberly zealous among the professionally Learned' he suppressed the details of who constituted this group: 'the established Clergy and . . . their Brethren who differ from them in [?notions/matters] of Church government, rather than points of Doctrine' (*TF* ii. 153, n. 2).

If a subscription scheme offered one means of securing a

---

[15] See Appendix.

suitable audience, hard reasoning offered another. Ironically, it is the much deplored intellectual laziness of the reading public which provides a safeguard against the dangers of readerly error, for if this laziness is so pervasive, 'it must surely be absurd to apprehend a preponderance of evil from works which cannot act at all except as far as [they] call the reasoning faculties into full co-exertion with them' (*TF* ii. 52). One suspects, however, that there was little comfort in this idea; for a natural pedagogue like Coleridge, bent upon rectifying the erroneous thinking of the age, it offered as little real comfort as the prospect of writing for those who, like the water lilies, really had no need of his labours.

It seems likely that this pedagogic intention was responsible for the curious amalgam in Coleridge's prose of (high) brow-beating his readers whilst pandering to them at the same time; repeatedly warning of the strenuous thinking which will be required of them, he often settles in the end for an anti-intellectual appeal to the emotions. The conviction that opinions should always be brought to the test of subjective experience and self-knowledge had always been at the forefront of his first conception of *The Friend*. 'Of this work', he wrote, 'every page has & will come from my Heart's Heart' (*CL* ii. 1053). A year later, in 1805, he vowed in his notebooks that he would write as truly as possible 'from *Experience* actual individual *Experience*', for it was experience which was needed 'to give a *light* and *shade* in the mind, to give to some ideas a greater vividness than others, & thereby to make it a thing of Time and outward reality—practical . . .' (*CN* ii. 2526). In keeping with his determination to counteract the habit of neglecting feeling and experience in the formation of intellectual convictions, Coleridge announced as his metaphysics in *The Friend* 'the referring of the Mind to its' own Consciousness for Truths indispensible to its' own Happiness' (*TF* ii. 73). Such truths were often described by him as 'practicable', an important word signifying strong internal convictions, felt first upon the pulse before being comprehended by the intellect. The concept of free will was one such truth: a truth, 'not only suitable to, but needful for' his nature (*CL* ii. 807). Here, in the appeal to personal need and experience rather than intellectual proof, lies the key to much of Coleridge's method in *The Friend*.

An instance of the tension between intellect and feeling can be seen in his well-known distinction, first developed in *The Friend*, between Attention, which is generally required from readers, and Thought, that 'most difficult and laborious Effort' which can only be demanded at moments of great intellectual difficulty. When we turn to the definition of Thought, however, it is experiential assent rather than intellectual exertion which seems to be required: 'the voluntary production in our own minds of those states of consciousness, to which, as to his fundamental facts, the Writer has referred us' (*TF* ii. 277). This 'voluntary' activity resembles other of Coleridge's injunctions to activity in that it invites readers to engage in an active receptivity. We should come to the text, not with skeptical and questioning minds, but with open, affectionate, and believing hearts. The ideal reader was not 'a quibbler in mock-logic' but 'a Reasoner, who *seeks* to understand, and looks into himself for a sense, which my words may excite in him, not *to* my words for a sense, which they must against his own will *force* on him' (*CL* ii. 1194). Coleridge's Reasoner, in so far as he is also a Seeker, achieves inner illumination at that moment when he assents to the truth of the text. In the opening number of *The Friend*, for instance, it is of the utmost importance that we find an emotional 'yea' within ourselves to certain 'universal persuasions', such as the existence of Conscience and free will, the latter being that 'grand *postulate*' which is 'not susceptible of any proof from without . . . for how can that, which is to explain all things, be susceptible of an explanation?' (*TF* ii. 279). Philosophically and intellectually, these notions are fraught with difficulty, but we need only turn inwards to establish their universal truth:

Conclusions drawn from facts which subsist in perpetual flux, without definite place or fixed quantity, must always be liable to plausible objections, nay, often to unanswerable difficulties; and yet having their foundation in uncorrupted feeling are assented to by mankind at large, and in all ages, as undoubted truths. As our notions concerning them are almost equally obscure, so are our convictions almost equally vivid, with those of our life and individuality. Regarded with awe, as guiding principles by the founders of law and religion, they are the favourite objects of attack with mock philosophers, and the demagogues in church, state, and literature; and the denial of them has in all times, though at various intervals, formed heresies and systems, which, after their day of wonder, are regularly exploded and again as regularly revived, when they have re-acquired novelty by courtesy of oblivion.   (*TF* ii. 6–7.)

Intellectual complexity disappears when it collides with feeling; furthermore, the convictions arising from inner feeling would, Coleridge believed, be more readily acknowledged if his readers resembled him in maturity, inwardness, humility, and self-awareness. Only fellow-sufferers will be admitted to a consensus of truth:

Suffice it for the present to affirm, to declare it at least, as my own creed, that whatever humbles the heart and forces the mind inward, whether it be sickness, or grief, or remorse, or the deep yearnings of love (and there have been children of affliction, for whom all these have met and made up one complex suffering) in proportion as it acquaints us with 'the thing, we are', renders us docile to the concurrent testimony of our fellow-men in all ages and in all nations.
(*TF* ii. 7.)

The need for consensus rather than controversy made Coleridge cautious in his choice of words, and in Number 1 in particular, the language is of such studied neutrality that it is often difficult to see what Coleridge is talking about. If this sometimes looked too much like equivocation, there was always the plea that words with too definite or precise a meaning hindered the all-important activity of a reader arriving at a position of assent. In 1812, when looking over a particular obscure and rhapsodic passage in *The Friend* concerning the Law of Conscience, and its injunction that we 'attribute Reality . . . to the Ideas of Soul, the Free Will, Immortality and God', Coleridge inserted a footnote earnestly entreating the Reader 'not to be dissatisfied either with himself or with the Author, if he should not at once understand the preceding paragraph; but rather to consider it as a mere annunciation of a magnificent Theme, the different parts of which are to be demonstrated and developed, explained, illustrated, and exemplified in the progress of the Work' (*TF* ii. 81 n.). Many of the more obscure passages of *The Friend* require this initial act of faith on the part of the reader, a willingness to suspend intellectual enquiry and surrender oneself up to the mysterious twilight of Coleridge's terms. That he considered this mystification a necessary part of the process of illumination can be seen in his claim that 'Ignorance seldom *vaults* into knowledge, but passes into it through an intermediate state of obscurity, even as Night into Day through Twilight' (*TF* ii. 81 n.). It was here, in this intermundium of obscurity, that Coleridge located the emotive power of language. Believing that terms of 'too great definiteness' ran the risk of consuming 'too much of the vital & idea-creating force' (*CN* i. 1016), he preferred to work with a set of key terms which were capable of drawing after them a magnetic field of vast and dim associations. Curiously, the strategy employed here resembles that of the demagogue, with his slogans of 'The Rights of Man' and 'The Sovereignty of the People', a social phenomenon feared by Coleridge and denounced in *The Friend*: 'To leave a general confused impression of something great, and to rely on the indolence of men's understandings and the activity of their passions, for their resting in this impression, is the old artifice of public Mountebanks, which, like strategems in war, are never the less successful for having succeeded a thousand times before' (*TF* ii. 47).

An example of the way in which key terms operate is to be found in a later addition to a letter written in 1798 and published in *The Friend*. This letter describes the first time Coleridge ever left England, crossing in a small packet-boat to Hamburg. The word 'Ocean' was, he tells us, one to which he had 'associated such a feeling of immensity' that, when out of sight of all land, he felt 'exceedingly disappointed . . . at the narrowness and *nearness*, as it were, of the circle of the Horizon'. So little, he added, 'are images capable of satisfying the obscure feelings connected with words' (*TF* ii. 193). Conversely, as we have already seen in the case of free will, obscure words or notions tend to combine with vivid convictions and strong feelings. But as in the case of obscure feelings, obscure notions must be worthy objects of the emotive power they generate. While the intellect must be habituated to 'clear, distinct, and adequate conceptions concerning all things that are the possible objects of clear conception', obscure notions and vivid feelings must be reserved solely for those objects 'which their very sublimity renders indefinite, no less than their indefiniteness renders them sublime: Being, Form, Life, the Reason, the Law of Conscience, Freedom, Immortality, God! To connect with the objects of our senses the obscure notions and consequent vivid feelings, which are due only to our ideas of immaterial and permanent Things, is profanation relatively to the heart, and superstition in the understanding' (*TF* ii. 71–2). Sublimity and indefiniteness, and their inextricable nexus: this is the locus of language's power, the place where the religious and emotional energies of the reader converge. And in this moment, when the mind leaves off its restless desire for clarity and is transported instead to a belief in its greatness, the sense of sublimity is contingent upon a 'temporary oblivion of the worthless "thing, we are" '. The effect is similar to that induced by the tragedies of the 'elder Dramatists', when we suspend the incidentals of our individual selves and lull them to sleep 'amid the music of nobler thoughts' (*TF* ii. 217–18). To complain of obscurity and imprecision, to resist believing before understanding, is to reveal oneself as deaf to the highest of harmonies.

4
Metaphysics and
The New Theodicy

We know too well, that it is not the mere notion, however clear, that restrains or impels us; but the feelings habitually connected with that notion. The Drunkard is convinced that his Drams are poison; yet takes them. For once that a deep conviction is the parent of a Habit, a Habit is an 100 times the parent of the Conviction . . . Hence, the sophistry may be shewn of Rousseau's Plan of Education—in which an intellectual conviction is always to precede the appropriate action. Mere knowledge of the right, we find by experience, does not suffice to ensure the performance of the Right—for mankind in general. How indeed should it, if mankind need instruction? that is, if they are sick & weak in their moral Being; when it is the very prime & the essential character of a Soul made perfect that the Knowledge of the Right is to Him the adequate, & the soul adequate, motive to the perform-ance—i.e. to do our Duty exclusively because it is our duty.—Much less shall we <be> led to our Duty by calculations of pleasant or harmful consequences.

Coleridge's *Notebooks*, 1810

AT some point during the composition of *The Friend*'s early numbers, Coleridge complained in his notebooks of 'accredited facts, almost universally considered as universal Experience, which yet neither or ever were actually experienced' (*CN* iii. 3556). Chief amongst these, and a principal target of *The Friend*, was the widely held utilitarian belief that 'self-interest in a more or less gross form is the true Spring (Triebfeder und Bewegungsgrund) of human Actions—that Actions are mainly if not exclusively determined by calculations of Hope & Fear &c' (*CN* iii. 3556). Such a view was, to Coleridge's mind, entirely spurious, because it took no account of what naturally concerned him deeply, the capacity for acting on irrational and self-destructive impulses—the fact that 'even where our understandings are in the Light . . . our organization is depraved, & our volitions imperfect' (*CL* i. 396). This blindness to our 'inherent depravity' was formed from 'the habit of judging of a thing not by our own feelings but by what we believe will be the judgment of others . . . & the habit of referring to notions formed from books for the truth & nature of characters & passions found in books, instead of trying them by our experience & actual Observation' (*CN* iii. 3556).

One of the most helpful correctives to a philosophy based on self-interest was Kant's concept of morality as the unconditional obedience of the will to pure Reason. The truly moral act in Kantian ethics is that which is performed, not out of any inclination, or with a view to one's self-interest, but performed *unconditionally*, that is, for the sake of the moral law. This pure conception of doing one's duty for duty's sake provided Coleridge with his most powerful weapon against the bookish notions of the utilitarians. Characterizing the morality of self-interest as 'imaginary' and 'ideal'—a mere phantom of the brain, unconnected with the way in which we actually behave[1]—Coleridge offers us Kant's sublime conception of Duty as a far more powerful spring to action, and one which says far more about our true nature and destiny. But it is precisely this latter feature of Kant's ethics—the fact that his system addresses itself to the *ideal* in each and every one of us—which prompts Coleridge's reservations when he turns to consider the working out of this principle in actual practice.

In a letter to Sir George Beaumont, written two months before he sailed for Malta, Coleridge excitedly announced that his latest project 'Comforts and Consolations' would contain 'a new Theodicee, & what will perhaps appear to many a new Basis of Morals', adding that the portions he had written of this work were 'a pure Strain of Music' (*CL* ii. 1053). Although Kant's name is never mentioned in *The Friend*, the

---

[1] For an excellent discussion of Coleridge's pragmatic attack on utilitarian theory, see Laurence Lockridge, *Coleridge the Moralist* (Ithaca, NY, and London, 1977), 244–50.

influence of his ethical writings is clearly discernible in the first two subjects of the Prospectus:

The true and sole Ground of Morality, or Virtue, as distinguished from Prudence.
The Origin and Growth of moral Impulses, as distinguished from external and immediate Motives. (*TF* ii. 18.)

The distinction between morality and prudence properly stands at the head of *The Friend*'s catalogue of subjects, for Coleridge intended to offer his readers a morality untainted by the prudential, utilitarian ethics currently in vogue. In this, he was following Kant's procedure in *Groundwork of the Metaphysic of Morals* (1785), a work which broke with popular eighteenth-century utilitarianism (loosely, the belief that an action is good if it produces pleasant, or good results) in order to substitute an objective and formal rule of moral conduct. This rule bids us to act only on that maxim through which we can at the same time will that it should become a universal law (*Groundwork*, p. 29).

The utilitarianism which Coleridge opposed is characterized by him as the system of 'enlightened Selfishness' taught by the eminent theologian William Paley (*CL* iii. 216). Instead of preaching the gospel message, 'Love your neighbour as yourself and God above all', Paley and his imitators taught: 'Act & feel so & so towards God & your neighbour because you love yourself above all' (*Marginalia*, i. 171–2). To place the essence of moral good in self-interest was, in Coleridge's view, to annihilate the Idea of Virtue. Partially sighted as we are, and far removed from the perfection demanded of us by God, the Paleyans would, with their doctrines, 'convert the temporary Curtain before the window into a windowless Wall—a perpetual exclusion of Light' (*CL* iii. 153).

At pains to contrast his own rigorous moral thinking with the prudential and expedient thinking of his age, Coleridge determined that *The Friend*'s first essay would be on 'the nature and importance of *Principles*. The blindness to this I have long regarded as the Disease of this discussing, calculating, *prudential* age—and to prove this & to shew it's consequences in morality, taste, and even in the common goings-on of daily

Life is my paramount Object for the whole work.' (*CL*
iii. 129.) That the distinction between principles and prudence
is really a Kant-like distinction between Reason and Understanding becomes clear in the following restatement of his
plan for Number 1: 'My first Essay will be on the Nature and
the Importance of *Principles*—i.e. of the pure REASON, which
dictates unconditionally, in distinction from the prudential
understanding, which employing it's mole Eyes in an impossible calculation of Consequences perverts and mutilates
its own Being, untenanting the function which it is incapable of
occupying.' (*CL* iii. 146.) The polemical exaggeration of this
can be attributed to Coleridge's desire to promote his new
journal. A more temperate distinction between Reason and
Understanding, and one which allows him to argue for a
politics based on an expedient calculation of consequences, is
to be found in a letter Coleridge wrote to Thomas Clarkson a
few months after returning from Malta. Assigning to each
'Faculty of the Soul' its proper sphere, he states that, while the
Understanding 'apprehends and retains the mere notices of
Experience . . . with the anticipation of meeting the same
under the same circumstances', the Reason concerns itself
with 'all such notices, as are characterized by UNIVERSALITY
and NECESSITY . . . [those] which are evidently not the effect
of any Experience, but the condition of all Experience, & that
indeed without which Experience itself would be inconceivable'
(*CL* ii. 1198). Translated into ethical terms, the Understanding
is 'the Faculty of adapting means to ends' while Reason
furnishes 'that by which we pre-determine the final End' (*TF*
i. 442 n.).

   The second subject of *The Friend*'s Prospectus, 'The Origin
and Growth of moral Impulses, as distinguished from external
and immediate Motives' is not very perspicuous.[2] That it also
forms part of Coleridge's attempt to recast contemporary
notions of Virtue in Kantian terms can, however, be
demonstrated from one of several notebook jottings on the
Groundwork made in 1803. To Kant's rule that 'It is not
enough that we act in conformity to the Law of moral

---

[2] For Jeffrey's objection to 'moral Impulses', see p. 49 above and *CL* iii. 150.

Reason—we must likewise FOR THE SAKE of that law' Coleridge added the following gloss: 'it must not only be our Guide, but likewise our Impulse—Like a strong current, it must make a visible Road on the Sea, & drive us along that road gemäss—um desselben willen' (*CN* i. 1705). That Coleridge's distinction here between Guide and Impulse mirrors Kant's distinction between an external conformity and a more profound, internal relationship to the law is confirmed by Coleridge's insertion of the German 'gemäss— um desselben willen' ('in accordance with—for the sake of the same').[3]

Kant's distinction reveals a minute attention to our inner moral life, and it was this feature of his work which struck Coleridge as so superior to other systems of morality. According to Kant, a man's moral worth lies not in what he can see—the good or bad consequences of his actions—but in the principle, or maxim, lying behind the action, out of sight. Following Kant, Coleridge is to argue in *The Friend*: 'If Man be a free Agent, his Good and Evil must not be judged of according to the nature of his *outward* Actions, or the mere *legality* of his Conduct; but by the final Motive and Intention of the Mind.' (*TF* ii. 281.) Virtue finds expression, not in what we *do*, but in what we are: in the principle, or 'final Motive of an intelligent Will' (*TF* ii. 281).

This emphasis on inner being rather than external doing was of great personal importance to Coleridge, making its first appearance in a notebook entry on the character of Southey, written at the same time as his earliest thoughts about 'Comforts and Consolations'. It would, Coleridge argues, be a very salutary exercise in charity and kindness to abide by the reflection 'that the Almighty will judge us not by what we *do*, but by what we *are*; and in forbidding us to judge each other has manifestly taught us by implication, that we cannot without hazard of grievous error & without hazard of grievous Breach of Charity deduce the latter from the Former' (*CN*

---

[3] Rosemary Ashton interprets this gloss quite differently, seeing it not as a restatement, but as 'a qualification' of Kant's insistence on obedience to the moral law for the sake of the law (*The German Idea: Four English Writers and the Reception of German Thought 1800–1860* (Cambridge, 1980), 45). .

i. 1605). It was always Coleridge's hope to be seen for what he
was in himself. Unable to prove himself in action, and yet
anxious to vindicate his inner moral life, he insisted that his
friends focus on the value and integrity of motives and
intentions. In a letter to Poole, written shortly before he spoke
of the 'new Theodicee' underpinning his 'Comforts and
Consolations', he urged: 'make your Esteem strictly &
severely proportionate to the *Worth* of the agent, not to the
value of the action/ & to refer the latter wholly to the Eternal
Wisdom & Goodness, to God, upon whom it wholly depends,
& in whom alone it has a moral Worth' (*CL* ii. 1037).

In so far as Kant's distinction offered Coleridge a mode of
self-defence from the negative judgements of friends, it was a
fitting foundation to a work affording comforts and consolations. That this very personal creed was carried over from the
original project into the heart of *The Friend* can be seen in his
letter to the Quaker Thomas W. Smith. In this letter, written
during an anxious time of doubt and self-searching, Coleridge
reveals his motive for going on with *The Friend*:

I . . . shall deem myself amply remunerated if in consequence of my
exertions a Few only of those, who had formed their moral creed on
Hume, Paley, and their Imitators, with or without a belief in the
facts of mere historical Christianity, shall have learnt to value
actions primarily as the language & natural effect of the state of the
agent; if they shall consider what they *are* instead of *merely* what they
do; so that the fig-tree may bring forth it's own fruit from it's own
living principle, and not have the figs tied on to it's barren sprays by
the hand of outward Prudence & Respect of Character.

(*CL* iii. 216.)[4]

To the question 'Would not the whole moral code remain the
same on the principle of enlightened Selfishness, as on that of
Conscience, or the unconditional obedience of the Will to the
pure Reason?' Coleridge replied, 'All possibly might remain
the same, only not the men themselves for whom the moral
Law was given' (*CL* iii. 216). In other words, although an
action prompted by self-interest may be indistinguishable in
appearance and effects from an action performed out of duty,
in terms of the inner, moral life, there is a world of difference

---

[4] The substance of this letter reappears in *The Friend* (*TF* ii. 314–15).

between the man who listens to and obeys the moral law out of duty, and he who allows other, prudential considerations to prevail.

It is a mistake to say that Coleridge 'early rejected' the categorical imperative as 'humanly unrealistic, a "stoic principle"' (*CN* iii. 4017 n.). On the contrary, he was profoundly drawn to this idea, identifying the 'unconditional Obedience of the Free Will to the Law of pure Reason' with the inward Christ (*CN* ii. 2664).[5] The Quaker belief in an inner Light was yet another expression of the same idea, an idea precious to Coleridge and one which seemed to have been realized to perfection by certain exemplary, Christ-like figures. In the Journal of the eighteenth-century Quaker John Woolman, Coleridge marvelled at the sight of a man living his life in strict conformity with the moral law, manifesting in all his actions 'unfeigned listening and obedience to the Voice within' (*CL* iii. 156). Amongst Coleridge's contemporaries, too, there was the inspiring example of the abolitionist Thomas Clarkson. 'If ever human Being did it', Coleridge wrote, Clarkson 'listened exclusively to his Conscience, and obeyed it's voice at the price of all his Youth and manhood, at the price of his Health, his private Fortune, and the fairest prospects of honorable ambition' (*CL* iii. 119). Men like Woolman and Clarkson manifested 'God*like*-ness', a word used by Coleridge in 1796 in an attempt to explain to the atheist John Thelwall what St Peter meant when he spoke of the human aspiration to be 'partakers of the divine nature'. 'God*like*-ness' required a man to act 'from a love of order, & happiness, & not from any self-respecting motive—from the *excellency*, into which you have exalted your *nature*, not from the *keenness* of *mere prudence*' (*CL* i. 284). A reference to Kant elsewhere in this letter as 'the most unintelligible Emanuel Kant' reveals the provenance of Coleridge's distinction.

That every man had within him the potential for 'God*like*-ness' was one of those beliefs 'needful' to Coleridge's nature, for his conscience was habitually oppressed by his 'non-performance' of what he had engaged to do (*CL* iii. 90). All

---

[5] The importance to Coleridge of the idea of 'the God within us' is noted by Whalley (*Marginalia*, i. 178–9 n.).

too often he had 'felt, spoken, and acted, against the *Light*' (*CN* iii. 4013), so much so in the case of opium that he came to see his addiction as a habit which undermined not just his body, but his spirit too. Each dose was a 'Savage Stab! that transpierces at once Health and Conscience' (*CN* iii. 3352). Never free from temptation, he rarely achieved the true tranquillity of a perfectly gratified conscience, a state of mind he Quakerishly described as 'the Blessedness of walking altogether in Light' (*CL* iii. 131). In *A Brief Account of the Rise and Progress of the People called Quakers* (1694), one of Coleridge's favourite Quaker texts, and an important key to our understanding of Number 1, William Penn wrote of two groups of men. There were those who claim fellowship with God, 'yet walk in darkness (viz. in disobedience to the light in their consciences)', and there were those who 'love the light, and bring their deeds to it, and walk in the light, as God is light' (*A Brief Account*, 66). In a notebook entry of 1810, Coleridge attempted to describe the almost supernatural sense of peace and calm consequent upon the knowledge of having acted in perfect harmony with the light. A conviction of God dwelling within arose as one of the

Effects . . . of the *moral* Being after difficult Conquest, the total State of the Spirit after the victorious Struggle, in <which> and by which *the* WILL has preserved its perfect Freedom by a deep and vehement Energy of perfect Obedience to the pure, practical Reason, or Conscience! Thence flows in upon and fills the Soul that Peace, which passeth Understanding!   (*CN* iii. 3911.)

That the triumph should reside in a sense of conflict overcome only strengthened the case for the form in which Kant had cast his categorical imperative. Its rigour seemed to Coleridge to be peculiarly fitted to man's weak and erring nature:

Ours is a life of Probation/ we are to contemplate and obey *Duty* for its own sake, and in order to this we—in our present imperfect state of Being—must see it not merely abstracted from, but in direct opposition to the *Wish*, the *Inclination*/ having perfected this the highest possibility of human nature, he may then with safety harmonize *all* his Being with this—he may love. To perform Duties absolutely from the sense of Duty is the *Ideal*, which perhaps no human Being ever can arrive at, but which every human Being ought to try to draw near unto—This is—in the only wise, & verily, in a most sublime sense—to see God face to face/ (*CN* ii. 2556.)

And even though, for the most part, the perfectly gratified conscience remained an elusive goal, the power it exerted over the imagination formed an essential part of our moral and intellectual growth. To possess such happiness was, Coleridge wrote, an 'instinctive craving', a yearning of the moral being after an 'unknown Bliss, or Blessedness—known only & anticipated by the Hollowness where it is'. Like the plant which 'in its dark Chamber turns & twists its stem & grows toward the Light-Cranny', the sensation of the want supplies 'the sense of the Object wanted' (*CN* iii. 3911).

The consciousness of striving was a necessary part of being on guard against the complacent and self-deceived stupors which counterfeited true tranquillity. In the 'Ode to Tranquillity', republished in Number 1, two counterfeits are identified, 'Satiety' and 'Sloth' (*TF* ii. 14). But there were others; in fact, such were Coleridge's vigilance and self-scrutiny that he was skilled at detecting these false paradises. There was, for instance, the stupor of 'absolute Abstraction':

> For not to *think* of what I needs must *feel*,
> But to be still and patient all I can;
> And haply by abstruse Research to steal
> From my own Nature all the natural Man;
> This was my sole Resource, my only Plan!
> And that which suits a Part infects the Whole,
> And now is almost grown the Habit of my Soul.
>
> (*CL* ii. 1201)

There was also, of course, the escape of an opium-induced stupor, and an old habit exacerbated by his drug addiction of substituting elaborate intentions for the deeds themselves: 'often the very fullness & vividness of the purpose & intention to do a thing imposes on the mind a sort of counterfeit feeling of quiet, similar to the satisfaction which the having done it would produce' (*CL* v. 139).

Thus, the stringency of Kant's categorical imperative was attractive to Coleridge for very personal reasons. He also believed that the 'suitableness of pure Virtue to human

Feelings' consisted, quite simply, in the 'likeness & affinity' of this Virtue with strong and enduring emotions: 'those Feelings that prompt to action & sustain under Pain/ Dignity, Hope &c' (*CN* i. 1713).

On a less experiential and more philosophical level, Coleridge adduced three arguments to explain why the formula of a duty performed for duty's sake was preferable to that which attempted to lead us to duty 'by calculations of pleasant or harmful consequences' (*CN* iii. 4017). First, the projection of consequences was speculative and impractical: a criterion 'neither tenable in Reason nor Safe in Practice' because 'purely *ideal*' (*TF* ii. 313). Whereas Kant's notion of virtue furnished 'a principle common to the Knowing & to the Simple', Paley's prudence demanded a 'high degree of Knowledge and Calculation' (*CN* iii. 3482). Instead of the certainty of listening to 'the plain, positive Injunction of Conscience', those who calculated consequences had to keep their eyes fixed 'on a Dæmon in the Distance, now flattering, now threatening them with obscure gestures, the interpretation of which forms their daily & hourly Superstition' (*Marginalia*, i. 223). Second, even when an action's consequences could be reliably calculated, it did not follow that this certainty would have any influence on the agent. This last point is made in a semi-autobiographical passage in *The Friend* concerning a Sot and a Prostitute.[6] In this passage, Coleridge illustrates the uselessness of the ethics of self-love by dramatizing man's perverse capacity for acting against his best interests. Although through knowledge gained by experience, the mature man 'shuns the beautiful Flame' while the infant eagerly grasps at it, there are occasions when the sense of 'a disproportion of certain after harm to present gratification' fails to have any influence whatsoever over our actions. The prospect of immediate gratification overrides the certain knowledge of future self-harm:

many a Maiden, who will not grasp at the fire, will yet purchase a wreathe of Diamonds at the price of her health, her honor, nay (and

---

[6] For an illuminating account of this section of *The Friend*, see Arden Reed, 'Coleridge, the Sot, and the Prostitute: A Reading of *The Friend*, Essay XIV', *Studies in Romanticism*, 19 (Spring 1980), 109–28.

she herself knows it at the moment of her choice), at the sacrifice of her Peace and Happiness. The Sot would reject the poisoned Cup, yet the trembling hand with which he raises his daily or hourly draught to his lips, has not left him ignorant that this too is altogether a Poison. (*TF* ii. 71.)

From his own experience of addiction, Coleridge knew all too well that knowledge of the evil consequences to come was impotent to further the practice of self-denial; such knowledge was one of the hard prices paid down for addiction. Writing of the fact that opium suspended the agony only to aggravate it further, he added:

and I know it—and the knowlege, and the fear, and the remorse, and the wilful turning away of the eye to dreams imperfect, that float like broken foam on the sense of the reality, and only distract not hide it, these are the wretched & sole Comforts, or rather these are the hard prices, by which the Armistice is accompanied & paid for. O who shall deliver me from the Body of this Death? (*CN* ii. 3078.)

Finally, and most obviously, the criterion of general consequences did not recognize the important distinction drawn by Kant between the truly moral act and an external conformity to the law. Confounding morality with legality, Paley and his imitators drew the attention away 'from the *Will*, that is from the inward motives and impulses which constitute the Essence of *Morality*, to the outward Act'. Thus, Coleridge argued, is the Virtue commanded by the Gospel downgraded to 'the mere Legality, which was to be enlivened by it' (*TF* ii. 314).

For all these reasons, Kant's categorical imperative was a far superior ethical rule to the arbitrary one offered by Paley's utilitarianism. It also provided a much needed test of motivation in the arena of strong feelings:

We ought not to relieve a poor man merely because our feelings impel us; but because these feelings are *just* & *proper* feelings. My *feelings* might impel me to revenge with the same force, with which they urge me to charity—/ I must therefore have some rule by which I may *judge* my feelings—& this Rule is '*God*'. (*Marginalia*, i. 751.)

The habit we see here of adopting Kant's architectonic whilst simplifying his ideas and absorbing them under his own emotive and explicitly Christian way of thinking, is a recurring feature of Coleridge's ethical writing in these middle years. It is also to be seen in the letter to Poole quoted earlier:

make your Esteem strictly & severely proportionate to the *Worth* of the agent, not to the *value* of the action/ & to refer the latter wholly to the Eternal Wisdom & Goodness, to God, upon whom it wholly depends, & in whom alone it has a moral Worth.　　(*CL* ii. 1037.)

To begin in Kant and end in God was Coleridge's way of softening and personalizing the Kantian ethic. It was also his way of testing Kant. Thus, in the notebooks, we often find Coleridge transposing the German philosopher into a biblical context. In one entry, the first four Commandments are completely recast in Kantian terminology. Whereas Paley and his followers had failed to do justice to the Decalogue, Kantian terms bestowed a glory on the Commandments by revealing their form and adding 'the principle to the Deed'. Thus are they made to appear in Coleridge's eyes complete, absolute, and of 'eternal Obligation':

1st Commandment—Unconditional Obedience of the Will to the pure Reason, or Conscience/ the *Reality* of which is *God* . . . Let the Will obey the pure Reason *exclusively* & *unconditionally*. Hence, it is a *command*—not an inducement. Do it—not for this reason or for that reason—but to fulfil the Law for the sake of the Law. It is its own *motive*—it is reason itself.—

2. Preserve the pure Reason pure—& debase it not by any mixture of *sens*uality—the sensuous Imagination. To consecrate & worship the eternal distinction between the Noumenon and the Phænomenon/ and never to merge the former in the latter.

3. Preserve the faculty of Discourse—the sermo interior and exterior—the discursive faculty, or understanding, as well as the discourse, or power of Speech, in strict awe & allegiance to the pure Reason—All idle sophisms, all sophistications of the mind tampering with the Conscience, by consequences, pretended *calculations*, and eudæmonism/ all forbidden. Awe—religious Awe—the silence of unconditional Obedience, in silence watching & listening for, & in silence & promptness obeying.

4. Not only to obey the pure reason in all our doings & sayings; but to consider it, of itself, as an object of our care & solicitude—&

therefore solemnly to devote a portion of our time to the principle
itself, & the modes of developing, & strengthening our sense of it—
(*CN* iii. 3293.)

In another entry we find the suggestion that, taken together,
Kantian and biblical commands make up the head and heart
of religion: 'In the Intellect—"Be able to *will*, that thy maxims
(rules of individual conduct) should be the Law of all
intelligent Being." In the Heart—or practical Reason—Do
unto others, as thou would'st be done by.' (*CN* ii. 3231.)
Heart and Intellect, 'Passion and order aton'd! Imperative
Power in Obedience!' Together, they play 'the first and
divinest Strain of Music' (*CN* ii. 3231).

The music of Kant and Christianity is probably the 'pure
Strain of Music' which Coleridge claimed to Beaumont he was
composing for his 'Comforts and Consolations', a work which,
true to the two parts of its title, was to embody practical and
saving truths as well as the more speculative consolations of
the new theodicy. *The Friend* inherited the hybrid nature of this
original project. It was to be both empirical and ideal:
concerned with '*what we are, and what we are born to become*' (*TF*
ii. 17). The importance of holding the empirical and ideal in
conjunction can be seen in Coleridge's definition of Christianity
as 'a divine *Religion*, which acknowledges the *existing* state of
human nature with more than all the *Historic* Truth of the
Epicurean Philosophy, and yet establishes an *Ideal* of Virtue in
all the severity of the Stoic—at once avoiding the baseness of
the one, and the bloating visionariness of the other' (*CL*
iii. 154).

The need for a balance between the reality and the ideal of
human nature leads us to Coleridge's reservations regarding
Kant's moral imperative. From a later passage in *Aids to
Reflection* (1825), it becomes clear that the earlier charge of
visionariness is a reference to Kant's denial of the place of
affections in the moral life:

Of the sects of ancient philosophy the Stoic is, perhaps, the nearest
to Christianity. Yet even to this sect Christianity is fundamentally
opposite. For the Stoic attaches the highest honour (or rather,
attaches honour solely) to the person that acts virtuously in spite of
his feelings, or who has raised himself above the conflict by their

extinction; while Christianity instructs us to place small reliance on a virtue that does not begin by bringing the feelings to a conformity with the commands of the conscience. Its especial aim, its characteristic operation, is to moralize the affections.   (*AR*, p. 65.)

The nearness, yet distance, of the stoical system to that of Christianity conveys Coleridge's essential ambivalence towards Kant's moral ideal. Although, in his own case, he was drawn to Kant's rule through a sense of personal weakness, he rejoiced at the sight of the 'humanly happy' man who 'in enjoyment *finds* his Duty' (*CN* ii. 2556). Wordsworth was such a man, for the exact performance of his duty coincided with love and poetry, the deepest sources of pleasure in his life. Just before leaving for Malta Coleridge had written: 'blessed are you, dear William! whose Path of Duty lies thro' vine-trellised Elm-groves, thro' Love and Joy & Grandeur' (*CL* ii. 1060).

In Coleridge's own life, too, his love for Sara Hutchinson was experienced as a prompt to Duty. As we have already seen, Sara bodied forth Virtue in a lovely form, bringing about a miraculous 'Incarnation & Transfiguration of Duty as Inclination'.

That Coleridge instinctively repudiated Kant's denial of feeling can be seen in the 1796 letter quoted above (p. 69), for while the architectonic of Kant's philosophy is clearly there, the aspiration to 'Godlikeness' requires us to act 'from a love of order, & happiness' (*CL* i. 284). The inclusion of happiness here as a motive to action spells the beginning of his uneasiness with Kant's rigorous ethic of a duty performed for duty's sake.

Gradually Kant's denigration of love emerged as the principal flaw of his system. In 1803 Coleridge complained of the way in which Kant 'very unfairly explains away the word Love into Beneficence' (*CN* i. 1705), and by 1817 this had hardened into the claim that his '*stoic* principle' is 'false, unnatural, and even immoral' because it would persuade us 'that a man who disliking, and without any feeling of Love for, Virtue yet *acted* virtuously, because and only because it was his *Duty*, is more worthy of our esteem, than the man whose *affections* were aidant to, and congruous with, his Conscience'

(*CL* iv. 791–2). More subtle, because more tentative, is the earlier notebook musing: 'N.B. will not a pure will generate a feeling of Sympathy/ Does even the sense of Duty rest satisfied with mere *Actions*, in the vulgar sense, does it not demand, & therefore may produce, Sympathy itself as an Action/ ?—This I think very important/—Nay, it is proved by Scripture' (*CN* i. 1705). Just as in 1796, 'the absurdities and wickedness' of William Godwin's system were to be compared unfavourably with 'that perfect canon' of Christ (*CL* i. 267), Kant is here brought to the test of Scripture and found wanting. What was needed was a system of morality which would satisfy the heart as well as the head, one which united 'the intention and the motive, the warmth and the light, in one and the same act of mind': 'Such a Principle may be extracted, though not without difficulty and danger, from the ore of the stoic Philosophy; but it is to be found unalloyed and entire in the christian System, and is there called FAITH.' (*TF* ii. 320.)[7]

The objection that Kant undervalued feeling, and that his system was inferior to the Gospel, was one of the first to be made when his moral philosophy was introduced into England. In *The Monthly Review* of 1794, J. L. Ewald's *Letters to Emma, concerning the Kantian Philosophy* is described as a work which offers 'a comparative view of the moral philosophy of the gospel, and that of Professor Kant':

The former is comprehensive, yet suited to every capacity; its principles are addressed to the affections of man as well as to his understanding; it allows the operation of self-love, and excludes only selfishness; it unites self-interest with social good, supplies the most powerful motives to virtue, and teaches man to act from principles of universal benevolence. The latter, he observes, is unintelligible to the majority of mankind; and even those who profess to comprehend it must acknowledge that it is addressed to the understanding, and not at all to the affections; and that, though it may furnish rules, it does not suggest motives to a virtuous conduct. In short, Christian morality is admirably adapted to direct the practice of all, in every relation of life; whereas that of Prof. *Kant* is suited only to speculative

---

[7] The search for a faith at once practical and speculative, affording warmth to the light of intellectual conviction, was a favourite theme (see *TF* ii. 71, *CL* ii. 1196, and *CN* i. 467).

metaphysicians, who will admit nothing except what can be directly deduced from the most abstract principles of objective reason.

(*MR* xiv. 544–5.)

The other objection arising from this passage—that Kant's moral philosophy is formal and ideal, an abstract rule rather than a practical guide to action—also receives quite detailed attention in this review. To those who extolled the categorical imperative as a 'most sublime and comprehensive precept of practical morality, calculated to improve human nature into a resemblance of the divine', Ewald replied that it was not intended in this way as a *practical* principle, 'but only as relating to the pure abstract philosophy of morals . . . and as an universal law for all intellectual beings' (*MR* xiv. 544).[8]

Coleridge's unremitting attention to the gap between our actual and potential selves led him to adopt similar reservations about the practical application of Kant's moral law. All credit was due to the German philosopher for educing the *form* of Virtue, providing man with an ideal of conduct bespeaking the highest expectation of human behaviour; but it was no easy matter to pass from the form of moral perfection to the content of one's particular duties. The difficulty of doing so was to be clearly seen in the examples of moral action provided by Kant in the *Groundwork*. At least one of these examples struck Coleridge as 'Strange nonsense!', provoking him to conclude that Kant and his followers were 'miserable Reasoners, in Psychology, and particular Morals—bad analysts of aught but Notions, equally clumsy in the illustration and application of their Principles—so much indeed as often to shake my Faith in their general System' (*CN* i. 1705 n.).[9]

It is perhaps not surprising that Kant's examples elicited

[8] That Coleridge would have been familiar with these *Monthly Review* articles on Kant is aptly demonstrated by D. Stansfield in her study, *Thomas Beddoes M.D. 1760–1808: Chemist, Physician, Democrat* (Holland, 1984), 93–4, 116–17, 138–9.

[9] John Stuart Mill similarly complained of the deployment of the moral law in the *Groundwork*, claiming that when Kant 'begins to deduce from this precept any of the actual duties of morality, he fails, almost grotesquely' ('Utilitarianism', in *Essays on Ethics, Religion and Society*, x, *Collected Works of John Stuart Mill*, General Editor, J. M. Robson (Toronto, 1965–), 207).

this reaction, for his moral law was strictly anti-empirical, taking its inspiration, not from a study of human nature in particular, but from that which must be valid for all rational creatures. Writing of the popular moralists of his day, Kant complained: 'it never occurs to these writers to ask whether the principles of morality are to be sought at all in our acquaintance with human nature (which we can get only from experience); nor does it occur to them that if this is not so . . . they had better adopt the plan of separating off this enquiry altogether . . . as a metaphysic of morals; of bringing this to full completeness entirely by itself' (*Groundwork*, pp. 74–5). For this reason, although his moral law was the rule by which all questions of right and wrong action were to be decided, it was not sufficient of itself to direct us in the minutiae of our day-to-day lives. To aid us in this, we need the additional guidance of the understanding, the faculty of adapting means to ends.

While Kant excludes empirical considerations from his moral philosophy, he gives them full play in his political writings, and it is this separation of spheres which forms the basis of *The Friend*'s moral and political philosophy. In the next chapter, we see Coleridge's Kantian reservations about the *efficacy* of the moral law reflected in his reluctance to espouse unequivocally the affirmative and perfectionist Quaker doctrine of the inner Light.

5

Coleridge's Quaker Subscribers

> Sara H[utchinson] tells me that he has rec'd several
> letters of thanks—one enclosing £20 and another from a
> quaker a Stranger enclosing £10
>
> John Monkhouse to Thomas Monkhouse, 26 June 1809

IT is a striking feature of *The Friend* that a large number of its subscribers were Quakers.[1] Of the five hundred or so names that have come down to us, nearly sixty are Quakers—over a tenth of the total number of subscribers—and I suspect that there are others who cannot be positively identified.[2] In this chapter I shall explain first how so many pacifist Quakers came to sign up for a vigorously anti-Napoleonic, pro-war journal. Second, I shall describe Coleridge's attitude towards Quakerism, focusing particularly on his ambivalent feelings towards the sect in 1809. Finally, I shall indicate some of the ways in which Coleridge's Quaker readership affects the general shape and content of *The Friend*. The opening number, for instance, written at the home of the Quaker Thomas Wilkinson, must be one of the most riddling and obscure essays ever written by Coleridge, and I shall argue that here.

---

[1] Rooke identifies only twenty-two Quakers (see Appendix E, *TF* ii. 407–67). Because her concern was to focus attention upon the many establishment figures who subscribed to *The Friend*, she was slow to spot the Quakers behind the many unidentified names and addresses recorded in Coleridge's notebooks and letters. In one case, for instance, she simply fixed upon the wrong man: Richard Phillips is mistakenly identified as Sir Richard Phillips, bookseller and proprietor of the *Monthly Magazine* (*TF* ii. 451). The address reveals that the Phillips on Coleridge's list was not a knight but a very prominent London Quaker—and one who was, furthermore, both a friend and relative of other well-known Quakers on the subscriber list. See the *Memoir of the Life of Richard Phillips by his daughter* (London, 1841), and the Dictionary of Quaker Biography (see n. 2 below).

[2] The Dictionary of Quaker Biography is in the process of being completed by the Librarians at Friend's House, London. It has been extremely useful for identifying Quaker subscribers—see the Appendix to this book—but it is at present incomplete.

as elsewhere in *The Friend*, the difficulty of accommodating two audiences—Quakers and non-Quakers—was partly responsible for the woeful indirectness and equivocation of his writing.

Coleridge owed his Quaker subscribers to the indefatigable efforts of Thomas Clarkson. Although he was not himself a Quaker,[3] Clarkson was intimately connected with the Society of Friends through his work as an abolitionist. In little more than a year, however, relations between the two men became strained, and what had begun as a promising financial venture ended as a source of great and lasting bitterness to Coleridge. The course of this friendship can be traced in the pages of *The Friend* as the suppressed ambivalence of Coleridge's attitude towards Quakerism gives way, in later numbers, to a pointed attack on several of the Quakers' most fundamental tenets.

If, at the outset, Coleridge had reservations about Clarkson's scheme, these were offset by a number of palpable advantages. It was reasonable for him to believe, for example, that sober and religious-minded Quakers would respond well to the serious tenor of *The Friend*; and for an author as susceptible as Coleridge to the anxieties of authorship—the bewildering 'impracticability of suiting every Essay to every Taste' (*TF* ii. 152)—it must have been encouraging to think that at least one section of his readers formed a homogeneous group with predictable tastes.

Furthermore, he was no doubt aware that the total number of *The Friend*'s Quaker readers would, in the end, be much higher than the initial figure suggested by his subscriber list; for although it is impossible to measure how far a periodical might be passed from hand to hand, it is certain that this practice is most common amongst small and related family groups, such as those which make up the Society of Friends. Clarkson claimed of the Quakers that there was no society 'where the members of it have such frequent intercourse with each other, or where they are so connected in the bonds of

---

[3] Barbara Rooke and David Erdman refer to Clarkson as a Quaker (*TF* vol. i, p. xxxviii and *EOT* iii. 71), but there is no evidence to suggest that he ever joined the sect; see Griggs's *Friend of Slaves*, pp. 30, 35, 88.

brotherly love';[4] and Anne Ogden Boyce, in her *Records of a Quaker Family*, provides us with an example of this familial spirit. Her three maiden aunts, Elizabeth, Mary, and Hannah Richardson, were sent *The Friend* by their cousin, Jonathan Priestman, who was a subscriber, and their eagerness to read the work caused Elizabeth to scold her cousin for not having sent it along earlier: 'I have looked into a few numbers of *The Friend*, and every time I have done so, I have felt surprised that thou wast not in the practice of bringing them to us as thou received them, so that we could have discussed them together. How did this happen?' Elizabeth clearly felt that Coleridge had important things to say, and her biographer remarks that there were many Friends at that time 'who wished to have the opportunity of reading weekly the opinions of Coleridge on literature, philosophy and public affairs'.[5]

With their complex network of related family groups and their frequent meetings, the Quakers provided Coleridge with a perfect working model of how he wanted *The Friend* to be supported. Ideally, the periodical was to be circulated on an informal and intimate basis, amongst subscribers of two kinds—friends, and friends of friends, the latter being people who did not know Coleridge personally but who had been carefully chosen by those who did.[6] Coleridge's hope was that 'there might be found throughout the Kingdom a sufficient number of meditative minds' to see him over the hurdle of his first twenty numbers; and once this small nucleus of readers was established, he envisaged them swelling his list of subscribers by recommending *The Friend* 'to men of kindred judgements among their acquaintances' (*TF* ii. 152).

There were also sound economic reasons for obtaining Quaker support. In the latter half of the eighteenth century, commerce had made rich men of many Quakers, and Coleridge hoped to take advantage of this new prosperity. Similarly, Wordsworth wrote to Clarkson in 1814 to secure for

---

[4] *Portraiture*, iii. 5.

[5] Anne Ogden Boyce, *Records of a Quaker family: The Richardsons of Cleveland* (London, 1889), 100, 277.

[6] Defending himself against the charge of hurrying out the Prospectuses, Coleridge begged Stuart to consider 'how large a proportion of my Subscribers are procured by private Friends' (*CL* iii. 176).

The Excursion a favourable mention in *The Philanthropist*,[7] 'because it circulates a good deal among Quakers, who are wealthy and fond of *instructive* Books' (*MY* ii. 181).

With the publication in 1806 of his *Portraiture of Quakerism*, followed by his *History of the Abolition of the Slave Trade* (1808), Clarkson himself was building a profitable literary career upon his relationship with Quakers. Two factors ensured that he made money on his books. First, by setting up subscription schemes and selling the works directly to readers, Clarkson saved the 27.5 per cent normally charged by the booksellers.[8] Second, he bolstered the number of his subscribers by promoting his books through the Quakers' highly organized and efficient programme of monthly, quarterly, and yearly meetings. Whereas for most authors, the getting of subscribers involved an enormous amount of time and energy, Clarkson's readership was an assured one. As historian of the abolition movement and apologist for Friends, he harnessed the Quaker network to forward his business concerns as an author.[9]

It was rumoured among Friends that Clarkson had made profits 'upwards of £1000' on his *Portraiture* (LSF Matthews MSS, Box A). The exact amount is not known, but it is certain that his labours were very handsomely rewarded. Dorothy Wordsworth congratulated her old friend Catherine Clarkson on the 'famous sum' of £600 for the first edition (*MY* i. 51), and several months later she mused: 'We may now fairly call you rich people, for if God preserve your husband's health what should hinder him from going on as he has begun; another subject will surely arise when he has finished his present work' (*MY* i. 156). The 'present work' referred to here was the *History*, and Dorothy's prediction about the advent of

---

[7] *The Philanthropist, or Repository for Hints and Suggestions calculated to promote the Happiness and Comfort of Men* (London, 1811–19), produced by the Quaker William Allen.

[8] See *Friend of Slaves*, pp. 89–90.

[9] Clarkson's business dealings with Quakers can be traced in his letters amongst the Lloyd papers at the Library of the Society of Friends, Friends' House, London; shelfmark: LSF Lloyd MSS 2/204–10. He was an extremely shrewd and enterprising businessman, with an extraordinary ability to devote himself entirely to the task in hand. His expertise in launching subscription schemes was much in demand; see his wife's complaint, *Friend of Slaves*, p. 81.

'another subject' was later fulfilled in Clarkson's biography of the seventeenth-century Quaker, William Penn.[10]

Southey, for one, was so impressed by Clarkson's success with the *Portraiture* that he planned to emulate his achievement with the first volume of the *History of Brazil*.[11] In May 1807 he expressed confidence that his history would bring in 'more considerable profits' than had ever yet fallen to his share (Warter, ii. 10), and later in the year he explained how this would be done. He planned to print the volume on his own account and then 'follow the example of my friend Clarkson, and dispose of any considerable number of copies myself . . . Upon this I shall consult Clarkson, who is as willing as he is able to befriend me in this matter.' (Warter, ii. 43). In the end, the scheme came to nothing, and later, when Southey saw Coleridge's difficulties in collecting subscriptions for *The Friend*, he rather hypocritically exclaimed: 'Never was anything so grievously mismanaged as the 'Friend'. Because he would have all the profit he would publish for himself; thus has he the whole trouble of collecting his money, the whole responsibility, instead of having a publisher to look to.' (Warter, ii. 189.) Like Southey himself in 1807, Coleridge was inspired by Clarkson's example to secure the whole profits to himself by setting up independently of publishers and booksellers.[12] It was for this reason that he went to stay with Clarkson at Bury St Edmunds in mid-July 1808, immediately before starting out on his journey to Grasmere.

Coleridge's visit to Bury was very timely. Arriving soon after the appearance of Clarkson's *History*, Coleridge took the opportunity of doing what he could to promote his friend's book. Although the work was selling extremely well by subscription,[13] Clarkson's state of mind at this time was 'very irritable', causing his wife to be fearful 'of the effect of any

---

[10] *Memoirs of the Private and Public Life of William Penn* (2 vols.; London, 1813).

[11] The time was ripe for such a history. In 1807, the Portuguese royal family sought refuge from Napoleon in Brazil; see Kenneth Curry, *Southey* (London and Boston, Mass., 1975), 126.

[12] Of the booksellers in particular, Coleridge had 'quite a horror', viewing their mode of trading in London as 'absolute rapacity' (*CL* iii. 213).

[13] Clarkson boasted that thousands of copies had been solicited before the work was advertised (*Friend of Slaves*, pp. 95–6).

severe review' (Allsop, ii. 112). Her fears were justifiable, as only a year before, the *Edinburgh Review* had abused the *Portraiture* as 'intolerably dull and tedious' (*ER*, April 1807, 85–102). In order to forestall a second round of such criticism, Coleridge wrote a very favourable account of the *History* and then persuaded Jeffrey to publish it (*CL* iii. 116–19).

With Clarkson 'gratified and satisfied' by the effect of this review (Allsop, ii. 113), Coleridge began to be optimistic about his own literary and financial prospects. Counting on Clarkson to do what he could for him, Coleridge hoped that by selling a thousand copies of *The Friend*, he would net for himself seven or eight hundred pounds a year (*CL* iii. 198). Although this may sound like a very high sum, it was, in fact, a rather conservative estimate: Clarkson believed that Coleridge would make this amount on only six hundred copies (WL MS A/Clarkson/15).

After staying with the Clarksons for two weeks, until the end of July, Coleridge travelled north as far as Leeds where he was quite seriously ill—probably as the result of trying to give up opium.[14] Clarkson wrote to him at the inn where he was staying, expressing sorrow at hearing of his illness and offering him money for the completion of his journey. Coleridge was to obtain this from John Broadhead, a Quaker who had 'greatly interested himself' in the sale of the newly published *History*, and who would therefore be able to supply all Coleridge's wants, 'whether they be £5 or whether they be £10'; and as his letter drew to a close, Clarkson urged Coleridge to spend some time with Broadhead, adding, 'I have no doubt, that more than ever you will love that Society, which presents the most perfect Pattern of moral Conduct, and of that which Man is capable of being brought to, upon Earth.' (WL MS A/ Clarkson/6.)[15] This letter supports the suggestion that Clarkson and Coleridge had been discussing the Quakers at Bury, and that Coleridge had professed warm feelings towards

[14] See *CN* iii. 3352, 3354.

[15] The principal source of our information about Broadhead is to be found in an obituary written for *The Annual Monitor or new letter case and memorandum book*, no. 19 (York, 1831), 8–11. He was the author of tracts on temperance, industry, and economy; his reputation was such that his advice and help were often sought by both friends and strangers.

them. It is also clear that Clarkson hoped Broadhead's virtuous life would be an inspiring example to Coleridge of the possibility of acting in perfect obedience to the voice within. As it happened, Clarkson's recommendation was a fortunate one, for the Quaker managed to get Coleridge back on his feet and send him on his way again (*TF* ii. 471–2).

The meeting with Broadhead was the first of several Quaker episodes on Coleridge's journey from Bury. While at Leeds, he reread his favourite Quaker authors, George Fox, William Penn, and the diarist John Woolman, and several of his notebook entries are inspired by Quakerish religious sentiments, and written in their distinctive idiom.[16] But perhaps the most remarkable feature of his journey was a visit to Ackworth, the Quaker school twelve miles south-east of Leeds (*CN* iii. 3349).[17] This suggests a considerable softening of attitude towards the principles of Nonconformist education, for only months before this visit, Coleridge had caused great offence to Friends by publicly attacking the Quaker educational theorist Joseph Lancaster, and eulogizing his Anglican rival, Dr Andrew Bell.[18] Other Quakers he met include Lindley Murray, whose grammatical treatises were in use at Ackworth during this period,[19] and Pim Nevins, who lived with his family in Leeds (*CL* iii. 121 n.). Finally, when he felt well enough to continue his journey north, he travelled in company with a young Quaker from Kendal, one Isaac Wilson.[20]

[16] *CN* iii. 3352–6; several of these entries relate to Coleridge's repeated efforts to master his opium habit.

[17] It is almost certain that Broadhead engineered Coleridge's visit to Ackworth, as he was a zealous supporter of the school: 'For a period of more than thirty years previous to his decease, he [Broadhead] was the faithful, zealous, active friend and supporter of the Institution at Ackworth. He was thoroughly acquainted with the discipline and economy of the Institution and manifested his solicitude for its welfare.' (*Annual Monitor*, no. 19, p. 10.)

[18] Coleridge claimed that as a result of his controversial lecture, he was menaced by the 'Bullies of Lancaster's Faction', one of whom was a Quaker zealot (*CL* iii. 98, 105). The best account of this lecture is Henry Crabb Robinson's letter to Catherine Clarkson, 7 May 1808, *Coleridge's Shakespearean Criticism*, ed. T. M. Raysor (2 vols: London, 1930), ii. 13–15.

[19] Murray was a friend of Clarkson's and lived near York. Coleridge made a memorandum to send for his works (*CN* iii. 3350).

[20] See the postscript to Broadhead's letter to the Wordsworths (*TF* ii. 471–2). Isaac Wilson is to be found in the Dictionary of Quaker Biography.

Clarkson's letters to Coleridge, written during the six months between December 1808 and the appearance of *The Friend*'s first number, reveal, among other things, that he was busy procuring subscribers from his circle of Quaker friends (WL MS A/Clarkson/6–15). Coleridge sent Clarkson a parcel of 200 Prospectuses, the largest number to be sent to any of his friends (see *CL* iii. 169–70). These Prospectuses were not, however, entirely to Clarkson's taste, and he lost no time in communicating his displeasure. The words 'Dress, Dancing and Music' were to be struck out from *The Friend*'s list of proposed subjects, and the reason Clarkson gave for this was that 'Quakers, to whom I might hand the Prospectus, might take fright—and be fearful, lest their children should see these essays, presuming that you might take the fashionable side of the Question' (WL MS A/Clarkson/8). In their dress Friends strove to be as simple as possible and in strict Quaker households dancing and music were proscribed pastimes. Clarkson's anxiety about the Prospectuses was such that a month later he wrote again to Coleridge, saying that if any came to him with the words still remaining, he would rub them out with his own pen (WL MS A/Clarkson/10). Clearly, Clarkson would have difficulty soliciting subscriptions if *The Friend* appeared to take the wrong stand on sensitive aspects of Quaker discipline. Coleridge deleted the offending words, but he was annoyed that he should feel obliged to make these alterations,[21] and this annoyance is the first sign that he was not prepared to meet *all* the Quakers' demands.

Clarkson felt that comparatively little success was to be had by writing to potential subscribers; it was far better to see people and converse with them, and for this reason London was obviously the best place for him to be. He proposed to be there at the end of December, and, just before leaving, wrote Coleridge a bullying letter about the latter's 'nearly finished' poem on the Abolition movement: if only he had finished the poem, it could have appeared in Robert Bowyer's forthcoming

---

[21] His annoyance can be heard in his letters to Wilkinson and Nevins. To the former he wrote: 'Now surely anything common to Dress or Dancing with Architecture, Gardening, and Poetry could contain nothing to alarm any man who is not alarmed by Gardening, Poetry, etc' (*CL* iii. 156; see also *CL* iii. 158–9).

Poems on the Abolition of the Slave Trade, a book which was certain to go 'into the Hands of the first People in the Kingdom'. Its appearance there, Clarkson wrote, 'would have paved *the way among numbers for the Purchase of your weekly Publication*' (WL MS A/Clarkson/9; Clarkson's emphasis). He even prevailed upon Bowyer to stop the press for three weeks in the hope that the poem would be finished. If Clarkson could remind his Quaker friends of what Coleridge was himself anxious to have publicized—his life-long commitment to the cause of Abolition[22]—then clearly he would be in a stronger position to promote *The Friend*.

In his letters Clarkson made it quite clear that he saw *The Friend* standing or falling by his ability to attract subscriptions: writing from London on New Year's Day 1809, he warned his friend that if he failed to send on the Prospectuses to him before he left London, 'the Work might go off, as far as I am concerned, for another year' (WL MS A/Clarkson/9). Clarkson asked Coleridge to send his two hundred Prospectuses to him care of William Allen, the prominent Quaker scientist and philanthropist with whom he often stayed when he was in London. Allen was a subscriber to *The Friend*; he was also one of the founding members of the Periodical Publications Committee, a committee set up by Friends in 1806, 'to consider of the best means for promoting the sale and circulation of such Books as tend to explain, and defend, our principles' (LSF Birkbeck, Misc. Papers, Box F.2). The members of this committee were free to expend 'such sums in Advertisements, or otherwise as they may see expedient', and in 1809 half of this ten-man committee subscribed to *The Friend*: in addition to William Allen, the subscribers were Luke Howard (clerk of the committee in 1809), Joseph Foster, Frederick Smith, and Richard Phillips. With such powerful Quakers behind him, Coleridge could look forward to a large and profitable circulation—providing only that his paper prove acceptable to Friends.

Clarkson was on intimate terms with each of these prominent London Quakers, and we can be sure that he was

---

[22] See his letter to Clarkson of 3 Mar. 1808 (*CL* iii. 78–9).

now willing to do for Coleridge whatever he had done in the past to promote his own works. Certainly, in his letters, he promised to do as much as he could, and his influence was such that there was some justification for his belief that the success of *The Friend* depended upon his efforts. We shall later see that Coleridge shared this belief for when it became clear to him that many subscribers had no intention of paying their subscriptions his first impulse was to blame Clarkson. Writing to Lady Beaumont in January 1810, a time when his hopes concerning *The Friend* were 'at dead low water', he exclaimed of Clarkson and his subscribers, 'What *minds*, or rather what *bodies*, I had to deal with' (*CL* iii. 275); and a week later, in a letter to Thomas Poole, he singled out the Quakers for special abuse: 'It would make you sick were I to waste my paper by detailing the numerous instances of meanness in the mode of payment & discontinuance, especially among the Quakers.' (*CL* iii. 280.) The bitterness he felt against them in 1810 for *The Friend*'s financial failure still makes itself heard five years later in *Biographia Literaria*. 'One gentleman', he wrote (and the reference is clearly to Clarkson), 'procured me nearly a hundred names for THE FRIEND, and not only took frequent opportunity to remind me of his success in his canvas, but laboured to impress my mind with the sense of the obligation, I was under to the subscribers . . . Of these hundred patrons ninety threw up the publication before the fourth number, without any notice.' (*BL* i. 175–6.) The depth and endurance of Coleridge's resentment here is a measure of the hopes he had once held in Clarkson's scheme.

Clarkson's business scheme for *The Friend* was a sound one; on this ground alone, it was unfair of Coleridge to blame him for *The Friend*'s financial losses. What made the accusation even more unfair was the fact that Clarkson's scheme could never have overcome the major obstacle of Coleridge's ambivalence towards Quakerism. Once, in the 1790s, the Quakers had come close to embodying the egalitarian teachings of Christ upon which Coleridge had hoped to build his programme of social reform. Now, in 1809, these tenets provoked a clash between religious idealism and political pragmatism.

In the 1790s in Bristol, as a young radical and outspoken critic of both the war and the slave trade, Coleridge must have encountered many Quakers in the circle of Dissenters and Liberals in which he moved; and there can be little doubt that the Quaker communities of Pennsylvania were the inspiration for the Pantisocratic scheme.[23] It could even be argued that Coleridge's uneasiness as an activist, and his growing dissatisfaction with rational dissent—with the Godwinites and the Unitarians—led him to identify the Quakers with that 'unresisting yet deeply principled Minority' of reformers referred to in his *Lectures on Revealed Religion* (*Lects. 1795*, p. 218). As his dislike and fear of the political scene began to dampen his zeal for immediate action, the quietist tendencies of Quaker reformism—its muted emphasis upon universal love, and its belief in preaching the Gospel rather than political rights—became increasingly attractive. This quietist strain of Christianized radicalism issued, eventually, in a wholesale rejection of political controversy. Towards the end of 1796, he piously wrote to the Quaker banker Charles Lloyd that 'politicians and politics' were 'a set of men and a kind of study . . . highly unfavourable to all Christian graces' (*CL* i. 240); and a couple of months later, immersed in the *Life* of the Quaker John Woolman, he exclaimed, 'I should almost despair of that Man, who could peruse the Life of John Woolman without an amelioration of Heart' (*CL* i. 302).[24]

Years later, Coleridge spoke of his life-long search for a 'vital head-and-heart FAITH' (*CL* ii. 1190), 'a moral Religion of practical Influence' (*CL* ii. 1196); and in the *Biographia*, he praised George Fox as one of the mystics who had helped him

[23] It is worth noting that in 1795, Coleridge quoted from Jean-Pierre Brissot's *New Travels in America*, a book which is full of praise for the Quaker communities of Pennsylvania (*Lects. 1795*, p. 47). The Quakers are presented as proof that 'a whole people with good morals' is not a chimera, and that such men can exist quite happily without government; see J. P. Brissot *New Travels in the United States of America. Performed in 1788*, trans. [Joel Barlow] (London, 1792), pp. xxix, 181–210, 262–431, and Sister Eugenia Logan, 'Coleridge's Scheme of Pantisocracy and American Travel Accounts', *PMLA*, 65 (1930), 1078–9.

[24] Coleridge's reading of Woolman at this time was due to the influence of his lodger Charles Lloyd, son of the Birmingham Quaker and banker. Lloyd was a disaffected Quaker, but this did not stop him from giving Woolman's works to friends as 'a keepsake'; see Charles Lamb's letters to Coleridge (Marrs, i. 96–7, 103–4).

'keep alive the *heart* in the *head*' (*BL* i. 152), thereby saving Coleridge from the atheistical and lifeless doctrines of Unitarianism, a creed which now seemed nothing but 'a physical Theory to gratify ideal curiosity' (*CL* ii. 1196). In retrospect, his rejection of radical Unitarian politics appeared as one of the most important steps in his 'final re-conversion to the whole truth in Christ' (*BL* i. 205); even at the time, the recoil had seemed like a reversion to his true self, a re-centering of his 'immortal mind'

> In the deep Sabbath of meek self-content;
> Cleans'd from the vaporous passions that bedim
> God's Image, sister of the Seraphim.
> ('Ode to the Departing Year', *PW* i. 168)

Closing his ears to the cries of the reformers, he described himself as wrapping his face in a mantle and waiting with 'a subdued & patient thought . . . to hear "the still small Voice" which is of God' (*CL* i. 395).

But the Quakerish mood of this reaction against politics was a transient one; by 1802, Coleridge was arguing on the side of war, and his earlier affection for Quakerism had become mingled with a thoroughgoing dislike of the contemporary sect. Towards the end of 1802, he wrote to his Unitarian friend John Prior Estlin:

> My creed is very simple—my confession of Faith very brief. I approve altogether & embrace entirely the *Religion* of the Quakers, but exceedingly dislike the *sect*, & their own notions of their own Religion.—By Quakerism I understand the opinions of George Fox rather than those of Barclay—who was the St Paul of Quakerism.
> (*CL* ii. 893.)

This was exactly the view of Southey: while the simple religion of the first Quakers came close to his ideal of genuine Christianity, he disliked the contemporary sect for its new theologizing habits.[25] In 1808 he wrote, 'I incline to Quakerism, and if the present Quakers abstained from insisting on articles

---

[25] It is not surprising that Southey and Coleridge should hold similar views on Quakerism, since both came under the influence of Thomas Clarkson. Geoffrey Carnall, in his excellent biography, *Robert Southey and his Age, The Development of a*

of faith, and left those points which are not explained in the
Gospel, untouched, with the same reverence as their fathers
do—I should perhaps call myself a Quaker' (Curry, i. 468).

Coleridge often complained that contemporary Quakerism
had fallen away from an old ideal. When *The Friend* had failed
and he was complaining about the 'meanness' of his Quaker
subscribers, he simply added, as though there was no more to
be said on the issue: 'So just was the answer, I once made
in the presence of some '*Friends*' to the ? What is genuine
Quakerism? Answer. The Antithesis of the present Quakers.'
(*CL* iii. 280.) For both Coleridge and Southey, the distinction
between a 'true' as opposed to a 'modern' Quakerism allowed
them to shift ground when it suited them: they tended to
praise as true those aspects of Quakerism which seemed
closest to their own ideas of genuine Christianity, and reject as
accretions many of the beliefs and practices which marked
Quakers off from other Christians.[26] But whereas Southey
claimed that he would have joined the sect were it not for the
fact that contemporary Quakers had fallen away from their
old simplicity and openness, Coleridge argued that, *because*
there was no difference between the ideal Christian and the
ideal Quaker, the true Quaker was neither more nor less than
the true Christian. In other words, he denied that the Quakers
had grounds for holding themselves aloof from other Christians.
Singling out all that he thought best about the Christianity
practised by the Quakers, Coleridge was tempted to say, in
effect, 'This is the heart of Quakerism and this belongs to all of
us as non-Quaker Christians.' This refusal to make a
distinction between Quakers and non-Quaker Christians
explains why Coleridge bridled at the assumption that *The
Friend* was to be a specifically Quaker journal; it also explains
his seeming unawareness of the difficulties which lay ahead of
him.

Conservative Mind (Oxford, 1960), 74 ff., argues that the first fruit of Southey's
friendship with Clarkson can be seen in his 1803 review of Myle's *History of the
Methodists*. There Southey had written, 'a greater blessing for mankind cannot be
desired or devised, than that the system of George Fox should become the practical
system of the Christian world'.

[26] For instances of this distinction in Southey, see Curry, i. 471, 474. For
Coleridge, see *CL* ii. 893, iii. 156, 158, and *CN* iii. 3910.

Coleridge's denial of any special status to the Quakers sprang partly from anti-sectarian feeling; but it was also a truly historical way of viewing Quakerism, for the early Friends did not see themselves as a sect but as a movement.[27] Modelling their religion upon that of the early Christians, they styled themselves 'primitive Christians' and denied that there was anything innovative about their faith and practice. Quakerism, it was claimed, was no more than 'a new nickname for old Christianity'.[28] But Coleridge's faithfulness to the self-image projected by the early Quakers was unacceptable to modern Friends because he used it to deny the very basis of their existence as a sect. And the offence must have been all the greater given that the Quakers had come to see themselves as a people apart, a special and exclusive group called forth by God to bear witness against the ways of the world.

Coleridge added to his dislike of sectarianism an instinctive distrust of simplicity and universalism. Doctrinally, Quakerism was a minimalist faith: it simply called upon all men, whether Christian or not, to recognize the voice of God within them; and because the Quakers believed that the inner Light was 'God's Talent to All: A Faithful and True Witness and Just Monitor *in every Bosom*',[29] hierarchy had no place in their Society, and they rejected the notion of a priesthood. As W. H. Barber has pointed out, in an article demonstrating the affinities between Quakerism and the Enlightenment, it was this tolerance and breadth of vision which so fascinated Voltaire when he first encountered the Quakers in England.[30] For Coleridge, of course, the fact that the Quakers made such an impression on the French deist could only confirm him in

[27] An excellent discussion of this subject is to be found in R. T. Vann, *The Social Development of English Quakerism: 1655–1755* (Cambridge, Mass., 1969), ch. 4, 'The Idea of Membership', 123 ff. and ch. 6, 'From Movement to Sect', 197 ff.

[28] One of William Penn's tracts was entitled *Quakerism a new nick-name for old Christianity* (1672). Penn also claimed that the Quakers 'did not consider how to contradict the World, or distinguish themselves as a *Party* from others; it being none of their Business, as it was not their *Interest*: No, it was not the Result of Consultation, or a framed design by which to declare or recommend Schism or Novelty' (*A Brief Account*, p. 52).   [29] *A Brief Account*, p. 29.

[30] 'Voltaire and Quakerism: Enlightenment and the inner light', *Studies on Voltaire and the Eighteenth Century*, 24 (1963), 81–109.

his suspicion of the '*potential* infidelity' lurking behind their doctrinal liberalism.[31] Equally worrying was the socially subversive impact of Quakerism as an *imperium in imperio*. Forming socially distinctive communities based upon egalitarian beliefs, the Quakers challenged the Coleridgean clerisy, 'the successive Few in every age' to whom, he believed, we owe our ameliorated condition (*TF* ii. 52).

Given Coleridge's religious and political reservations about the way in which Quakerism had developed historically, it was inevitable that he should feel in two minds about his Quaker readers. We have seen their financial importance to him, and have also noted his genuine admiration for those features of the religion which had remained constant to his ideal of primitive Christianity. But his dislike of the contemporary sect meant that, whilst keen to have Quakers sign up for *The Friend*, he had no intention of alienating other readers on their account. Perhaps the best symbol of his willingness to go so far but no further with Quakerism can be seen in the name he gave his new periodical. We do not know when Coleridge settled upon 'The Friend' as his title, but it was at some time either during or after his visit to the Clarksons in July 1808.[32] His choice was, in part, a symbolic concession to the Quakers, and it had its desired effect: one of Coleridge's non-Quaker subscribers informed him that the title had excited 'no little curiosity' amongst the sect in Yorkshire (*TF* vol. i, p. xxxix). But 'The Friend' was a safe title too, for it had been used before as a periodical name;[33] furthermore, it fitted nicely into the general pattern of eighteenth-century titles (such as *The Lover*, *The Batchelor* and

[31] In *The Statesman's Manual*, Coleridge attacks Lancaster, the Quaker educationalist, for disseminating the ' "*liberal idea*" of teaching those points only of religious faith, in which all denominations agree' (*LS*, p. 40).

[32] The title makes its first appearance in Coleridge's notebooks in an entry headed 'Hints for the Friend' (*CN* iii. 3407).

[33] In the Bodleian Library there are three eighteenth-century periodicals called *The Friend*. The earliest is a weekly essay which appeared every Sunday in 1755. Then in 1774, another anonymous journal called itself *The Friend: or, Essays Instructive and Entertaining for Youth of Both Sexes: on the most important subjects: exemplified with stories from Real Life*. The third is, like the first, a weekly essay, but it is not anonymous: *The Friend: A Weekly Essay* by William Fox, Attorney at Law (London, 1796).

The Guardian),[34] and it was not unlike other names with which Coleridge was toying at this time—*The Advocate* and *The Upholder* (*CN* iii. 3366, 3390). It is my own belief that Coleridge's choice was influenced by what Clarkson says about the word 'Friend' in his *Portraiture*. In the introduction to this work he refers to the title 'Friend' as 'a beautiful appellation, and characteristic of the relation which man, under the Christian dispensation, ought uniformly to bear to man' (vol. i, p. viii). Later, Clarkson identifies the two quite different ways Quakers use the term: 'They use the word Friend as significative of their own union, and, when they speak to others, as significative of their Christian relation one to another.' (i. 328.) So, when one Quaker speaks to another, the term Friend simply denotes a fellow member of the sect; but it is also used of non-Quakers, signifying a broad Christian fellowship where friendship is envisaged as the highest relationship possible between men. The Quakers' wider use of this term would have been especially gratifying to Coleridge, for his early, idealizing conception of friendship remained as the basis for much of his later moral and political thinking:

The ardour of private Attachments makes Philanthropy a necessary *habit* of the Soul. I love my *Friend*—such as *he* is, all mankind are or *might be*! The deduction is evident—. Philanthropy (and indeed every other Virtue) is a thing of *Concretion*—Some home-born Feeling is the *center* of the Ball, that, rolling on thro' Life collects and assimilates every congenial Affection. (*CL* i. 86.)[35]

Thus, the double aspect of the word 'Friend' suited Coleridge's purposes exactly, for he wanted to stand both inside and outside the Quaker circle; whilst happy to have Quakers respond to his title's special appeal, he was equally keen to insist that his periodical was written for all Christian believers.[36]

---

[34] See the Alphabetical List of Periodicals published by G. S. Marr in *The Periodical Essayists of the Eighteenth Century* (London, 1923), 260–4.

[35] Rooke tentatively suggests that the 'key' to the meaning of Coleridge's title lies in this 1794 letter to Southey (*TF*, vol. i, p. xxxix).

[36] Coleridge made it quite clear to his Quaker friend Pim Nevins that his periodical was to be a work 'addressed to *all men*' (*CL* iii. 158).

With the publication of the first, Kendal, Prospectus, Coleridge was instantly taken to task by the Quaker Thomas Wilkinson, the man whom Dorothy Wordsworth was to dub 'The Father of *The Friend*' (*MY* i. 356). Although we do not possess Wilkinson's letter, we can reconstruct the nature of his 'doubts and apprehensions' from Coleridge's reply (*CL* iii. 155–7).[37] Wilkinson was dissatisfied with the Prospectus because he expected to find there a statement of the Quakers' most cherished belief: that all men have the Light of Jesus within. Instead, he found the rather vague and non-committal statement that *The Friend* would provide 'Sources of Consolation to the afflicted in Misfortune, or Disease, or speculative Gloom, from the Exertion and right Application of the Reason, the Imagination, and the moral Sense' (*TF* ii. 18, n. 5). Wilkinson's expectations were disappointed: Coleridge was bidding for the attention of Friends, and yet his Prospectus did not give so much as a hint of any commitment to Quaker doctrine.[38] Wilkinson even seems to have doubted whether Coleridge planned to discuss the subject of religion at all. To this objection Coleridge replied: 'I neither intend to omit, nor from any fear of offence have scrupled to announce my intention of treating, the subject of religion. I had supposed that the words 'speculative gloom' would have conveyed this intention' (*CL* iii. 155). He then went on to make the rather extraordinary claim that he had been induced to omit 'the principle of internal guidance' from the Prospectus because he feared he might be mistaken for a Quaker. It was the absence of this principle which led Wilkinson to believe that Coleridge 'denied the existence of an internal monitor' (*CL* iii. 155–6).

Coleridge was shocked by this assumption, and he cited John Woolman's *Life* in support of his claim that he *did* believe in the inner Light:

[37] James Dyke Campbell attempted to do this in a brief article entitled 'Coleridge on Quaker Principles', *The Athenaeum* 3438 (16 Sept. 1893), 385–6.

[38] Samuel Tuke, a Quaker friend of Wilkinson's, also disliked the Prospectus. Writing to Wilkinson in Mar. 1809, he enquired if Coleridge was 'going forward with his projected paper "The Friend" ', adding, 'I did not like the Prospectus' (LSF, Thomas Wilkinson MS/20).

Oh that in all things, in self-subjugation, unwearied beneficence, and unfeigned listening and obedience to the Voice within, I were as like the evangelic John Woolman, as I know myself to be in the belief of the existence and the sovran authority of that Voice! When we meet, I will endeavour to be wholly known to you as I am, in principle at least. (*CL* iii. 156.)

The nervous movement of the entire letter to Wilkinson reflects Coleridge's dilemma. He wanted to convince Wilkinson of his unshakeable belief in a principle he had deliberately dropped from his Prospectus; and though admitting that he dropped it for fear of sounding like a Quaker, he is none the less anxious to reassure Wilkinson of his oneness with him in the Quaker faith.

Coleridge's selective approach to Quakerism makes itself felt behind his conditional avowal of the Quaker faith: 'if', he claimed to Wilkinson, the works of William Penn 'contain a faithful statement of genuine Christianity according to your faith, I am one with you'. A much more direct and striking avowal of Quakerism is declared in the postscript, but it arises out of a very thorny passage of self-defence. To Wilkinson's accusation that he had been *merely pretending* to be sympathetic to Quakerism in order to increase his subscriber list, Coleridge replied:

P.S. Do you not know enough of the world to be convinced that by declaring myself a warm defender of the Established Church against all sectarians, or even by attacking Quakerism in particular as a sect hateful to the bigots of the day from its rejection of priesthood and outward sacraments, I should gain twenty subscribers to one? It shocks me even to think that so mean a motive could be supposed to influence me. I say aloud everywhere, that in the essentials of their faith I believe as the Quakers do, and so I make enemies of the Church, of the Calvinists, and even of the Unitarians. Again, I declare my dissatisfaction with several points both of *notion* and of *practice* among the present Quakers—I dare not conceal my convictions—and therefore receive little good opinion even from those, with whom I most accord. (*CL* iii. 157.)

Coleridge was determined to show Wilkinson that he *did* believe in the existence of an internal monitor, and it is possible that his stay with him was connected with this purpose. Nor was Wilkinson the only Quaker to whom Coleridge declared his intention of affirming the inner Light: to Pim Nevins he promised that the existence and divine nature of the Voice within would be one of the foundation stones of *The Friend* (*CL* iii. 158).

The opening essay of *The Friend* reveals, however, that Coleridge did not 'say aloud everywhere' what he was prepared to admit in his letters: that in the essentials of their faith he believed as the Quakers did. In fact, the obscurity of Number 1 is such that it is very difficult to tell from moment to moment what it is that Coleridge is talking about. Sometimes he seems to be discussing Reason, or conscience; at other times his unnamed subject sounds like free will, or man's innate knowledge of good and evil. An example of the way in which Coleridge manages to keep his terms as open as possible can be seen in the following passage, where he appeals mysteriously to certain unspecified 'universal persuasions', amongst which we must place:

the sense of a self-contradicting principle in our nature, or a disharmony in the different impulses that constitute it—of a something which essentially distinguishes man both from all other animals, that are known to exist, and from the idea of his own nature, or conception of the original man.   (*TF* ii. 7.)

Such evasiveness was, I believe, partly the result of two pressures, both of which relate to his Quaker readership. The correspondence with Wilkinson had impressed upon Coleridge that the Quakers would only be satisfied by some reference to the inner Light. At the same time, however, because he did not want to be seen to be writing for Quakers alone, he was determined to avoid what he called 'peculiar & sectarian phraseology' (*CL* iii. 158). Faced with such a dilemma, Coleridge resorted to subterfuge: he cunningly slipped in an allusion which was designed to be recognized by Quakers, but not by anyone else. This allusion was to one of the best known expositions of the inner Light, from William Penn's Preface to George Fox's *Journal*, the very text which Coleridge had cited to Wilkinson as one of his favourite Quaker tracts (see *CL*

iii. 156). In his preface, Penn writes that the 'Light of Christ within' is the Quakers' '*Fundamental* Principle, which is as the *Corner stone* of their Fabrick . . . the *Root* of the goodly Tree of Doctrines that grew and branched out from it'.[39] Coleridge clearly adopts these images in the opening paragraph of Number 1 where he refers mysteriously to a subject, 'trite indeed and familiar as the first lessons of childhood; which yet must be the foundation of my future Superstructure with all its ornaments, the hidden Root of the Tree, I am attempting to rear, with all its Branches and Boughs' (*TF* ii. 6).[40] Given Coleridge's desire to write for both Quakers and non-Quakers, a strong echo of Penn's inner Light which none the less stops short of declaring itself is exactly what we might expect to find in *The Friend*'s opening number. The echo served another purpose as well. Coleridge's own terms for the Voice or Light within were *conscience*, or the *effective Reason*, and the allusion was one way of bringing the Quakers round to seeing an affirmation of their own distinctive beliefs behind these orthodox equivalents.

The second source of Coleridge's uneasiness in Number 1 lies in his reservations about the efficacy of the Light, and the status of its authority in relation to God. In his letter to Wilkinson Coleridge offered the example of John Woolman's perfect obedience to the Light as a vindication of its sovereign authority. His own experience was, however, very much at odds with this conviction; knowing how easily the dictates of conscience were overturned, Coleridge often felt less than confident about the Light's *effective* authority. In a memorable aphorism on man's moral nature, he summarized his feelings thus: 'We can scarcely think too highly of the potential in us, or too humbly of the Actual.'[41]

Also, when thinking about the Light as God's Reason, Coleridge's habit was to draw a distinction between a practical and a theoretical view of the faculty. In a notebook

---

[39] *A Brief Account*, p. 36.

[40] Hooker's tree of English conservatism may also have been an influence here; see below, pp. 108–9.

[41] Marginal note on Schlegel's *Athenaeum*, quoted by Kathleen Coburn, *Experience into Thought: Perspectives in the Coleridge Notebooks* (Toronto, 1979), 80.

entry of 1805, we find him meditating on two analogies, the
first being that of watches and the sun, the second being men's
consciences and God's Reason:

Never goes quite right, any one; no two go exactly the same, they
derive their dignity and use as being Substitutes and Exponents of
heavenly motions/ but still in a thousand instances they are & must
be our instructors, by which we must act, in practice presuming a
co-incidence, while theoretically we are aware of incalculable
Variations.   (*CN* ii. 2661.)

Man's conscience is no more than a substitute, an
inaccurate indicator of God's Reason.[42] However, at the same
time as Coleridge opens the gap between the human and
divine, he attempts to bridge it by asserting a discontinuity
between what we know to be true of the limitations of
conscience, and what we must in practice presume of its
authority. Although conscience can only give us a very
approximate idea of God's Reason, we are none the less
obliged to fall back on it as our only guide.

The voice of conscience is sovereign, then, not because it is
God's voice speaking within, nor because it is always
effective—the diseased will militates against that; it is
sovereign because it behoves us to regard it as authoritative.
Given the complex tissue of feelings surrounding Coleridge's
thinking about the conscience, it is not surprising that when
he finally ushers the term into Number 1, he fails to recapture
the confident and affirmative spirit of his letters to Wilkinson
and Nevins, where the inner Voice had been spoken of as
'divine', and imbued with 'sovran authority'. In Number 1 he
writes:

It is still the great definition of humanity, that we have a conscience,
which no mechanic compost, no chemical combination, of mere
appetence, memory, and understanding, can solve; which is indeed
an *Element* of our being!—a conscience, unrelenting yet not absolute;
which we may stupify but cannot delude; which we may suspend,
but cannot annihilate; although we may perhaps find a treacherous

---

[42] Nor do the dictates of one man's conscience necessarily coincide with those of
another: 'no two go exactly the same'.

counterfeit in the very quiet which we derive from its slumber, or its entrancement.   (*TF* ii. 8.)

Each assertion brings with it a qualifying clause; and in the attempt to hold together the theoretical and practical aspects of conscience, a gap appears between Coleridge's desire to make high claims for the faculty and his awareness of its fallibility in practice. On balance, it could be claimed that the qualifying clauses work for, and not against, the authority of conscience: the conscience may not be absolute, but it cannot be deluded or annihilated. Nevertheless, the passage comes to rest rather gloomily on the fact that a slumbering or entranced conscience is a good counterfeit of an annihilated one.

Coleridge's guardedness about the authority of our inner monitor was to have repercussions on his political arguments in *The Friend*, shaping his anti-individualism and his tendency to think about man under two quite separate headings, that is, as a private individual and as a citizen of the state. As we shall see in Chapter 7, Coleridge's restricted application of the principles of pure Reason to the sphere of the moral life is tantamount to a rejection of the Quakers' habit of regarding the inner Light as a rule of conduct in all matters.

After his stay with Wilkinson, Coleridge returned to Grasmere: the first two numbers had been published, and the third was already at the printer's (*MY* i. 355). He did not again come under Quaker influence, and consequently he strained less and less to make special allowances for their views. Apart from two flattering asides in Numbers 4 and 5 (both references to Clarkson and the Quakers as fighters against slavery),[43] there is little to suggest that catering for the Quakers still occupied the foreground of Coleridge's thinking; in fact, a new *anti*-Quaker note is sounded in Number 6.

Anger with Clarkson was the principal cause of Coleridge's sudden, overt hostility towards Quakerism. By the middle of June 1809, Coleridge was in need of more paper: he had

---

[43] 'What have not Clarkson, Granville Sharp, Wilberforce, and the Society of the Friends, effected for the English Nation, imperfectly as the intellectual and moral faculties of the People at large are developed at present?' (*TF* ii. 69); see also *TF* ii. 53.

enough for Number 3, but not enough to continue *The Friend* with any regularity. Consequently, he wrote to Clarkson to see what he could do (*CL* iii. 212). According to a letter from Coleridge to Stuart, written three months later, Clarkson replied by penning 'one of the most unfeeling letters, that ever man received'. Denying to Stuart that he had ever applied to Clarkson for money, Coleridge immediately gives the lie to this statement by launching into a bitter attack on Clarkson for squandering away 'his Wife's property as well as [his] own on very worthless Objects but on the other hand Objects and Persons whose Obligations to him feed and flatter his ostentation & love of feeling his superiority & power' (*CL* iii. 222). The refusal of a further loan from Clarkson was pain-ful enough in itself,[44] but Coleridge was much more deeply wounded by what he took to be Clarkson's suggestion that subscribing to *The Friend* was tantamount to subscribing to a charity. Writing to Lady Beaumont in the last few months of *The Friend*, Coleridge exclaimed,

what *minds*, or rather what *bodies*, I had to deal with, your Ladyship will find no difficulty in conjecturing from a phrase contained in a letter to me from Mr Clarkson, to whose application I owed from sixty to seventy Names . . . 'You ought to consider, that THE FRIEND is a very *dear* work—what if I had charged a shilling per sheet for *my* work?—and that fifty two shillings a year is a serious sum for a person to *bestow* upon one Author.' Pity that Mr C. had not added—'when there are so many other *Objects* of Distress that have equal or stronger claims on the charitable'.   (*CL* iii. 275–6.)[45]

This is a fairly accurate account of what Clarkson had written. Furious with Coleridge for advertising a new edition of his poems at the end of Number 2, Clarkson had begged him to concentrate on one thing at a time, pointing out at the same time that most of *The Friend*'s subscribers would be unable to afford a second work, and that those who could afford it had 'great Calls upon them, so that they would think 50 Shillings a

---

[44] Clarkson had written, 'I can neither give, lend, nor borrow. I have given, lent and borrowed for others to the last Shilling' (WL MS A/Clarkson/15).

[45] This is the core of Coleridge's later, and highly embellished account of *The Friend*'s publication in *Biographia Literaria*.

year quite sufficient to give to one Persons work. They would like to have liberty for other works . . . than to be thus confined.' (WL MS A/Clarkson/15.) In his anxiety to persuade Coleridge of the importance of concentrating on *The Friend*, Clarkson did not hold back from saying that some of his subscribers were 'even now doubtful whether they should continue the Work'.

This remarkable piece of tactlessness—prompted, no doubt, by disappointment with *The Friend*'s opening numbers—undermined Coleridge's confidence in Clarkson's subscribers at an early stage. As *The Friend* proceeded, and Coleridge became more and more convinced that his readers were dropping away on all sides, his attitude towards his Quaker subscribers hardened. Freed from any sense of obligation to Clarkson, he no longer took care to step his way around controversial issues. Perhaps the most sensitive of these was pacifism; on this subject more than on any other, Coleridge's antagonism towards Clarkson and the Quakers can be clearly heard.

Few testimonies were as precious to Quakers as their pacifist rejection of all forms of violence; and the subject of the Quakers' peace principle forms an important part of Clarkson's *Portraiture*. In a chapter on the conflict between the policy of the world and the policy of the gospel, Clarkson frankly states that wars have nothing to do with Christianity: 'To confess . . . that wars must be, is either to utter a libel against Christianity, or to confess that we have not yet arrived at the stature of real Christians' (iii. 97). Citing a number of early Church authorities, Clarkson argues that a distinction was habitually made between soldiers and Christians; he also demonstrates the way in which primitive Christians, and the Quakers who modelled themselves upon them, grant the widest application possible to the biblical command, 'Love thy Enemy'. No geographical boundaries should fix 'the limits of love and enmity between man and man' (iii. 35), and no distinction is to be made between public and private enemies, such that it is lawful to kill one's country's enemies, but unlawful to kill one's neighbour. For Quakers, wartime killing carried as heavy a burden of justification as civil murder.

The rousing of *The Friend*'s war-cry in Number 6 followed

soon after the arrival of Clarkson's offensive letter.[46] In this number, Napoleon is described as a force of pure evil, the leader of an army whose lawless violence can only be stemmed by a nation united in opposition; mixed and scattered virtues, 'at civil War with themselves, or at best perplexing and counteracting each other', provide no defence whatsoever against Napoleon's 'giant and united Vices'. It was Britain's misfortune that

in the present Hour of Peril we may hear even good Men painting the horrors and crimes of War, and softening or staggering the minds of their Brethren by details of individual wretchedness; thus under pretence of avoiding Blood, withdrawing the will from the defence of the very source of those blessings without which the blood would flow idly in our veins, and lest a few should fall on the Bulwarks in glory, preparing us to give up the whole State to baseness, and the children of free Ancestors to become Slaves, and the Fathers of Slaves.   (*TF* ii. 84.)

The generosity of Coleridge's opening description of the advocates of peace as 'good Men' is suddenly exploded by the suggestion that their concern for human life is a 'pretence', a cover beneath which they engage (whether consciously or not) in politically subversive activities. Nor does Coleridge leave us in any doubt as to the identity of these peace men. Writing admiringly of Machiavelli's political aphorisms, he goes on to argue that the weightier of these should be collected together into a book, which should then be prefixed with the motto: ' "The Children of Darkness are wiser in their Generation than the Children of Light" ' (*TF* ii. 85).

By Number 12, Coleridge had thrown off all restraint upon the subject. To those who argued that men should make ploughshares rather than arms, and that soldiers and sailors would be 'better employed' in peaceable activities than 'in fighting or in learning to fight', he replied,

When the fifteen millions, which form our present Population, shall have attained to the same purity of Morals and of primitive christianity, and shall be capable of being governed by the same

---

[46] Coleridge claimed to Lady Beaumont that Clarkson's letter arrived after the appearance of Number 5 (*CL* iii. 275).

admirable Discipline, as the Society of the Friends, I doubt not that we should be all Quakers in this as in the other points of their moral Doctrine. But were this transfer of employment desirable, is it *practicable* at present, is it in our power? These Men *know*, that it is not. What then does all their Reasoning amount to? Nonsense.

(TF ii. 169.)

At first Coleridge sounds as though he is reaffirming his earlier approval of the essentials of Quaker faith; indeed, David Erdman cites the phrases 'purity of Morals' and 'admirable Discipline' as evidence of Coleridge's enduring sympathy for Quakerism (*EOT* iii. 71). But what begins as approbation of the fact that the Quakers' desire for peace rather than war is right in principle ends in the contemptuous sneer of the practical man for those who hope to change the world. Nor does Coleridge stop at the charge of impracticability: he goes beyond this to say that the Quakers knowingly and cynically pursue goals which make nonsense of all their efforts.

The argument against peace on the grounds of its impracticability is joined by a host of other claims as Coleridge becomes more aggressively outspoken and patriotic. For instance, the cry for peace becomes associated in later numbers with a lack both of manliness,[47] and of a proper nationalistic spirit. Patriotism is described in elevated, Burkean terms as 'a necessary link in the golden chain of our affections and virtues' (*TF* ii. 323), and nationalism is prized above an arid and meaningless cosmopolitanism. In a discussion reminiscent of the 1790s debate between private attachment and universal benevolence, Coleridge weighs up the claims of nationalism and cosmopolitanism; and just as he had earlier attacked the notion of a universal benevolence which excluded private affection, he now turns away 'with indignant scorn' 'from the false Philosophy or mistaken Religion, which would persuade him that Cosmopolitism is nobler than Nationality, and the human Race a sublimer object of love than a People' (*TF* ii. 323). The ideal Patriot should turn his back on those

---

[47] In Number 22, Coleridge refers to the 'unmanly impatience for Peace' which prevailed in England at the time of the Treaty of Amiens (*TF* ii. 300).

who aspire to be the friends and benefactors of the whole human race—an aspiration dear to the Quakers, and one fuelled by their belief that we are 'all children of the same parent and therefore brothers to each other'.[48] The visionary hope of 1795, of the coming of that 'glorious period when Justice shall have established the universal fraternity of Love' (*Lects. 1795*, p. 13), has been replaced by a patriotic ideal: the soldier whose greatest act of love is to 'force a passage for his Comrades by gathering up the Bayonets of the Enemy into his own breast: because his Country "*expected every Man to do his duty!*" ' (*TF* ii. 323.) Convinced that the war against Napoleon was a 'blessed' one for Britain (*CL* iii. 58), Coleridge joined the ranks of those who interpreted the call for peace as proof either of blindness or cowardice, or, worse still, of an attachment to the enemy's cause.

Thus, we see Coleridge move in *The Friend* from a position of uneasiness and equivocation to a direct assault on the Quakers' pacifism and their steadfast refusal, even in a time of national crisis, to compromise their religious principles. The hardest hit of all occurs in Coleridge's allegorical defence of Britain's seizure of the neutral Danish fleet in 1807 (*TF* ii. 328–33). Depicting Denmark's neutrality in the war as treacherous to England's security, Coleridge ends his allegory by personifying Denmark as a Quaker:

'if I were out on a shooting Party with a Quaker for my companion, and saw coming on towards us an old Footpad and Murderer, who had made known his intention of killing me wherever he might meet me; and if my companion the Quaker would neither give me up his Gun, nor even discharge it as (we will suppose) I had just before unfortunately discharged my own; if he would neither promise to assist me nor even promise to make the least resistance to the Robber's attempt to disarm himself; you might call me a Robber for wresting this Gun from my companion, though for no other purpose, but that I might at least do for by myself, what he *ought* to have done, but *would* not do either for, or with me!'   (*TF* ii. 332–3.)

---

[48] See Clarkson's *Portraiture*, iii. 34–5.

6

The Conservative Tradition: Hooker and Burke

There is, by the essential fundamental Constitution of things a radical infirmity in all human contrivances, and the weakness is often so attached to the very perfection of our political Mechanism, that some defect in it, something that stops short of its principle, something that controls, that mitigates, that moderates it, becomes a necessary corrective to the Evils that the Theoretick Perfection would produce . . . Prudence (in all things a Virtue, in Politicks the first of Virtues) will lead us rather to acquiesce in some qualified plan that does not come up to the full perfection of the abstract Idea, than to push for the more perfect, which cannot be attain'd without tearing to pieces the whole contexture of the Commonwealth, and creating an heart-ache in a thousand worthy bosoms.

Edmund Burke to Charles-Jean-François Depont,
November 1789

IT was Coleridge's intention in Number 9 of *The Friend* to develop 'from its' embryo Principles the Tree of French Liberty, of which the Declaration of the Rights of Man, and the Constitution of 1791 were the Leaves, and the succeeding and present State of France the Fruits' (*TF* ii. 123). According to Coleridge, the chief planters of this tree of French liberty were Rousseau and the French economists. These were the men who, as ideologues of the French Enlightenment, attempted to build society on the simplest of bases: on natural law and on the universals of abstract reason. Holding elevated and optimistic beliefs about the power of each and every man's reason, these *philosophes* argued for an inalienable sovereignty inherent in every rational being; and from this they deduced that 'the People itself is its' own sole rightful Legislator' (*TF* ii. 128).

To the Enlightenment's universalist and rationalist political theory, Coleridge opposes a concrete, conservative body of thought, one which is rooted in the historical and the particular rather than in the general and speculative. Abstract ideas of Right—such as those embodied in the concepts of the General Will and of the inalienable sovereignty of the People—were alluring at first glance, but ultimately they cleared the way 'for military Despotism, for the satanic Government of Horror under the Jacobins, and of Terror under the Corsican' (*TF* ii. 128).

Coleridge prefaces his essay with a long quotation from the opening chapter of Richard Hooker's *Of the Lawes of Ecclesiasticall Politie* (1593).[1] Hooker was one of Coleridge's favourite writers,[2] and he had recently been rereading his treatise on Law as part of his preparation for *The Friend* (*CN* iii. 3574). This treatise is an elaborately constructed defence of the Church of England against its Puritan critics, and the passage which Coleridge selects for quotation warns of the dangers of questioning what has been long established, and of seeking to resolve all difficulties by reference to a single rule. Characterizing Truth as complex and difficult of access— 'obscure, dark and intricate'—Hooker argues that we can only penetrate to its depths by dint of great intellectual effort. Laws are similarly elusive and mysterious. Although attractive and familiar enough on a superficial view, like a beautiful tree, laws have a root 'in the bosom of the Earth concealed; and if there be occasion at any time to search into it, such labour is then more necessary than pleasant, both to them which undertake it and for the lookers on' (*Lawes*, I. 1.2, as quoted in *TF* ii. 122). Thus, those who seek out and attempt to tamper with the root can only ever be an expert and intrepid minority,

---

[1] Only the first four Books were printed in 1593. Book V appeared in 1597, Books VI and VII in 1648 and all eight Books in 1662. For the publishing history of this work, see vol. i of *The Folger Library Edition of the Works of Richard Hooker*, general ed. W. Speed Hill, vols. i– (Cambridge, Mass., 1977–). References to the *Lawes of Ecclesiasticall Politie* will appear as *Lawes*, followed by book and chapter and section numbers.

[2] For Coleridge's admiration of Hooker, see *TF* ii. 26, 150 and *Marginalia*, ii. 1131, 1146.

and even these must approach their task with infinite caution and reverence.

Unlike the massive and ancient tree of English law, the roots of which lie buried in the accumulated wisdom and experience of past ages, the tree of French liberty is imagined in *The Friend* as an upstart growth, sprung from the shallow despotism of abstract Reason. Coleridge's appropriation of Hooker's tree metaphor is a way of saying that the earlier writer's work is itself a part of the established wisdom lying behind English law. It is also a hint to his readers of the provenance of his arguments for uprooting the theories of Rousseau and the French economists.

The opening gambit of Hooker's work was to challenge what he saw as the Puritans' mistaken reliance upon Scripture as the sole law to be followed in all things:

> For whereas God hath left sundry kindes of lawes unto men, and by all those lawes the actions of men are in some sort directed: they hold that one onely lawe, the scripture, must be the rule to direct in all thinges, even so farre as to the *taking up of a rush or strawe*.
>
> (*Lawes*, II. 1.2.)

Rejecting the Puritans' formula for conduct as too simple, Hooker argues that man is subject to several different kinds of law, according to the different aspects of his being:

> as the actions of men are of sundry distinct kindes, so the lawes thereof must accordingly be distinguished. There are in men operations some naturall, some rationall, some supernaturall, some politique, some finally Ecclesiasticall. Which if we measure not ech by his owne proper law, whereas the things themselves are so different; there will be in our understanding and judgement of them confusion. (*Lawes*, I. 16.5.)

It is part of the purpose of Hooker's treatise to eliminate this confusion by declaring 'what lawe is, how different kindes of lawes there are, and what force they are of according unto each kind' (*Lawes*, Preface 7.2).

Of the general categories of law drawn up by Hooker,[3] the

---

[3] Hooker lists six different categories of Law (*Lawes*, I. 3.1).

two most important are the laws of Reason, and positive, or
human, laws. These are the two areas of law which relate most
directly to man, and the distinction which is drawn between
them provides part of the background of Coleridge's elabora-
tion in Number 9 of the realms of Reason and Understanding,
of principle and prudence.[4]

For Hooker the law of Reason 'which men commonly use to
call the law of nature' (*Lawes*, I. 8.9) is the universal moral
law which God lays down for all men, and which all men are
capable of understanding through the faculty of Reason. With
the exception of children, innocents, and madmen, in all men
'there is that light of reason, whereby good may be knowne
from evill, and which discovering the same rightly is termed
right' (*Lawes*, I. 7.4). In so far as this law is derived from
God's eternal law, it is divine in nature; it is also binding upon
all men because it comprises a series of self-evident propositions which every man possessed of Reason is capable of
discovering for himself. In fact, so self-evident are these truths
of Reason that Hooker adopts an anti-rationalist position to
drive the point home:

The maine principles of reason are in themselves apparent. For to
make nothing evident of it selfe unto mans understanding were to
take away al possibility of knowing any thing. And herein that of
Theophrastus is true, *They that seeke a reason of all things do utterly
overthrow reason.* In every kind of knowledge some such grounds there
are, as that being proposed the mind doth presently embrace them
as free from all possibilitie of error, cleare and manifest without
proofe.   (*Lawes*, I. 8.5.)[5]

But while it is easy to discern the first principles of this law of
Reason, other, more specific maxims can only be known by
deduction:

The first principles of the law of nature are easie, hard it were to
finde men ignorant of them: but concerning the duty which natures
lawe doth require at the handes of men in a number of thinges

---

[4] In a marginal note on the *Lawes*, Coleridge remarked that Hooker was one of the
many forerunners of Kant in his recognition of a distinction between Reason and
Understanding (*Marginalia*, ii. 1152).

[5] For Coleridge's interest in the quotation from Theophrastus, see *CN* iii. 3574
and *TF* i. 464.

particular, so far hath the naturall understanding even of sundry whole nations bene darkned, that they have not discerned no not grosse iniquitie to bee sinne.   (*Lawes*, I. 12.2.)

Once we descend from the general, universal realm into that of the particular, we enter a twilight region of error and uncertainty where complexity and diversity reign supreme, and where nothing can be resolved by reference to simple, absolute rules. It is at this point in his argument that Hooker develops his concept of human, or positive law.

As a result of 'the staines and blemishes . . . springing from the root of human frailtie and corruption' (*Lawes*, Preface 3.7), Hooker believed that we are incapable of observing all the precepts of Reason, and must necessarily live under the compulsion of positive law. Also, quite apart from the difficulties arising from our weak and erring nature, the laws of Reason are strictly limited in so far as they concern themselves with general principles; unable to take account of the contingencies of human life, they are particularly ill-suited to the needs of 'politic societies'. Those who set too much store by abstract and general principles show themselves to be ignorant of 'what restraintes and limitations all such principles have, in regarde of so manifold varieties as the *matter* whereunto they are appliable doth commonlie afford' (*Lawes*, V. 9.2). And because these varieties are 'not knowne but by much experience', the exercise of adducing the proper limits and application of principles 'requireth more sharpnes of witt, more intricate circuitions of discorse, more industrie and depth of judgment then common habilitie doth yeeld' (*Lawes*, V. 9.2). Until their limits be fully known,

generall rules . . . are, by reason of the manifolde secret exceptions which lye hidden in them, no other to the eye of mans understandinge then cloudie mistes cast before the eye of common sense. They that walke in darknes knowe not whether they goe. And even as little is theire certaintie whose opinions generalities onlie doe guide. With grosse and popular capacities nothinge doth more prevaile then unlimited generalities, because of theire playnenes at the first sight; nothinge lesse with men of exact judgment, because such rules are not safe to be trusted over farre.   (*Lawes*, V. 9.2.)

Whereas general laws of Reason are permanent and unchanging, human laws, especially those which Hooker describes as 'meerly' human,[6] are subject to alteration according to what is 'fit and convenient' (*Lawes*, I. 10.10), or 'as the matter it selfe is concerning which they were first made' (*Lawes*, I. 15.1). The notion of expedience as the standard for judging human law, and the belief that good human laws should be flexible enough to adapt to changing circumstances, are central to Hooker's conception of man-made law. Expanding on these ideas, he holds 'that lawe-makers must have an eye to the place where, and to the men amongst whome; that one kinde of lawes cannot serve for all kindes of regiment' (*Lawes*, I. 10.9). Similarly, the lawmaker who wants to 'judge rightlie of thinges done'

must joigne with his formes and conceiptes of generall speculation the matter wherein our actions are conversant . . . For in as much as the hand of justice must distribute to *everie particular* what is due, and judg what is due with respect had no lesse of particular circumstances then of generall rules and axiomes, it cannot fit all sorts with one measure, the wills counsels qualities and states of men beinge divers.

(*Lawes*, V. 81.4.)

Hooker's emphasis upon the variety and changeableness of human nature and affairs, his rejection of abstract, universal rules and his repeated insistence upon the importance of 'particular circumstances' all emerge as features of *The Friend*'s political philosophy. Like Hooker, Coleridge believes that man needs to live under positive law; because his nature is not primarily rational but 'mixed'—made up of 'something besides Reason' (*TF* ii. 132)—he needs more guidance than that which is given by laws of Reason. Moreover, whereas angels and glorified spirits embody pure Reason, man's reason is always under constraint, for it must 'cloath itself in the Substance of individual Understanding and specific Inclination, in order to become a Reality and an Object of Consciousness and Experience' (*TF* ii. 132).

Imitating Hooker's twofold distinction between human and natural law, Coleridge contrasts laws which flow from the

---

[6] The distinction between 'mixedly' and 'meerly' human laws appears in *Lawes*, I. 10.10.

pure Reason and are 'immutable', with 'Regulations dictated by Prudence' which have passed away, 'and while they lasted, were binding only for that one State whose particular Circumstances rendered them expedient' (*TF* ii. 128). Fully endorsing Hooker's rule that diversity reigns supreme in political and social affairs, Coleridge repeatedly warns his readers of the dangers of applying broad general rules without due regard to varied circumstances. For instance, in Number 7, he writes, 'A Constitution equally suited to China and America, or to Russia and Great Britain, must surely be equally unfit for both, and deserve as little respect in political, as a Quack's panacæa in medical, Practice.' (*TF* ii. 105.)

Coleridge also adopts Hooker's hierarchy of law, in which to move from laws of Reason to human laws is to 'descend unto probable collections what is convenient for men'; in moving down, we find ourselves 'in the territorie where free and arbitrarie determinations, the territorie where humane lawes take place' (*Lawes*, I. 8.11). In imitation of this, Coleridge sets up a disjunction in Number 9 between a 'magic Circle of the pure Reason' and a 'Sphere of the Understanding and the Prudence' (*TF* ii. 127). As the phrase 'magic Circle' suggests, Coleridge follows Hooker in assigning to the laws of Reason a somewhat limited and specialized field in which to operate. Although principles deduced from Reason are central to a proper understanding of a man as a moral being and as an end in himself, Coleridge makes it absolutely clear that these same principles are of little use in thinking about man as a social and political being. In a passage reflecting Coleridge's desire to grant all and nothing to Reason, we read:

That Reason should be our Guide and Governor is an undeniable Truth, and all our notion of Right and Wrong is built thereon: for the whole moral Nature of Man originated and subsists in his Reason. From Reason alone can we derive the Principles which our Understandings are to apply, the Ideal to which by means of our Understandings we should endeavour to approximate. This however gives no proof, that Reason alone ought to govern and direct human beings, either as Individuals or as States. It ought not to do this, because it cannot. The Laws of Reason are unable to satisfy the first conditions of Human Society. (*TF* ii. 131.)

A further instance of Coleridge's ambivalence towards Reason can be found in his claim that, while the 'measure of the Understanding and of all other Faculties of Man, is different in different Persons . . . Reason is not susceptible of degree'. Although, on this basis, he asserted the spiritual equality of all men—'In respect of their Reason all Men are equal' (*TF* ii. 125)—in practical terms this same assertion gives rise to the exclusion of Reason from the sphere of man's social and political life. No field of human activity

which subsists wholly in degrees, the changes of which do not obey any necessary Law, can be Subjects of pure Science, or determinable by mere Reason. For these things we must rely on our *Understandings*, enlightened by past experience and immediate Observation, and determining our choice by comparisons of Expediency. (*TF* ii. 129.)

Just as Hooker's 'generall rules' could prove 'no other to the eye of mans understandinge then cloudie mistes cast before the eye of common sense' (*Lawes*, V. 9.2), so too those lofty, spiritual attributes of Reason are shown to be impediments to the construction of *The Friend*'s practical political philosophy.

For Hooker, the great variety of human laws is testimony to the fact that they are concerned not with absolutes, but with contingencies; unlike the laws of Reason which 'do bind men absolutely, even as they are men' (*Lawes*, I. 10.1), human laws relate to men as members of a social order. This distinction between man considered in himself and man considered as a social and political creature finds a central place in *The Friend*, with Coleridge quoting in Number 4 the all-important conclusion to Hooker's first Book:

For as Hooker has well observed, the law of men's actions is one, if they be respected only as men; and another, when they are considered as parts of a body politic.   (*TF* ii. 57.)[7]

For this reason, Hooker argued, it is 'both commonly sayd, and truely, that the best men otherwise are not alwayes the best in regard of societie.' (*Lawes*, I. 16.6.) This rather

---

[7] 'the law of mens actions is one, if they be respected only as men; and another, when they are considered as parts of a politique body' (*Lawes* I. 16.6).

startling deduction, with its implied distinction between the morally good man and the politician, does not appear in *The Friend* because Coleridge is at pains to demonstrate the opposite point: that no distinction can rightly exist between the honest man and the true patriot (*TF* ii. 327). Nevertheless, as we shall see later, Coleridge's adoption of Hooker's sense of the 'moral differences' between private and public life is far from trouble-free, entailing considerations which, even when glozed over by Coleridge's moral rhetoric, are yet sufficiently perplexing to set up disquieting reverberations throughout his text.

A number of other features of Hooker's work can be traced in *The Friend*. For example, Coleridge employs Hooker's notion of consent to sanction the authority inherent in human law.[8] If there be any difference, Coleridge writes, 'between a Government and a band of Robbers, an act of consent must be supposed on the part of the People governed' (*TF* ii. 103). In Book I of his treatise, Hooker had made it clear that laws derive their ultimate validity from the consent of the people who are to be governed by them: 'Lawes they are not therefore which publique approbation hath not made so' (*Lawes*, I. 10.8); and since, by nature, men 'have no ful and perfect power to commande whole politique multitudes of men; therefore utterly without our consent we could in such sort be at no mans commandement living' (*Lawes*, I. 10.8). Although this notion of consent looks like an eminently liberal idea, it in fact forms the keystone of Hooker's conservatism and of his defence of the established Church. Since a law is the deed of the whole body politic, of which all men are members, every man has a duty to observe that law;[9] thus, the Puritans were duty-bound to conform to the laws of the established Church as laid down by those who had lived before them. The passage quoted above continues:

[8] For an excellent discussion of Hooker's notion of consent, see W. D. J. Cargill Thompson, 'The Philosopher of the "Politic Society": Richard Hooker as a Political Thinker' in *Studies in Richard Hooker*, ed. W. Speed Hill (Cleveland and London, 1972), 40.

[9] 'A lawe is the deed of the whole bodie politike, whereof if ye judge your selves to be any part, then is the law even your deed also' (*Lawes*, Preface 5.2).

And to be commanded we do consent, when that societie whereof we are parte hath at any time before consented, without revoking the same after by the like universall agreement. Wherefore as any mans deed past is good as long as him selfe continueth: so the act of a publique societie of men done five hundreth yeares sithence standeth as theirs, who presently are of the same societies, because corporations are immortall: we were then alive in our predecessors, and they in their successors do live still.   (*Lawes*, I. 10.8.)

The marginal note which Coleridge appended to this passage, establishing the parallel in his mind between Hooker's notion of consent and Kant's Idea of the social contract, is a sign of his approval: 'an ever originating Social Contract *is* an Idea, which exists and works continually and efficaciously in the Moral Being of every free Citizen' (*Marginalia*, ii. 1148).[10]

Hooker's concept of shared agreements, linking together past and present, led him to his deep reverence for long-established habit and custom. We should

be slow and unwillinge to chaunge without verie urgent necessitie the ancient ordinances rites and longe approved customes of our venerable predecessors . . . That which wisdome did first begin and hath bene with good men longe continewed, chalengeth allowance of them that succeede, although it plead for it selfe nothinge . . . there are fewe thinges knowne to be good, till such time as they grow to be ancient.   (Lawes, V. 7.3.)

This classic statement of conservatism went hand in hand with a rejection of individualism. According to Hooker, individual judgement is a decidedly inferior guide to that offered by traditional laws and customs which have been agreed upon not 'by one, or two, or few, but by all' (*Lawes*, I. 8.9). Arguing that the dictates of individual Reason must bow before a collective, public, and historical Reason, Hooker castigated those who 'breede disturbance' by 'following the law of private reason, where the law of publique should take place' (*Lawes*, I. 16.6). Such 'patrons of libertie', as Hooker

---

[10] The belief in an original social contract as an event or historical fact struck Coleridge as an absurd theory: 'no more than a means of simplifying to our Apprehension the ever-continuing causes of social union, even as the Conservation of the World may be represented as an act of continued Creation' (*TF* ii. 102).

sarcastically called the Puritans, set up their own private judgement above all other authority, proclaiming that the laws of those in command were void 'in as much as everie man is left to the freedom of his owne minde in such thinges as are not either exacted or prohibited by the law of God' (*Lawes*, V. 71.4). In response to this plea for the unfettered exercise of private judgement, Hooker argued that:

Those thinges which the Law of God leaveth arbitrarie and at libertie are all subject unto possitive lawes of men, which lawes for the common benefit abridg particular mens libertie in such thinges as farre as the rules of equitie will suffer. This wee must either maineteine or els overturne the world and make everie man his own commaunder.   (*Lawes*, V. 71.4.)

In the stormy 1790s, the ascendancy of the individual conscience over established custom and habit was a popular theme of reactionary writing; in the Prospectus of *The Antijacobin* (1797), individualism is cited as one of the besetting vices of the new radical philosophy:

We have yet to learn the modern refinement of referring in all considerations upon human conduct, not to any settled and preconceived principles of right and wrong, not to any general and fundamental rules which experience, and wisdom, and justice and the common consent of mankind have established, but to the internal admonitions of every man's judgment or conscience in his own particular instance.[11]

This distrust of individualism as a subversive, jacobinical principle is also present in *The Friend*, but whereas *The Antijacobin* displays a universal suspicion of the claims of conscience,[12] Coleridge is careful not to confine its claims, except in the realm of politics. His account is more subtle and complex, turning, as we shall see, upon a Hooker-like and Kantian distinction between a realm of spriutal freedom and a realm of political necessity.

[11] The writer was George Canning; see *Burke, Paine, Godwin and the Revolution Controversy*, ed. Marilyn Butler (Cambridge, 1984), 216; hereafter cited as *Revolution Controversy*.

[12] In the passage quoted from the Prospectus, Canning was actually speaking of morals (*Revolution Controversy*, p. 216).

From this brief account of Hooker's *Lawes of Ecclesiasticall Politie* it is clear that his work influenced Burke's political thought. Throughout Burke's writings, and particularly in his *Reflections on the Revolution in France* (1790), we find the same distrust of naked, individual Reason, and the recommendation that we rely instead on the collected Reason of ages: 'We are afraid to put men to live and trade each on his own private stock of reason; because we suspect that this stock in each man is small, and that the individuals would do better to avail themselves of the general bank and capital of nations, and of ages.' (*Reflections*, p. 183.) Hooker can also be heard in Burke's concept of one generation binding another in such a way as to preclude radical reform. Where the state is concerned, 'no man should approach to look into its defects or corruptions but with due caution' for it constitutes a partnership 'not only between those who are living, but between those who are living, those who are dead, and those who are to be born' (*Reflections*, pp. 194–5).[13] Thus every lawmaker and reformer should exhibit reverence and respect towards the state; using an image loaded with emotional and ideological significance for his theory of the family as the basis of social life, Burke appeals to the reformer to handle the state with that 'tender parental solicitude which fears to cut up the infant for the sake of an experiment' (*Reflections*, p. 277).

Burke also inherited Hooker's characterization of politics as a practical science, concerned with the immediate, the actual, and the concrete. Abhorring abstract or speculative notions of political right, he stood forth as the champion of a statesmanship based on expediency and circumstance:

Circumstances (which with some gentlemen pass for nothing) give in reality to every political principle its distinguishing colour, and discriminating effect. The circumstances are what render every civil and political scheme beneficial or noxious to mankind.

(*Reflections*, p. 90.)

---

[13] Wordsworth echoes this idea in *The Prelude*. 'There is', he writes, 'One great society alone on earth/ The noble living and the noble dead' (X, 11, 968–9). See also *The Convention of Cintra, The Prose Works of William Wordsworth*, ed. W. J. B. Owen and J. W. Smyser (3 vols.; Oxford, 1974), i. 339.

This is a recurrent theme of Burke's writings in the 1790s. In his *Letter to a Member of the National Assembly* (1791), we read:

I must see with my own eyes, I must, in a manner, touch with my own hands, not only the fixed, but the momentary circumstances, before I could venture to suggest any political project whatsoever. I must know the power and disposition to accept, to execute, to persevere. I must see all the aids, and all the obstacles . . . I must see the things; I must see the men.   (*LMNA* iv. 384.)

And because existing institutions were the growth of generations of experience, reformers should feel dwarfed and humbled in their presence:

The science of government being therefore so practical in itself, and intended for such practical purposes, a matter which requires experience, and even more experience than any person can gain in his whole life, however sagacious and observing he may be, it is with infinite caution that any man ought to venture upon pulling down an edifice which has answered in any tolerable degree for ages the common purposes of society, or on building it up again, without having models and patterns of approved utility before his eyes.
(*Reflections*, p. 152.)

It was because France ignored the complexity of government, treating it as a simple, theoretical game, subject to universal rules, that her progress had been so stormy. For Burke, France's political misfortunes were all attributable to a single source: 'that of considering certain general maxims, without attending to circumstances, to times, to places, to conjunctures, and to actors' (*LMNA* iv. 386). In connection with this emphasis upon the tangible, he frequently uses the word 'experience'. His doctrine of 'experience and nothing but experience' is, in the words of one recent critic, 'a way of knowing the world nonabstractly. It conveys that special power on institutions hallowed by time and on affections endeared by custom. It is the mode of practice rather than of theory'.[14] Not that Burke wants to overthrow the role of abstract ideas altogether, for to do so would be to dismiss

[14] James K. Chandler, *Wordsworth's Second Nature: A Study of the Poetry and Politics* (Chicago, 1984), 40–1; further references to this important study of Wordsworth's Burkeanism will appear as Chandler.

principles,[15] but the aspiration for 'Theoretick Perfection' in Government must always be held in check by 'something that controls, that mitigates, that moderates it'.

Finally, Hooker and Burke share the ideal of a unified church integrally joined to a unified commonwealth. Church and State are part of a single whole, an organic and hierarchic society sharing common underlying principles. As an extension of this idea, religion is seen to have a social function as well as a spiritual end. For Burke, true religion is 'the basis of civil society' (*Reflections*, p. 186); for Hooker, it is 'the roote of all true vertues and the stay of all well ordered common-wealths'.[16] Nevertheless, built into this rhetoric of unity is the important proviso that ecclesiastical and civil life are concerned with different values and different spheres of activity. A difference consists, Hooker writes, 'in the matter about which the actions of each are conversant' (*Lawes*, VII. 14.13); and in *Reflections* Burke clears a space between civil and religious life by claiming of pulpit politics that the 'cause of civil liberty and civil government gains as little as that of religion by this confusion of duties' (*Reflections*, p. 94).

Coleridge's firm repudiation of novelty in morality and politics,[17] his opposition to a priori conceptions of political right, his dislike of abstract notions in statesmanship, and his rejection of the doctrine that absolute sovereignty resides in the will of the people—all these can be traced to a common tradition of English conservatism. Over and above this, however, we find in *The Friend* a number of specific debts to Burke: Coleridge's characterization of Rousseau as the intellectual father of the French revolution, his view that Rousseau's

---

[15] We are reminded of the subtlety of Burke's position in Chandler, p. 33.

[16] These words form the title of the opening chapter of Book V of *Lawes*. In connection with this point, see also *Lawes*, V. 1.2.

[17] 'how shall I avert the scorn of those Critics who laugh at the oldness of my Topics, Evil and Good, Necessity and Arbitrement, Immortality and the ultimate Aim. By what shall I regain their favour? My themes must be *new*, a French Constitution; a Balloon; a change of Ministry; a fresh Batch of Kings on the Continent, or of Peers in our happier Island . . . Something new, however, it must be, quite new and quite out of themelves: for whatever is within them, whatever is deep within them, must be as old as the first dawn of human Reason' (*TF* ii. 73).

philosophy flattered 'the pride and vanity of men' (*TF* ii. 140), and his sarcastic attitude towards the 'enlightened' eighteenth century.[18]

The Friend's admiring reference to Burke's presiding genius as 'keen-eyed yet far-sighted' (*TF* ii. 21) suggests that he possessed political shrewdness and moral vision, a combination of gifts which sorted well with Coleridge's dual commitment to what we are, and to what we are capable of becoming. Even more pertinent to his purposes in *The Friend* is his presentation of Burke's career as similar to his own. In Number 2, where Coleridge refutes the charge of his earlier radicalism, he prefaces his self-defence with a conservative passage from one of Burke's early speeches when 'he was the most beloved, the proudest name' with the Friends of Liberty (*TF* ii. 22). Ostensibly, his strategy is to reveal Burke as a man who, like himself, had always held sufficiently large and progressive views to endear him to both political parties. The real point of the analogy is, however, a deeper one: that neither he nor Burke deserve the charge of apostasy because they had always been conservatives.

Burke's influence on the younger man was a long-standing one. At Cambridge, Coleridge's fellow undergraduates did not need to buy Burke's controversial pamphlets, for on the day they appeared, they were read and memorized by their enthusiastic friend; then, to the delight of the young men assembled in his rooms in the evening, he would repeat 'whole pages verbatim'.[19] That Burke's arguments made a deep impression on Coleridge at this time can be clearly seen in his early political writings. Perhaps the most conspicuously Burkean passage—and one whose message is still heard clearly in *The Friend*—is to be found in the introductory address to his *Conciones ad Populum* (1795). In this passage, Coleridge criticizes the Democrats on two accounts. The first charge against them concerned their tendency to condemn institutions without thinking, attributing to the system which

---

[18] 'The notion of our measureless superiority in Good Sense to our Ancestors, is somewhat less fashionable, than at the commencement of the French Revolution: we hear less of the jargon of *this enlightened Age*' (*TF* ii. 85). See also *TF* ii. 45, 52.

[19] E. K. Chambers, *Samuel Taylor Coleridge: A Biographical Study* (Oxford, 1938), 20.

they rejected 'all the evils existing under it' (*Lects. 1795*, p. 37). Burke had similarly fulminated against the revolutionaries' work of wholesale destruction. Bent on pulling 'every thing in pieces' and 'habitually employed in finding and displaying faults', these men disqualified themselves 'for the work of reformation' (*Reflections*, pp. 282–3). The second of Coleridge's charges against the Democrats concerned their penchant for judgements based on nothing more than untried theory. Contemplating truth and justice ' "in the nakedness of abstraction" ', they 'condemn constitutions and dispensations without having sufficiently examined the natures, circumstances, and capacities of their recipients' (*Lects. 1795*, p. 37).

The phrase ' "in the nakedness of abstraction" ' alludes to the well-known passage near the beginning of the *Reflections* where Burke declares that he 'cannot stand forward, and give praise or blame to any thing which relates to human actions, and human concerns, on a simple view of the object, as it stands stripped of every relation, in all the nakedness and solitude of metaphysical abstraction' (*Reflections*, pp. 89–90).[20]

Because he believed that the successful running of a society depended upon trained and experienced practitioners, Burke had little respect for political theorists and speculators; for men of letters who meddled with politics he had nothing but the most virulent contempt. Chief of the literary offenders were Voltaire and Rousseau. These writers, together with other figures of the French Enlightenment, were so completely taken up 'with their theories about the rights of man' that they seemed to Burke to 'have totally forgot his nature' (*Reflections*, p. 156). Rousseau's doctrines were singled out as particularly pernicious: paradoxical and immoral, they were the beliefs of a madman and an atheist (*Reflections*, p. 182).

A month after Burke's *Reflections* appeared, the National Assembly paid homage to Rousseau by voting that a statue be raised to him as the liberator of France.[21] For Burke, this was

---

[20] Cf. Wordsworth's use of the metaphor of nakedness to describe the Godwinian dream of Reason: '. . . the dream / Was flattering to the young ingenuous mind / Pleased with extremes, and not the least with that / Which makes the human reason's naked self / The object of its fervour' (*The Prelude* x, 815–19). See also *Excursion* v II. 560–3.   [21] Chandler, p. 98.

a very timely public gesture, lending credibility to his charge
that there existed a link between recent events in France and
the new 'atheisticall' philosophy. Emboldened, he hammered
the point home, denouncing modern French philosophers as
men who, 'ignoble, savage and hard-hearted', were undermining the foundations of Church and State. Rousseau's
'philosophy of vanity'—*The Social Contract* and *Émile*—had
become the 'canon of holy writ' for members of the National
Assembly; and the man himself was 'their standard figure of
perfection': 'His blood they transfuse into their minds and into
their manners. Him they study; him they meditate; him they
turn over in all the time they can spare from the laborious
mischief of the day, or the debauches of the night.' (*LMNA*
iv. 373.) Drawing inspiration and guidance from his writings,
the National Assembly attempted

to find a substitute for all the principles which hitherto have been
employed to regulate the human will and action . . . They have
therefore chosen a selfish, flattering, seductive, ostentatious vice, in
the place of plain duty. True humility, the basis of the Christian
system, is the low, but deep and firm foundation of all real virtue.
But this, as very painful in the practice, and little imposing in the
appearance, they have totally discarded.   (*LMNA* iv. 373.)

This censure of Rousseau and other French Enlightenment
philosophers exerted a powerful influence over later observers
of Jacobinism, assuming grotesque proportions in 1798 when
it was seriously argued by one writer that the revolution was
effected by an antichristian conspiracy of philosophers, bent
upon the subversion of the lower orders from their traditional
pieties. With Voltaire as their ringleader, these conspirators
acknowledged no other master but that of their own Reason.
Their collective teaching, contemptuously referred to as
'philosophism', was an arrogant, specious system of thought,
thoroughly inimical to the spirit of religion, and secretly
peddled throughout the countryside to all who could read, or
were willing to listen:

Philosophism is the error of every man who, judging of every thing
by the standard of his own reason, rejects in religious matters every
authority that is not derived from the light of nature. It is the error of

every man who denies the possibility of any mystery beyond the limit of his reason, of every man who, discarding revelation, in defence of the pretended rights of reason, their liberty and equality, seems to subvert the whole fabric of the Christian religion.[22]

Coleridge was not tempted to indulge in conspiracy theories; nor, in his reaction from radical politics, did he manifest a sudden and excessive dislike for 'visionary *philosophes*'.[23] Nevertheless, he shared Burke's profound distrust of French metaphysics and his wariness of prevailing public opinion. For Coleridge, a knowledge of contemporary speculative principles—the scheme or mode of moral and political thinking currently in vogue—was an important indication of the stability or otherwise of a society. In *The Friend* he referred to the wide diffusion throughout the public highways of pre-revolutionary France, not just of radical catchwords, but of endless disputations concerning 'the most abstract Principles of the universal Constitution' (*TF* ii. 107). He later came to Burke's conclusion that revolutions did not have their origins 'in the cabinets of statesmen, or in the practical insight of men of business, but in the closets of uninterested theorists, in the visions of recluse genius': 'all the *epoch-forming* Revolutions of the Christian world, the revolutions of religion and with them the civil, social, and domestic habits of the nations concerned, have coincided with the rise and fall of metaphysical systems' (*LS*, pp. 14–15).

   Taking *Reflections on the Revolution in France* as his model in Number 9, Coleridge aims his attack, as Burke had done, at the philosophical thought of Rousseau. He even follows Burke in matching Rousseau with an English counterpart—a sower

[22] *Memoirs, Illustrating the Antichristian Conspiracy: A Translation from the French of the Abbé Barruel* (Dublin, 1798), 4. Perhaps it was Coleridge's reading of this work which prompted him in 1799 to refer, resignedly, to the 'philosophisms' which 'fly to and fro—in serieses of imitated Imitations' (*CL* i. 538).

[23] In 1799, at the height of the Tory reaction, Coleridge wanted Wordsworth to write a blank verse poem 'addressed to those, who, in consequence of the complete failure of the French Revolution, have thrown up all hopes of the amelioration of mankind, and are sinking into an almost epicurean selfishness, disguising the same under the soft titles of domestic attachment and contempt for visionary *philosophes*' (*CL* i. 527). For Coleridge's characterization of himself as '*un Philosophe*', see *CL* i. 421 and his later revision of this letter for inclusion in *The Friend* (*TF* ii. 192).

of French revolutionary doctrine at home—but it is not Richard Price[24] (or any other Dissenter for that matter), but the country gentleman and so-called 'Father of Reform', Major John Cartwright. As was the case with Burke in his *Reflections*, Coleridge's attack on Enlightenment philosophy was provoked, not so much by the existence of mischievous political principles across the Channel, as by the propagation of these principles at home. The cry for parliamentary reform had been raised again in 1807, and was to culminate in a great demonstration of support in May 1809.[25] Coleridge opposed this call for reform;[26] in the speeches of men like Cartwright he believed he could hear a repetition of those abstract ideas of political right which had led to the excesses of the French Revolution. Although he admitted that there was some truth in the claim that the French code of revolutionary principles had been 'rejected as a *System*' in England (*TF* ii. 110), certain maxims and principles were sufficiently compelling to have maintained a life of their own. To Coleridge's mind, chief amongst these were the political principles derived from abstract notions of man's pure Reason.

Coleridge directed his arguments against Cartwright for two reasons. First, he rightly saw in Cartwright's reforming zeal a potential threat to the homogeneity of the governing élite; as a landowner and country gentleman, Cartwright must have seemed to Coleridge a betrayer of his class, a man whose actions signalled the breakdown of traditional social structures. Second, Cartwright was a safe person to attack precisely because he was *not* a dissenter. There is little doubt that Coleridge viewed English Dissent as the subversive home counterpart of French revolutionary doctrine, for he believed

---

[24] Burke believed that Price was the ringleader of those who wanted to reform the English state 'on the French model' (*The Correspondence of Edmund Burke*, ed. T. W. Copeland (10 vols.; Cambridge 1958–70), vi. 81).

[25] See S. Maccoby, *English Radicalism 1786–1832 from Paine to Cobbett* (London, 1955), 246. For general background to the reform movement in this period, see Michael Roberts, *The Whig Party 1807–1812* (London, 1939), 172–302, and G. S. Veitch, *The Genesis of Parliamentary Reform* (London, 1913), 343.

[26] In a letter to Daniel Stuart, written during the pause after the appearance of Number 2, Wordsworth wrote, 'I find Coleridge is decidedly against *Reform* and shall be very happy to hear what he has to say upon the subject which I believe he will not fail to do in the next or succeeding numbers of "The Friend" ' (*MY* i. 359).

that '*Unanglicanism*' or 'the mersion of derivative, official and representative Duties, Powers, and Privileges in *personal* rights is one of the principal ingredients in Jacobinism' (*CL* iv. 710). Yet much as he would have liked to follow Burke by striking out against a leading representative of this tradition, he fought shy of doing so, partly because a large number of Dissenters had signed up as subscribers, but mainly because he had been so closely associated with them in the past.

This early involvement with Dissent makes all the difference to Coleridge's account of Enlightenment philosophy, enabling him to adopt the tone of a sympathetic insider to the system he stands outside and criticizes; and it is on the basis of this sympathy and toleration that he seeks to establish himself as a more authoritative, because more balanced, critic than Burke. The difference between the two writers is seen most obviously in their treatment of their English opponents. Burke's attitude towards Price is one of withering contempt, and nowhere is this contempt more corrosive than in those few pages where abusive epithets are rained down upon the Dissenter's head for naïvely confounding the quite separate duties of the preacher and the politician: Price is a 'spiritual doctor of politics', a 'political Divine' who propagates 'political gospel' (*Reflections*, pp. 96–9).[27] For Coleridge, Cartwright is guilty of a similar confusion of the realms of morality and politics, but for this offence he is only mildly reproved. One epithet alone is bestowed upon him: that of the 'venerable State-Moralist', a term which conveys succinctly, but respectfully, 'the whole Error of his System' (*TF* ii. 137).

The gentlemanly and forbearing spirit of Coleridge's discussion of Cartwright underpins his claim that *The Friend*'s critique of revolutionary principles offers more rounded insights than the accounts given by other conservative writers. Unlike Burke, who had pitted himself from the start against all that the revolution stood for, Coleridge had been 'a sharer in the general vortex', one whose feelings and imagination had not remained 'unkindled' in the general conflagration of the 1790s

---

[27] For a good analysis of this aspect of Burke's rhetoric, see D. O. Thomas, *The Honest Mind: The Thought and Work of Richard Price* (Oxford, 1977), 316–17.

(*TF* ii. 146). This is admitted with some pride in *The Friend*, because it authorized him to testify to the power and attractiveness of Enlightenment modes of thinking. This testimony is put to very different uses in *The Friend*. First, it provided Coleridge with a strong argument in justification of his youthful errors. Second, it functioned as an essential part of a critical method committed to uncovering the 'whole Truth' about French Enlightenment philosophy. To this latter end, Coleridge argued that Rousseau's philosophy was mischievous, not because it was entirely misguided, but because it was composed of half-truths. Quoting from Wordsworth's *Prelude*, he suggests that, like others of their generation, they had approached 'the shield/Of human nature from the golden side/And would have fought, even to the death, to attest/The quality of the metal' which they saw (*TF* ii. 147). Until this golden side was conceded by anti-Enlightenment writers, their arguments would carry scant authority, for the only antidote to a system composed of both truth and falsehood was not to dismiss it out of hand, but to address both its good and bad points.

Burke himself was by no means impervious to the 'golden side' of Rousseau's writings. In a letter of 1791, he confessed that the Frenchman 'saw things in bold and uncommon lights';[28] and he was prepared to admit publicly that Rousseau's style was 'glowing, animated, enthusiastic', so much so that, when he was 'sometimes moral', he could be 'moral in a very sublime strain' (*LMNA* iv. 377). For the most part, however, his energies were spent in vilifying his opponent, and in the rare moments when he does concede something to the other side, there is no trace of the principle on which we see Coleridge proceeding: that the adoption of a more generous attitude increases rather than diminishes the scope and effectiveness of one's attack. According to *The Friend*, it was a 'bad policy to represent a political System as having no charm but for Robbers and Assassins, and no natural origin but in the brains of Fools or Madmen, when Experience has proved, that the great danger of the System

---

[28] *The Correspondence of Edmund Burke*, vol. vi, p. 81.

consists in the peculiar fascination, it is calculated to exert on noble and imaginative Spirits' (*TF* ii. 123). The anti-Jacobins of the 1790s relentlessly pursued this misguided policy. Cynically raising a 'panic of Property' for party purposes, they so hysterically distorted and falsified the system they attacked that they ended up believing their own lies: 'even', Coleridge writes, 'as our Bulls in Borrowdale sometimes run mad with the echo of their own bellowing' (*TF* ii. 143). The inevitable and disastrous upshot of this aristocratical frenzy was that it only confirmed the young radicals in their newly acquired faith.

Such, at least, was Coleridge's view of the radical decade, and he counted Burke amongst the most virulent of these anti-Jacobins. The anti-intellectualism and anti-rationalism of Burke's writings had always seemed to Coleridge to be serious flaws in his critique of radical thinking. In *The Watchman*, he included Burke amongst those who 'lampooned God Almighty for having made men rational!', and in general, he was disturbed by the 'throb and tempest of political fanaticism' at work in Burke's writings (*Watchman*, pp. 35, 31). Although his admiration of Burke only increased over the years, traces of the earlier reservations persist. In a very odd and enigmatic passage of *The Friend*, he alludes to a certain inconsistency in Burke's 'fundamental Principles', an inconsistency which takes the form, not of supporting different principles at different periods of his life, but of appealing to different principles within the space of a single work: 'If his Opponents are Theorists, *then* every thing is to be founded on PRUDENCE, on mere calculations of EXPEDIENCY . . . Are his Opponents Calculators? *Then* Calculation itself is represented as a sort of crime.' (*TF*, ii. 124.)

Although Burke defended his volatility 'on the pretext of balancing the too much on the one side by a too much on the other', this justification carried little weight with Coleridge who saw himself pursuing a cooler line of argument: that 'the whole Truth is the best antidote to Falsehoods which are dangerous chiefly because they are half-truths' (*TF* ii. 124).

Coleridge was particularly disturbed by Burke's portrait of

the rationalist as a dispassionate and heartless creature,[29] and his claim that the revolutionary philosophy was the 'offspring of cold hearts and muddy understandings' (*Reflections*, p. 171). Nothing seemed more exaggerated and wrong-headed than these two claims, and they were misrepresentations which seemed to carry as much danger in 1809 as they had done in the 1790s.[30] Speaking from his own experience, Coleridge claimed that the revolutionary philosophy was generated not by hard-hearted and unfeeling philosophers, but by young men like himself, generous and warm-hearted spirits who 'in the amiable intoxication of youthful Benevolence, are apt to mistake their own best Virtues and choicest Powers for the average qualities and Attributes of the human Character.' (*TF* ii. 123.) There were few points on which Coleridge was more insistent than this, a fact which can be attributed, most simply and obviously, perhaps, to his desire for self-vindication. This plea went hand in hand with an unshakable devotion to the generous ideal of human nature upon which Enlightenment political theory was built. For all the disastrous shortsightedness and impracticability of political doctrines derived from Reason and natural law, it none the less remained true that these concepts retained a certain abstract and ideal moral beauty. In a letter to the Beaumonts describing his youthful radicalism, Coleridge spoke of his earlier speculative principles as ' "Dreams linked to purposes of Reason" '.[31] He then went on to defend these shadowy ideals by suggesting that they made up the best part of his youth:

For what is the nature & the beauty of Youth? Is it not this—to know what is right in the abstract, by a living feeling, by an intuition of the uncorrupted Heart? To body forth this abstract right in beautiful

---

[29] 'Nothing can be conceived more hard than the heart of a thorough-bred Metaphysician. It comes nearer to the cold malignity of a wicked spirit than to the frailty and passion of a man' (*Letter to a Noble Lord* (1796) in *Works*, ed. Charles William, Earl Fitzwilliam, and Sir Richard Bourke (8 vols.; London, 1852, v. 241).

[30] Coleridge's anxiety about this aspect of Burke's propaganda can be traced from *The Watchman* through the notebooks to *The Friend* (see *Watchman*, pp. 33–4, *CN* i. 1623, ii. 2503 and n., *TF* ii. 72–3).

[31] Coleridge is casting himself here in the role of Rivers, the supremely rationalist and individualist hero of *The Borderers*: 'I had within me / A salient spring of energy, a fire / Of inextinguishable thought—I mounted / From action up to action with a

Forms? And lastly to project this phantom-world into the world of Reality, like a catoptrical mirror? Say rather, to make ideas & realities stand side by side, the one as vivid as the other, even as I have often seen in a natural well of translucent water the *reflections* of the lank weeds, that hung down from it's sides, standing upright, and like Substances, among the substantial water-plants, that were growing on the bottom.   (*CL* ii. 1000.)

Although the beautiful forms are known, in retrospect, to be no more than the reflections of lank weeds, they still exert their earlier fascination. The structure of feeling in this letter—the sense that Coleridge is standing both inside and outside his earlier experience—is repeated in a passage in *The Friend* on Pantisocracy. This youthful scheme, 'as harmless as it was extravagant', was to have combined 'the innocence of the patriarchal Age with the knowledge and genuine refinements of European culture'. Looking back on these impossible hopes from the distance of nearly fifteen years, Coleridge writes:

Strange fancies! and as vain as strange! yet to the intense interest and impassioned zeal, which called forth and strained every faculty of my intellect for the organization and defence of this Scheme, I owe much of whatever I at present possess, my clearest insight into the nature of individual Man, and my most comprehensive views of his social relations.   (*TF* ii. 146–7.)

Until this debt was acknowledged (and ironically, it was the radical Hazlitt who, as elegist of the 1790s, took up Coleridge's cause)[32] young men would continue to fall victim to their own ideal worlds. So sure of this was Coleridge that he claimed his labours in *The Friend* would be amply rewarded if he succeeded in arming 'a single man of Genius against the fascinations of his own ideal World, a single Philanthropist against the enthusiasm of his own heart!' (*TF* ii. 148.)

mind / That never rested—without meat or drink / I have lived many days—my sleep was linked / To purposes of reason—my very dreams / Assumed a substance and a character' (IV. ii. 118–25).

[32] Hazlitt's most moving tributes to the radical spirit of the 1790s are to be found in his essay on Godwin in *Spirit of the Age* and in his review 'Observations on Mr Wordsworth's Poem The Excursion' (Howe, xi. 16–19, iv. 119–20).

Coleridge believed he owed it to himself, and to others of his generation who had been similarly entranced, to reveal the source and power of this spell; he also owed it to the reformers of 1809 to expose the whole truth—and full danger—of the principles which they were promoting.

The same strategic openness to Enlightenment modes of thinking can be seen in the next chapter, as we follow Coleridge's arguments for a distinction between man's spiritual and political nature. And once again Coleridge's generosity towards the opposite point of view can be attributed to his earlier involvement with Dissent. In his book *Coleridge, Critic of Society*, John Colmer expresses puzzlement at what appears to be Coleridge's failure in *The Friend* to connect the principles of Rousseau and the French economists with those of the Dissenting tradition:

> to treat a demand for reform based on the confusion of religious and civil liberties as if it had its only origin in the theories of the Physiocrats was to ignore altogether the most characteristic feature of the English dissenting tradition, which was the transference of ideas of Christian liberties and moral freedom to the world of political action. It was surprising that Coleridge's earlier connexions with dissenting circles did not reveal the strength of this tradition, for his own Bristol lectures illustrate its influence.[33]

I would suggest that Coleridge did make the connection, but that he preferred to leave it unsaid.

[33] John Colmer, *Coleridge, Critic of Society* (Oxford, 1959), 105–6.

7

The Enlightenment Tradition:
Kant and Rousseau

Two excesses: to exclude reason, to admit nothing but
reason.

Blaise Pascal, Pensées

> 'Spite of proudest boast,
> Reason, best reason, is to imperfect man
> An effort only, and a noble aim;
> A crown, an attribute of sovereign power,
> Still to be courted—never to be won.
> —Look forth, or each man dive into himself;
> What sees he but a creature too perturbed;
> That is transported to excess; that yearns,
> Regrets, or trembles, wrongly, or too much;
> Hopes rashly, in disgust as rash recoils;
> Battens on spleen, or moulders in despair?
> Thus comprehension fails, and truth is missed;
> Thus darkness and delusion round our path
> Spread, from disease, whose subtle injury lurks
> Within the very faculty of sight.
> Yet for the general purposes of faith
> In Providence, for solace and support,
> We may not doubt that who can best subject
> The will to reason's law, can strictliest live
> And act in that obedience, he shall gain
> The clearest apprehension of those truths,
> Which unassisted reason's utmost power
> Is too infirm to reach.

Wordsworth, The Excursion

WHEN Kant first read Rousseau's works, he was inspired by
his passionate conviction of the ethical autonomy and dignity
of man; whereas once (he confessed) he had despised the

masses for their ignorance, a reading of Rousseau had put him right by teaching him 'to honour men'.[1]

A number of critics have demonstrated the influence of Rousseau's thought on Kant.[2] Recently, Charles Taylor has argued that Rousseau's recovery of the link between freedom and morality is similar in kind to the link established in Kant's moral philosophy between rationality and law. For both thinkers, freedom consists in obedience to a law which we prescribe to ourselves; and Rousseau's concept of the general will, which is the political embodiment of this idea, is seen to underlie Kant's account of the kingdom of ends.[3]

More generally, certain broad features of Kant's philosophy—his universalism, his concept of Reason, and his optimism about man—are seen by critics to shape and, in turn, be shaped by, the radical spirit of the French Enlightenment.[4] This pro-French bias did not go unremarked by Kant's British contemporaries. In a review of Kant's 'Project for a perpetual Peace' in 1797, it was noted that several passages glanced 'with disapprobation at the British system of policy' while others were partial to 'the views of the French'; and two years later, in the same periodical, William Taylor referred to the 'notorious Gallicanism' of Kant's opinions.[5] This Gallicanism is clearly implied by the language used to describe the new epistemology:

The essential difference between [Kant] and former philosophers, in their mode of searching for a general criterion of what is knowable, is

[1] Quoted by H. J. Paton, *The Categorical Imperative: A Study in Kant's Moral Philosophy* (London, 1946), 42.

[2] For a general account of this influence, see Ernst Cassirer, *Rousseau, Kant, Goethe: Two Essays*, trans. J. Gutmann, P. O. Kristeller, and J. H. Randall (Princeton, NJ, 1945); hereafter cited as Cassirer. A more recent and detailed study can be found in Howard Williams, *Kant's Political Philosophy* (Oxford, 1983), 128, 143, 162, 172.

[3] 'Kant's Theory of Freedom', *Conceptions of Liberty in Political Philosophy*, ed. Zbigniew Pelczynski and John Gray (London, 1984), 100–22; hereafter cited as *Conceptions of Liberty*.

[4] See Karl Mannheim, *Essays on Sociology and Social Psychology*, ed. Paul Kecskemeti (London, 1953), 84 and George Herbert Mead, *Movements of Thought in the Nineteenth Century*, ed. Merritt H. Moore (Chicago, 1936), 25–50.

[5] *MR* xxii (1797), 114; *MR* xxviii (1799), 65. The Abbé Barruel included Kant as a Jacobin and atheist in his *Memoirs, Illustrating the Antichristian Conspiracy* (see pp. 123–4 above). He was also to link Kant with Robespierre; see R. Wellek, *Immanuel Kant in England 1793–1838* (Princeton, NJ, 1931), 14–15.

this: *they* endeavoured to ascertain the possible extent of human knowledge from the nature and properties of the things to be known; *he* directed his enquiries immediately to the powers of the human mind, and, abstractedly from all particular knowledge, and individual objects, examined the properties of knowledge in general, or the common nature of all our knowledge.[6]

On one side, we have a Burkean language of empirical emphasis, where the philosopher's attention is directed to the particular and the individual; on the other side, we have Kant's theory of a mind 'abstractedly' at work, concerned with knowledge in general and the common nature of man.

Despite the affinity of Kant's work with the spirit of the Enlightenment, and with Rousseau in particular, there are certain aspects of his thought which put him at odds with this tradition. For our purposes, the most important of these lies in the distinction Kant draws in his political writing between the realms of politics and morality. This distinction constitutes a major objection to Rousseau's political theory, and it is adopted by Coleridge for his own critique of *Du Contrat social* (1762) in Number 9.

An essential part of Coleridge's effort to reveal the seductive heart of Enlightenment political philosophy lay in exposing the profound ethical view of man upon which it was based: not even Burke, who detested Rousseau's writings, could deny the presence in them of certain 'just notions' about man, and a tendency to be moral about these 'in a very sublime strain'. As Coleridge saw it, the problem was that these indisputable moral truths, or principles of Reason—the belief that every man is a free and rational being, possessing the inalienable right of 'determining his conduct by his own Will, according to his own Conscience' (*TF* ii. 125)—were enlisted by Rousseau and others in support of unacceptably democratic political conclusions; hence Coleridge's declaration towards the beginning of Number 8 that the most important goal of his political writing was the restoration of the principles of Reason to their proper sphere. It was his hope that 'by

[6] Review of 'Nitsch's View of Kant's Principles', *MR* xxii (1797), 16.

detecting the true source of the influence of these Principles [of Reason], we shall at the same time discover their natural place and object: and that in themselves they are not only Truths, but most important and sublime Truths, and that their falsehood and their danger consist altogether in their misapplication' (*TF* ii. 110).[7]

Coleridge believed that the principles of Reason were misapplied when laid down by theorists as the basis for settling questions of political right. Reason's true domain was not politics or government but morality, and the all-important distinction which Coleridge proceeds to draw in *The Friend* between these two spheres is the foundation upon which his entire discussion of Reason is to rest. Political theorists like Rousseau and Cartwright erred because they confounded 'the sufficiency of the Conscience to make every Person a *moral* and amenable Being, with the sufficiency of Judgement and Experience requisite to the exercise of *political* Right' (*TF* ii. 136). Within the bounds of the spiritual and moral self, the principles of Reason constitute 'the most important and sublime Truths' (*TF* ii. 110), but as soon as they stray beyond this sphere into the political arena, these same truths become dangerous falsehoods. Once this important point had been grasped by his readers, Coleridge believed that a just assessment of man's mixed nature would prevail:

the dignity of Human Nature will be secured, and at the same time a lesson of Humility taught to each Individual, when we are made to see that the universal necessary Laws, and pure IDEAS of Reason, were given us, not for the purpose of flattering our Pride and enabling us to become national Legislators, but that by an energy of continued self-conquest, we might establish a free and yet absolute Government in our own Spirits.   (*TF* ii. 110–11.)

Coleridge opens his attack on Rousseau's optimistic and rationalist philosophy with an enthusiastic paean to man's Reason. There are several explanations for this rather surprising opening. First, as we saw in the last chapter, Coleridge was anxious to adopt as generous a stance as

---

[7] This aim is in keeping with the article in his Prospectus, where he had promised sources of consolation from 'the Exertion and right Application of the Reason' (*TF* ii. 18).

possible towards his opponents. Second, he was by no means unsympathetic to the elevated, spiritual view of man's moral nature which he attributed to Rousseau. Third, and most importantly, he wanted to establish at the very outset of his essay this all-important distinction between man's *spiritual* and *political* nature; only after he has demonstrated and endorsed his view of man's *moral* nature does he move on to a discussion of man in the *political* realm, thus creating the desired distinction between these two spheres.

The structure of Coleridge's argument in Number 9, with its enthusiastic avowal of certain a priori principles concerning man's spiritual status, followed by a sober reassessment of these when transferred to the sphere of practical politics, is modelled upon a recurring feature of Kant's political writing. For instance, in his essay 'On the Common Saying: "This may be True in Theory, but it does not Apply in Practice" ' (1793), Kant argues that the civil state, 'regarded purely as a lawful state', is based on the following a priori principles:

1. The *freedom* of every member of society as a *human being*
2. The *equality* of each with all the others as a *subject*
3. The independence of each member of a commonwealth as a citizen.   (Reiss, p. 74.)

Together, these principles constitute Kant's concept of an original social contract. He is careful to add, however, that they are not 'so much laws given by an already established state as laws by which a state can alone be established in accordance with pure rational principles of external human right' (Reiss, p. 74). In keeping with the tension which appears here between what exists in fact and what exists only as a rational ideal, Kant develops his notion of an original social contract, 'by means of which a civil and thus completely lawful constitution and commonwealth can alone be established', only to conclude: 'we need by no means assume that this contract . . . actually exists as a *fact*, for it cannot possibly be so . . . It is in fact merely an *idea* of reason' (Reiss, p. 79). The notion of man's ontological freedom and autonomy which lies at the heart of the perfect civic constitution is abstracted by Kant from the realm of political reality, and refashioned as an Idea of Reason. These Ideas of Reason are rational ideals to which nothing in experience can ever correspond; they are important only to the extent that they form a test of the rightfulness of every public law (Reiss, p. 79).

Kant's distinction between an ideal moral world where freedom and equality hold sway, and a political world of inequality and coercion, is exactly mirrored by Burke's contrast between the 'true moral equality of mankind' and that 'real inequality, which it never can remove' (*Reflections*, p. 124). For Burke, the separation of spheres turns on a Hooker-like distinction between man as he is in himself, and man as a member of a political community. For Kant, it turns on a dualistic conception of man as both noumenon and phenomenon. As noumenon, man is free and capable of acting in obedience to the dictates of Reason; as phenomenon, he is subject to the laws of nature, and his actions tend to be determined by inclination and desire. In the *Groundwork of the Metaphysic of Morals*, man is viewed as subject to two different kinds of law. Regarding himself from two different points of view,

He can consider himself *first*—so far as he belongs to the sensible world—to be under laws of nature (heteronomy); and *secondly*—so far as he belongs to the intelligible world—to be under laws which, being independent of nature, are not empirical but have their ground in reason alone   (*Groundwork*, p. 113).

This habit of thinking about man under two quite different aspects gives Kant's political philosophy its distinctive blend of idealism and pragmatism. Depending upon whether he is working with a projection of what man is capable of in principle, or a conviction of what he tends to be like in practice, Kant's political theory manifests either progressive, liberal principles, or a more cautious acceptance of the existing social structure.

Coleridge was drawn to Kant's thought because he saw mirrored there his own dualistic conception of man. Although capable of the highest virtue because of our God-like faculty of Reason, we are none the less conscious of inner weakness, of 'the sense of a self-contradicting principle in our nature, or a disharmony in the different impulses that constitute it—of a something which essentially distinguishes man both from all other animals, that are known to exist, and from the idea of his own nature, or conception of the original man' (*TF* ii. 7). Higher than the animals because of our Reason and free will, we are none the less flawed and imperfect creatures, shut out from that condition of primal innocence embodied by Adam before the Fall. Yet God's original conception of Adam, making him 'just and right/ Sufficient to have stood,'[8] remains for Coleridge an informing ethical principle, an aspect of our being which must be taken into consideration in any truly complete account of man. Although weak and erring in practice, our inner knowledge of what we ought to be is the inspiring ideal by which we must live.

Keeping close to the shape of Coleridge's argument in Number 9, we shall see his ethical system simultaneously affirm and qualify the claims of mainstream Enlightenment thinking. We shall then see the disintegration of any 'Gallican' elements in his thinking as he moves into the realm of practical politicking. Relying on the distinction which he sets up between the realms of morality and politics, he attempts to invalidate Rousseau's *Social Contract* as political theory by arguing that his concept of general will is essentially no different from Kant's moral law.

For Coleridge, the dignity and worth of human nature spring from Reason and, intimately involved with man's possession of Reason, from his free will. Both these tenets—together with the series of linked truths which follow on from them—are laid down by him as undeniable. Celebrating the dual claim that all men possess Reason and possess it equally, he addresses the faculty in the following way: 'thou alone, more than even the Sunshine, more than the common Air, art given to all Men, and to every Man alike! To thee, who being one art the same in all, we owe the privilege, that of all we can become one, a living *whole*! that we have a COUNTRY!' (*TF* ii. 126.)

---

[8] *Paradise Lost: The Poems of John Milton*, ed. John Carey and Alistair Fowler (London, 1968), Book III, ll, 98–9.

Looked at from one point of view, Coleridge is here endorsing the potentially revolutionary doctrine of man's natural rights: his natural equality and oneness with others. In the *Rights of Man* (1791–2), for instance, Tom Paine had written in similar terms of *the unity of man*', 'by which I mean, that men are all of *one degree*, and consequently that all men are born equal, and with equal natural right . . . The Mosaic account of the creation . . . is full to this point, *the unity or equality of man.*'[9] This is the Quaker heart of Paine's radical philosophy,[10] the innate equality of all men answering to George Fox's teaching of the universality and equality of the Light. But it is important to note the way in which, in Coleridge's hands, this spiritual and individual unity is quietly absorbed into a higher unity than self; that of nationhood. A similar qualification of individual authority can be seen in William Penn, where he defends George Fox from those who rebelled against him for seeking '*Dominion* over Conscience'. A conservative rather than a radical Quaker,[11] Penn concedes that the nature of the Light is the same in all, and that it is therefore 'the Root of all True Christian Fellowship', but he balances these claims by arguing that this Fellowship is based, not on equality, but on subordination of each to all. In so far as the Quaker rebels 'would have had every man Independent, that as he had the Principle in himself, he should only stand and fall to that, and no Body else . . . they struck at the *Spiritual Unity*, which a people, guided by the same Principle, are naturally led into' (*A Brief Account*, p. 94). The principle of 'One in all' was an argument, not for anarchic individual self-assertion, but for self-restraint in the name of a higher spiritual unity.

The undeniable truths about man's moral and rational

[9] *Rights of Man*, introduction by Eric Foner, Penguin American Library edn. (Harmondsworth, 1984), 66.

[10] Paine's father was a Quaker (see *Rights of Man*, p. 8).

[11] In a chapter describing the more conservative Quakerism of the post-Reformation period, Barry Reay refers to Penn as 'patrician' (*The Quakers and the English Revolution* (London, 1985), 121). Additional references to Penn's conservatism are to be found in W. C. Braithwaite, *The Second Period of Quakerism* (Cambridge, 1961), 129, 337 and Howard Brinton, *Friends for 300 Years: Beliefs and Practice of the Society of Friends since George Fox started the Quaker movement* (London, 1953), 134.

nature which Coleridge seeks to establish in Number 9 are sketched in the following terms. All voluntary actions, having for their objects good or evil, are moral actions, and all morality is grounded in Reason. Every man is born with the faculty of Reason; all men, as rational beings, are therefore moral beings. From these truths Coleridge derives the sacred principle 'recognized by all Laws human and divine',

that a Person can never become a Thing, nor be treated as such without wrong . . . the distinction between Person and Thing consists herein, that the latter may rightfully be used, altogether and merely, as a *Means*; but the former must always be included in the *End*, and form a part of the final Cause.   (*TF* ii. 125.)

This principle of the sanctity of the individual as end-in-himself can be found throughout Rousseau's writings,[12] but the particular formulation which Coleridge gives to this idea is the one enunciated by Kant:

man, and in general every rational being, *exists* as an end in himself, *not merely as a means* for arbitrary use by this or that will: he must in all his actions, whether they are directed to himself or to other rational beings, always be viewed *at the same time as an end.*
(*Groundwork*, p. 90.)

This notion of man as an end-in-himself is central to Kant's moral philosophy. By means of this inspiring concept, he builds up a picture of man as a rational, moral, and autonomous being, capable of making and obeying universal law. By virtue of his rationality, each and every man 'has not merely a relative value—that is, a price—but has an intrinsic value—that is, *dignity*' (*Groundwork*, p. 96).

From the fact that every man possesses Reason, Coleridge moves on to deduce man's free will; and, as the faculty of Reason implies free will, Morality (i.e. the dictate of Reason) 'gives to every rational Being the right of acting as a free agent, and of finally determining his conduct by his own Will, according to his own Conscience' (*TF* ii. 125). For Rousseau,

---

[12] 'Man is too noble a being to serve simply as the instrument for others, and he must not be used for what suits them without consulting also what suits himself . . . It is never right to harm a human soul for the advantage of others' (*Nouvelle Héloïse*, V, letter 2; quoted in Cassirer, p. 33).

it was of the essence of man's nature to be free: to renounce liberty was to renounce being a man (*SC*, bk. I, ch. 4). It was freedom, too, which marked man off from all other animals, giving him a special status in the hierarchy of nature:

Nature commands every animal, and the beast obeys. Man feels the same impetus, but he realizes that he is free to acquiesce or resist; and it is above all in the consciousness of this freedom that the spirituality of his soul is shown. For physics explains in some way the mechanism of the senses and the formation of ideas; but in the power of willing, or rather of choosing, and in the sentiment of this power are found only purely spiritual acts about which the laws of mechanics explain nothing.[13]

Thus, the claim that every man possessed free will was based on each man's immediate recognition of the moral imperative constituted by his own conscience; and the fact that every man could testify to the existence of such an inner Law was substantial proof of the dignity of his spiritual nature.

Kant's philosophy is similarly inspired by a mystic conception of freedom. Second only to Reason, freedom is held as a postulate of the moral life: all rational beings possess a will which is capable of determining itself in accordance with and for the sake of the moral law.

The testimony of other writers to the *fact* of this freedom was of great value to Coleridge, for it was his own experience that we only begin 'to think of, & intellectually to know, our freedom when we have been made to feel its imperfections, & its loss'. Young men in good health, 'ignorant of the corruption & weakness of their own hearts, & therefore always prone to substitute the glorious *Ideal* of human nature for the existing reality' (*CN* iii. 3743), might deny the reality of free will, but eventually they come to acknowledge and accept 'the concurrent testimony of our fellow-men in all ages and in all nations' (*TF* ii. 7).

Coleridge celebrates man's moral freedom and autonomy in a passage which recalls the 'Profession of Faith of the Savoyard Vicar' in Rousseau's novel *Émile*. In this famous chapter, we read:

[13] *Second Discourse*, quoted by Roger D. Masters, *The Political Philosophy of Rousseau* (Princeton, NJ, 1968), 70.

Conscience! Conscience! Divine instinct, immortal voice from heaven; sure guide for a creature ignorant and finite indeed, yet intelligent and free; infallible judge of good and evil, making men like to God! In thee consists the excellence of man's nature and the morality of his actions; apart from thee, I find nothing in myself to raise me above the beasts—nothing but the sad privilege of wandering from one error to another.[14]

Substituting the term Reason for Conscience, Coleridge enters fully into Rousseau's hymn to man's spiritual nature, and the likeness between the two passages is enhanced when we put back into *The Friend* a sentence present in the draft but omitted from the printed version:

REASON! best and holiest gift of Heaven and bond of union with the Giver. The high Title by which the Majesty of Man claims precedence above all other living Creatures! Mysterious Faculty, the Mother of Conscience, of Language, of Tears, and of Smiles! [but for Thee, we [?roam/become] like the Brutes of the Field, goaded on by lawless Desires, or driven round in the unvarying circles of Instinct! and through Thee we are <made> but a little lower than the Angels!]   (*TF* ii. 125; *TF* i. 190, n. 2.)[15]

These passages from Rousseau and Coleridge are paralleled in turn by Kant's famous apostrophe to Duty in the *Critique of Practical Reason*:

Duty! Thou sublime and mighty name that dost embrace nothing charming or insinuating but requirest submission and yet seekest not to move the will by threatening aught that would arouse natural aversion or terror but only holdest forth a law which of itself finds entrance into the mind and yet gains reluctant reverence (though not always obedience)—a law before which all inclinations are dumb even though they secretly work against it.[16]

---

[14] *Émile*, trans. Barbara Foxley, introduction P. D. Jimack, Everyman's Library edn. (London, 1977), 254.

[15] Milton's account of God's creation of man in *Paradise Lost* is also an influence here: 'There wanted yet the master work, the end / Of all yet done; a creature who not prone / And brute as other creatures, but endued / With sanctity of reason, might erect / His stature, and upright with front serene / Govern the rest, self-knowing, and from thence / Magnanimous to correspond with heaven' (VII, ll. 505–11).

[16] *Critique of Practical Reason*, trans. Lewis White Beck (New York, 1956), 193. Cassirer pointed out the similarity between this passage and the passage quoted from

The affinity of feeling which exists here between Kant and Rousseau is further supported by their recognition of the gap between man's higher and lower natures; just as Kant concedes the secret workings of man's inclinations against the voice of Duty, Rousseau's Savoyard Vicar follows up his celebration of conscience with the claim that

it is not enough to be aware that there is such a guide; we must know her and follow her. If she speaks to all hearts, how is it that so few give heed to her voice? She speaks to us in the language of nature, and everything leads us to forget that tongue. Conscience is timid, she loves peace and retirement; she is startled by noise and numbers; the prejudices from which she is said to arise are her worst enemies. She flees before them or she is silent; their noisy voices drown her words, so that she cannot get a hearing; fanaticism dares to counterfeit her voice and to inspire crimes in her name. She is discouraged by ill-treatment; she no longer speaks to us, no longer answers to our call; when she has been scorned so long, it is as hard to recall her as it was to banish her. (*Émile*, p. 254.)

This is the conscience which we encountered in Number 1 of *The Friend*, the element of our being which we can stupefy and suspend, but never utterly annihilate, 'although we may perhaps find a treacherous counterfeit in the very quiet which we derive from its slumber, or its entrancement' (*TF* ii. 8).

Having described man as a rational and free being, and one who, by virtue of his Reason, is equal in worth to all other rational beings, Coleridge moves on to enquire about the kind of authority which, on the basis of this picture, one man is entitled to exercise over another. Rhetorically, he asks:

Who then shall dare to prescribe a Law of moral Action for any rational Being, which does not flow immediately from that Reason, which is the Fountain of all Morality? Or how without breach of Conscience can we limit or coerce the Powers of a Free-Agent, except by a coincidence with that Law in his own Mind, which is at once the Cause, the Condition, and the Measure of his Free-agency? (*TF* ii. 126.)

Émile; it was not without reason, he wrote, that 'all the accounts of the Kantian moral philosophy placed the famous apostrophe to duty . . . side by side with this passage from Rousseau's *Profession of Faith*' (Cassirer, p. 48).

The moral law which exists in the mind of every one of us is the cause, condition, and measure of our free will; and we can only justifiably curtail another's freedom by appealing to that law. The tension which Coleridge sets up here between freedom and law is carried further by his assertions that man must be both free and obedient: 'Man must be *free*; or to what purpose was he made a Spirit of Reason, and not a Machine of Instinct? Man must *obey*; or wherefore has he a Conscience?' (*TF* ii. 126.) These questions are resolved by the dictum that perfect freedom consists in obedience to the moral law: 'The Powers, which create this difficulty, contain its solution likewise: for *their* Service is perfect Freedom' (*TF* ii. 126).

Behind Coleridge's dictum lies the biblical reference to 'the perfect law, the law that makes us free' (James 1: 25). The idea of man's autonomy, of his being subject to a 'law of freedom',[17] that is, a law of his own making, is a commonplace of Christian thought, finding its *locus classicus* in Milton's concept of the Fall. In *Paradise Lost*, Adam 'fervently' impresses upon Eve that

> . . . God left free the will, for what obeys
> Reason, is free, and reason he made right . . .
>
> (IX. 351–2)

This belief that true freedom involves the obedience of will to Reason is reiterated by Michael when he speaks to Adam of that 'true liberty'

> . . . which always with right reason dwells
> Twinned, and from her hath no dividual being:
> Reason in man obscured, or not obeyed,
> Immediately inordinate desires
> And upstart passions catch the government
> From reason, and to servitude reduce
> Man till then free.
>
> (XII. 84–90)

In one of the key passages of *The Social Contract*, moral freedom is defined by Rousseau as 'obedience to a law which we

---

[17] James exhorts his listeners always to 'speak and act as men who are to be judged under a law of freedom' (James, 2:12).

prescribe to ourselves', whilst 'the mere impulse of appetite is slavery' (*SC* bk. I, ch. 8). Similarly, in the *Groundwork*, Kant claims that the will is only autonomous when it is not merely subject to universal moral law, 'but is so subject that it must be considered as also *making the law* for itself' (*Groundwork*, p. 93).

When Paine concluded Part I of his *Rights of Man* with the words, 'Reason obeys itself; and Ignorance submits to whatever is dictated to it', he was giving popular expression to this idea of man as his own law-giver; he was also, of course, giving the idea a subversive, political content. It is precisely this politicization of abstract moral truths which Coleridge opposes in Number 9, and it is at this point in his essay—at the moment when man's moral autonomy is proclaimed—that he launches his attack on revolutionary political philosophy. The universally binding truths of Reason which hold on the ethical plane cannot be simply translated into universally binding laws in the political sphere; in particular, it was a dangerous error to move (as he claimed Rousseau did) from an assertion of man's ethical autonomy to an assertion of political liberty.

In order to show the disastrous consequences of confusing political freedom with an internal, formal freedom, Coleridge presents us with a highly exaggerated version of the individualistic aspects of *The Social Contract*. For while it is true that Rousseau sees man as a rational, autonomous, and inviolable moral agent, making and obeying his own laws and existing independently of the commanding will of another, Coleridge was wrong to claim that this individualism is absolute and unchecked. We shall also see the unfairness of the conclusion which Coleridge draws from this exaggerated individualism: that Rousseau's political system lacks a central, coherent locus of power.

Roughly paraphrasing the arguments of *The Social Contract*, Coleridge claims that Rousseau's conviction of the inviolability of man's Reason or conscience was so all-embracing that it led him to deny absolutely the right of either an individual or a state to compel a man to do anything 'of which it cannot be demonstrated that his own Reason must join in prescribing it'. Even in the social state, the Reason of any one man cannot 'be rightfully subjugated to the Reason of any other' (*TF* ii. 126). Thus, no government was legitimate which did not derive its authority from the consent of the individual as such. In order to ask obedience from free rational beings, a society must, in Rousseau's view, 'be framed on such Principles that every Individual follows his own Reason while he obeys the Laws of the Constitution, and performs the Will of the State while he follows the Dictate of his own Reason' (*TF* ii. 126). The problem of finding such a perfect constitution of government forms the subject, Coleridge writes, of Rousseau's *Social Contract*. In support of this claim, he quotes and translates (in somewhat abbreviated terms) the famous lines from Book I, chapter 6:

Trouver une forme d'Association—par laquelle chacun s'unissant à tous, n'obeisse pourtant qu'à lui même, et reste aussi libre qu'auparavant. i.e. To find a form of Society according to which each one uniting with the whole shall yet obey himself only and remain as free as before.   (*TF* ii. 126.)[18]

Silently passing over the notion of 'each one uniting with the whole', Coleridge emphasizes yet again the absolute inalienability of every man's right in *The Social Contract* to 'retain his whole natural Independence, even in the social State':

He cannot possibly concede or compromise it: for this very Right is one of his most sacred Duties. He would sin against himself, and commit high treason against the Reason which the Almighty Creator has given him, if he dared abandon its' exclusive right to govern his actions.   (*TF* ii. 126–7.)

As far as it goes, this does not exaggerate the uncompromising terms in which Rousseau speaks of freedom in *The Social Contract*. Freedom is absolute liberty of self-government, the demand that each man be completely independent of the will of every other. As one recent critic has put it, so radical and

---

[18] Rousseau had actually written: 'Trouver une forme d'association qui défende et protège de toute la force commune la personne et les biens de chaque associé, et par laquelle chacun . . .' *Du Contrat social*, ed. C. E. Vaughan (Manchester, 1947), 13.

absolute was this emphasis that Rousseau could conceive no middle ground between liberty and slavery.[19] To be in any way dependent upon the will of another was to be a slave.

Nevertheless, by giving exclusive attention to the individualistic bias of *The Social Contract*, Coleridge fails to do justice to Rousseau's equally compelling account of the forces limiting and curtailing our natural freedom and independence. He says nothing, for instance, of the remarkable moral transformation which takes place when we pass from a state of nature to the civil state, a process in which instinct gives way to justice, and 'a stupid and unimaginative animal' is transformed into 'an intelligent being and a man' (*SC* bk. I, ch. 8). According to Rousseau, when we participate in the social contract, we exchange our 'natural liberty, which is bounded only by the strength of the individual' for 'civil liberty, which is limited by the general will' (*SC* bk. I, ch 8).[20] It is in this sense of exchanging one freedom for another that Rousseau can maintain that we remain in the social state 'aussi libre qu'auparavant' (*SC* bk I, ch. 6). Thus, when Coleridge asserts of *The Social Contract* that every one has an alienable right to retain their 'whole natural Independence, even in the social State' (*TF* ii. 126), he is in fact putting a very misleading construction upon Rousseau's concept of us remaining as free as before; for it is precisely our 'whole natural Independence' which we must surrender when we enter into the social contract; in Rousseau's words, the retention of any part of our 'state of nature' would necessarily render the association 'inoperative or tyrannical' (*SC* bk. I, ch. 6).

Coleridge also ignores the rather startling terms used by Rousseau to explain his notion of a civil liberty 'limited by the general will'. For Rousseau, the clauses of the social contract

[19] Stephen Ellenburg, *Rousseau's Political Philosophy: An Interpretation from Within* (Ithaca, NY, and London, 1976), 20. Patrick Gardiner, in an essay 'Rousseau on Liberty', also draws attention to Rousseau's notion of freedom as self-determination and self-mastery (*Conceptions of Liberty*, pp. 83–99).

[20] In the same chapter, but with a different emphasis, Rousseau writes: 'What man loses by the social contract is his natural liberty and an unlimited right to everything he tries to get and succeeds in getting; what he gains is civil liberty and the proprietorship of all he possesses' (*SC* bk. I, ch. 8).

can be reduced to a single one: 'the total alienation of each associate, together with all his rights, to the whole community' (*SC* bk. I, ch. 6). A strictly equal surrender of rights is made by each citizen. Every one 'gives himself absolutely' to the community; no individual, *qua* individual, may retain any rights whatsoever.[21] By this unconditional act of surrender, individual rights are alienated 'without reserve' in return for an equal share in the rights of the community as a whole. Thus natural equality is exchanged for a new form of civil equality:

the social compact sets up among the citizens an equality of such a kind that they all bind themselves to observe the same conditions and should therefore all enjoy the same rights.   (*SC* bk. II, ch. 4.)

In so far as those associating in the social contract share equally in the sovereign power, they are called citizens; to the extent that they are under the laws of the state, however, they are termed 'subjects' (SC bk. I, ch. 6). As generations of worried critics have pointed out, Rousseau does not hesitate to grant the political community unlimited powers over its subjects:

As nature gives each man absolute power over all his members, the social compact gives the body politic absolute power over all its members also; and it is this power which, under the direction of the general will, bears, as I have said, the name of Sovereignty.
          (*SC* bk. II, ch. 4.)

Coleridge was not impervious to the totalitarianism implicit in such an absolute conception of sovereignty,[22] but he passes over it in his desire to brand *The Social Contract* as a work of obsessive individualism. As a result of this distortion, he misleadingly characterizes Rousseau's political system as one

---

[21] 'for, if the individuals retained certain rights, as there would be no common superior to decide between them and the public, each being on one point his own judge, would ask to be so on all; the state of nature would thus continue, and the association would necessarily become inoperative or tyrannical' (*SC* bk. I, ch. 6).

[22] Elsewhere in his writings, Coleridge establishes a vivid connection between Jacobinism and the totalitarian state, where the individual is sacrificed to 'the shadowy idol of ALL.' (*LS*, p. 63; see also *EOT* ii. 388).

in which authority is atomized and dispersed amongst millions of individuals enjoying the same rights and subject to the same duties (*TF* ii. 131). Nothing could be more untrue than this claim that Rousseau's body politic is 'but an aggregate of Individuals' (*TF* ii. 126), for Rousseau's state has, in fact, a corporate identity and personality. The act of association creates a 'public person', 'a moral and collective body' with a common identity, life, and will (*SC* bk. I, ch. 6).

The role played by the general will in limiting and coercing an individual's freedom is baldly summed up in Rousseau's dictum that whoever refuses to obey the general will 'shall be compelled to do so by the whole body': 'This means nothing less than that he will be forced to be free; for this is the condition which, by giving each citizen to his country, secures him against all personal dependence' (*SC* bk. I, ch. 7). Nowhere does Coleridge comment upon this paradoxical idea of men being 'forced to be free' under the terms of the social contract. Somewhat ironically, the closest he comes to capturing the flavour of this idea is when he criticizes Rousseau for holding too restricted a view of the role of governments: the utmost power allowed by Rousseau to government consists solely, he writes, in preserving 'the Freedom of all by coercing within the requisite bounds the Freedom of each' (*TF* ii. 131).

Coleridge moves directly from his exaggerated account of Rousseau's individualism into an exposure of the wholly unsatisfactory nature of his concept of the general will, a task now made relatively simple by his silence concerning the anti-individualistic aspects of Rousseau's thought. Nothing seemed more absurd to Coleridge than the belief that when a group of people assemble together, their individual errors and pre-judices disappear, and a divinely inspired consensus, or general will arises. Yet on his own admission, it was a belief held, not just by Rousseau, but by Burke himself. Not only did Burke hold that, in parliamentary proceedings, ' "Prejudice corrects Prejudice, and the different asperities of party zeal mitigate and neutralize each other" ' (*TF* ii. 127), he also believed that it was easy ' "to distinguish what are acts of power, and what the determinations of equity and reason" '

(*TF* ii. 127).[23] Following Kant, who conceded the impossibility of ever knowing with complete certainty whether the determining motive of an action was or was not in accordance with the moral law, Coleridge doubted our ability to discriminate between political decisions which were expressions of the general will, and those which merely represented a collection of individual wills. Furthermore, the belief that individual errors would cancel each other out in deliberate assemblies seemed 'a mere *probability*, against which other probabilities may be weighed: as the lust of Authority, the contagious nature of Enthusiasm, and other of the acute or chronic diseases of deliberative Assemblies' (*TF* ii. 127).

In deciding which was the most likely probability in any given case, other considerations such as circumstances and expediency inevitably enter into our calculations, 'and thus', Coleridge argued, 'we already find ourselves beyond the magic Circle of the pure Reason, and within the Sphere of the Understanding and the Prudence' (*TF* ii. 127). Coleridge had little faith in the wisdom of popular assemblies, and he counted it as a disastrous flaw in the argument of *The Social Contract* that Rousseau shared his scepticism on this point. For, rather than deny the tendency of such assemblies to be carried away by passion and common error, Rousseau concedes that it is often difficult to secure the judgement prompting the general will 'from the seductive influences of individual wills' (*SC* bk. II, ch. 6): 'each individual, as a man, may have a particular will contrary or dissimilar to the general will which he has as a citizen. His particular interest may speak to him quite differently from the common interest' (*SC* bk. I, ch. 7). More frankly, he asks: 'How can a blind multitude, which often does not know what it wills, because it rarely knows what is good for it, carry out for itself so great and difficult an enterprise as a system of legislation? . . . The general will is always in the right, but the judgment which guides it is not always enlightened' (*SC* bk. II, ch. 6).

---

[23] Coleridge is quoting here from a Note to Burke's *Motion relative to the Speech from the Throne* (1784), *Works* iii. 534; see *CN* iii. 3609. Elsewhere, Burke seemed less confident: 'The will of the many, and their interest, must very often differ; and great will be the difference when they make an evil choice' (*Reflections*, p. 141).

From this admission of difficulty arises Rousseau's distinction between the general will and the will of all, the latter being the sum of particular desires selfishly pursuing ends harmful to the true interest of the state. It was in this distinction that 'the Falsehood or Nothingness of the whole System' became manifest for Coleridge:

For hence it follows, as an inevitable Consequence, that all which is said in the *Contrat social* of that sovereign Will, to which the right of universal Legislation appertains, applies to no one Human Being, to no Society or Assemblage of Human Beings, and least of all to the mixed Multitude that makes up the PEOPLE: but entirely and exclusively to REASON itself, which, it is true, dwells in every Man *potentially*, but actually and in perfect purity is found in no Man and in no Body of Men.   (*TF* ii. 127–8.)

As a piece of argument against *The Social Contract*, this is unconvincing for two reasons. First, Coleridge fails to show the way in which men are inevitably too self-interested for the operation of Reason; second, the assertion that Reason exists in man only as a potential is clearly brought in as a way of denying the truths of Reason any application in the world as it is. In the arguments that follow—in Coleridge's endorsement of a universal moral law and in his rejection of its political analogue, the general will—Kant's influence can be clearly seen.

The idea of Reason as a potential, a slowly developing, never-to-be-realized capacity in man, is derived from Kant's essay, *Idea for a Universal History with a Cosmopolitan Purpose* (1784). This short work can be read as Kant's response to *The Social Contract*; in it, he presents his reflections on the problem which Rousseau's treatise had set out to solve: how to achieve the perfectly just civil constitution.

The perfectly just civil society is, for Kant, the one which ideally rational men would construct if they were legislating members of a kingdom of ends, that is, acting only on those maxims which can at the same time be willed as universal laws. As such, it is a rational ideal, an aspiration for the species but something which can only be imperfectly realized in practice.[24] If the political writings of Abbé St Pierre and Rousseau had been ridiculed, it was (Kant thought) because they believed that the realization of their ideas was 'so imminent' (Reiss, p. 48).

In claiming that reason exists in man only as a potential, Coleridge echoes the first two propositions of Kant's essay:

> *First Proposition*: All the natural capacities of a creature are destined sooner or later to be developed completely and in conformity with their end.
> *Second Proposition*: In man (as the only rational creature on earth), those natural capacities which are directed towards the use of his reason are such that they could be fully developed only in the species, but not in the individual.   (Reiss, p. 42.)

Reason, Kant writes, 'requires trial, practice and instruction to enable it to progress gradually from one stage of insight to the next'. Accordingly,

every individual man would have to live for a vast length of time if he were to learn how to make complete use of all his natural capacities; or if nature has fixed only a short term for each man's life (as is in fact the case), then it will require a long, perhaps incalculable series of generations, each passing on its enlightenment to the next, before the germs implanted by nature in our species can be developed to that degree which corresponds to nature's original intention   (Reiss, pp. 42–3).

Because we are incapable as individuals of fulfilling 'nature's original intention', the laws of Reason by which we strive to be governed must be supplemented by positive, conventional laws.

Rather than find man's imperfections a hindrance to his rational development, Kant argued that if it were not for his social, self-seeking pretensions, man's excellent natural capacities 'would never be roused to develop'. Living 'an Arcadian, pastoral existence of perfect concord, self-sufficiency and mutual love', all man's talents 'would remain hidden for

[24] The problem of establishing a perfect civil constitution 'is both the most difficult and the last to be solved by the human race' (Reiss, p. 46).

ever in a dormant state, and men, as good-natured as the sheep they tended, would scarcely render their existence more valuable than that of their animals' (Reiss, p. 45). Coleridge's endorsement of Kant's optimistic teleology can be seen from his reply in Number 9 to those who argued for a society based on a strictly equal distribution of property. Such a state could not subsist without gross injustice, 'except where the Reason of all and of each was absolute Master of the selfish passions, of Sloth, Envy, &c; and yet the same State would preclude the greater part of the means, by which the Reason of man is developed' (*TF* ii. 132). Paradoxically, utopian aspirations for the perfect society are seen to work against the actual achievement of such a goal. For Kant, as for Coleridge, the way ahead lies not in radical reform but in a clear-eyed acceptance of our limitations and weakness.

Kant shared Rousseau's belief that man's development could be fulfilled only in society. Although enamoured of his unrestrained freedom and individuality, 'Man has an inclination to *live in society*, since he feels in this state more like a man, that is, he feels able to develop his natural capacities' (Reiss, p. 44). The only way in which a man could fulfil the end for which he was created—his rational nature—was to renounce his brutish freedom and seek calm and security within a law-governed constitution. Once enclosed within this civil union, his earlier asocial instincts, 'his self-seeking pretensions and insatiable desires for possession and power', were transformed in the same way as trees in a forest, which 'by seeking to deprive each other of air and sunlight, compel each other to find these by upward growth, so that they grow beautiful and straight—whereas those which put out branches at will, in freedom and in isolation from others, grow stunted, bent and twisted' (Reiss, p. 46).

It is at this point in Kant's essay, at the moment when he celebrates the concept of moral transformation so central to *The Social Contract*, that he reveals his most fundamental criticism of Rousseau's political philosophy. The problem lay in what Kant saw as the incorrigibility of man's nature. Although, as a rational creature, man 'desires a law to impose limits on the freedom of all, he is still misled by his self-seeking animal inclinations into exempting himself from the law where he can. He thus requires a *master* to break his self-will and force him to obey a universally valid will under which everyone can be free' (Reiss, p. 46). Thus far, Kant has said nothing which is not stated clearly in *The Social Contract*, but he then goes on to ask, 'where is he to find such a master? Nowhere else but in the human species. But this master will also be an animal who needs a master' (Reiss, p. 46). The impossibility of ever finding a supreme authority which would itself be just led Kant back to his earlier image of men as trees, only to conclude: 'Nothing straight can be constructed from such warped wood as that which man is made of' (Reiss, p. 46).[25]

Unlike Rousseau, who seemed to Coleridge to be unaware of the blow dealt to his concept of the general will by an admission of irredeemably recalcitrant individual wills, Kant was fully alive to the problem, and to the need for some kind of solution to it. He achieved this solution by treating the original contract (which is based on general will)[26] not as a fact, but as an idea of Reason, a hypothetical state of affairs towards which it is our duty to aspire.[27] The concept of general will obliges every legislator 'to frame his laws in such a way that they could have been produced by the united will of a whole nation, and to regard each subject, in so far as he can claim citizenship, as if he had consented within the general will . . . For if the law is such that a whole people could not *possibly* agree to it . . . it is unjust' (Reiss, p. 79). 'But', Kant continues, and this is where the obligations generated by a liberal hypothesis make way for an illiberal reality, 'if it is at least *possible* that a people could agree to it, it is our duty to consider the law as just, even if the people is at present in such a position or attitude of mind that it would probably refuse its

[25] Citing this remark in his essay 'Nationalism', Isaiah Berlin enlists Kant as an ally on the anti-rationalist, pluralist side (*Against the Current: Essays in the History of Ideas* (Oxford, 1981), 353.)

[26] The original contract is 'based on a coalition of the wills of all private individuals in a nation to form a common, public will for the purposes of rightful legislation' (Reiss, p. 79).

[27] For Coleridge's adoption of Kant's social contract theory, and his application of it to Hooker, see above, p. 116 and n. 10.

consent if it were consulted' (Reiss, p. 79). Relying upon arguments of this kind, Kant yokes together an ideal of republicanism with an autocratic reality:

It is the duty of monarchs to govern in a republican (not a democratic) manner, even although they may rule autocratically. In other words, they should treat the people in accordance with principles akin in spirit to the laws of freedom which a people of mature rational powers would prescribe for itself, even if the people is not literally asked for its consent.   (Reiss, p. 187.)

Instead of inviting all to participate equally in the running of the state, Kant's general will functions as an informing, liberal principle, providing a sanction for power to the autocrats already wielding the reins of government.

Behind Kant's pragmatic conservatism—his tendency to endorse the prevailing system of government—lay a belief in the sovereignty of law; and it was this belief which caused him to repudiate the citizen's right to rebellion. Although he made an exception of revolutionary France,[28] Kant held that to rebel against an established order, no matter how tyrannical, was to contravene the social contract and violate the very principles of right: 'revolution under an already existing constitution means the destruction of all relationships governed by civil right, and thus of right altogether' (Reiss, p. 162).[29] To recognize the sovereignty of law was to admit that certain political duties lay beyond the scope of conscience, namely, that in some circumstances, the strict requirements of individual virtue must bow before the claims of citizenship. The potential conflict here between internal and external duties—between acting virtuously (that is, in accordance with the dictates of one's conscience) and acting legally (that is, in accordance with the requirements of justice)—is fully investigated in Kant's *Metaphysic of Morals* (1797). Exploring the role of the categorical imperative in our day-to-day lives, Kant concludes that there must be a distinction between ethical legislation which 'makes an action a duty and also

---

[28] Kant's attitude to the French Revolution is discussed by Williams in *Kant's Political Philosophy*, pp. 208–14.

[29] For discussion of this point see *Conceptions of Liberty*, pp. 112–13.

makes duty the motive' and juridical legislation which 'does not include the motive in the law and so permits a motive other than the Idea of duty itself': 'The mere conformity or non-conformity of an action with the law, without reference to the motive of the action, is called its *legality* (lawfulness). But that conformity in which the Idea of duty contained in the law is also the motive of the action is called its *morality*.'[30] This distinction between the legality and morality of an action, and the recognition of a potential conflict between the two, is central to Coleridge's political thought in *The Friend*:

> every Depositary of the supreme Power must presume itself rightful: and as the source of law, not legally to be endangered. A form of government may indeed, in reality, be most pernicious to the governed, and the highest moral honor may await the patriot who risks his life in order by its' subversion to introduce a better and juster Constitution; but it would be absurd to blame the Law, by which his Life is declared forfeit. It were to expect, that by an involved contradiction, the Law should allow itself not to be Law, by allowing the State, of which it is a part, not to be a State. (*TF* ii. 57.)

Immediately after establishing Reason as a Kantian idea, Coleridge forges the link, so crucial to his argument, between Rousseau's general will and Kant's moral law. In doing so, he is not only amongst the first to reveal Rousseau's influence on Kant, but foremost in using this insight to demonstrate the essentially ethical nature of Rousseau's general will—the fact that 'it is a principle of moral conduct applied to political behaviour'.[31]

For Rousseau, when a man enters into the social contract and participates in the general will, he acts morally because he acts in accordance with universal law; he seeks, not his own selfish ends, but the good of the entire community: 'Then only, when the voice of duty takes the place of physical impulses and right of appetite, does man, who so far had considered only himself, find that he is forced to act on different principles, and to consult his reason before listening

---

[30] *The Doctrine of Virtue: Part II of the Metaphysic of Morals*, trans. introduction and notes Mary J. Gregor (Philadelphia, 1964), 16–17; hereafter cited as *Doctrine of Virtue*.

[31] See translator's introduction (*SC*, p. xxx).

to his inclination' (*SC* bk. I, ch. 8). The tension which
Rousseau sets up in *The Social Contract* between acting out of
private interest and acting in accordance with the general will
resembles Kant's distinction in the *Groundwork* between acting
from heteronomous motives (those dictated by inclination and
desire) and acting autonomously (out of a sense of duty, in
accordance with the moral law). For Kant, to act autonomously is to behave in such a way that the maxim of our
individual action can also be willed as universal law.[32]

The joining together of the general will and Kant's
categorical imperative was Coleridge's way of underpinning
his claim that Rousseau's political principles belonged more
properly to the sphere of a Kantian moral philosophy. Apply
Rousseau's political doctrines, Coleridge argues,

to any case, in which the sacred and inviolable Laws of Morality are
immediately interested, all becomes just and pertinent. No Power on
Earth can oblige me to act against my Conscience. No Magistrate,
no Monarch, no Legislature, can without Tyranny compel me to do
any thing which the acknowledged Laws of God have forbidden me
to do. So act that thou mayest be able without involving any
contradiction to will that the Maxim of thy Conduct should be the
Law of all intelligent Beings—is the one universal and sufficient
Principle and Guide of Morality.   (*TF* ii. 128.)

Then, as part of his explanation of how and why the
categorical imperative qualifies as the supreme moral principle,
Coleridge drives a wedge between morality and politics, for
the '*object* of Morality is not the outward act, but the internal
Maxim of our Actions' (*TF* ii. 128). What gives an action its
moral worth is not the value of any actual or intended results,
but the maxim, or subjective principle, in accordance with
which we act. Thus, in so far as we are concerned with the
formal aspect of moral action, no better test can be applied
than Kant's categorical imperative. But 'with what shew of
Reason', Coleridge asks, 'can we pretend, from a Principle by
which we are to determine the purity of our motives, to deduce
the form and matter of a rightful Government, the main office
of which is to regulate the outward Actions of particular

[32] For Kant's distinction between autonomy and heteronomy, see *Groundwork*,
pp. 94–5.

Bodies of Men, according to their particular Circumstances?'
(*TF* ii. 128.)

The claim that morality is concerned not with the outward
act but with the internal maxim of an action, is, of course, a
commonplace of Kant's philosophy. In his *Metaphysic of
Morals*, we find it laid down as a chapter heading that,

Ethics does not give laws for *Actions* (*Ius* does that), but only for the
Maxims of Actions.   (*Doctrine of Virtue*, p. 48.)

Whereas in matters of morality we are concerned, Kant
writes, with internal, subjective principles, 'not with the
actions we see, but with their inner principles, which we
cannot see' (*Groundwork*, p. 72), *Ius* is concerned with the
external rightness or wrongness of actions, considered without
regard to the motives which prompted them.

We first meet this distinction between *Ius* and Ethics in
Number 4 of *The Friend*, in the essay, 'On the Communication
of Truth'. According to Coleridge, a writer must be accountable for his works both as an individual and as a citizen: he
must be able to acquit himself before two different courts of
appeal (*TF* ii. 56–7). The first judge is his own conscience, the
faculty which concerns itself with the nature, not with the
results, of his action. The second judge is the state, before
whom the writer appears as a citizen. Unlike the first court,
the state 'concerns itself with the Conscience only as far as it
appears in the Action, or, still more accurately, in the fact'
(*TF* ii. 57). Thus, at an early stage in *The Friend*, Coleridge
lays the foundation of Kant's distinction between the realms of
morality and politics; and it is this Kantian distinction which
he uses in Number 9 to define his sense of why Kant's supreme
moral principle (and, by implication, Rousseau's general will)
is so misplaced in the political realm, a realm in which the
maxim of all law-making must be '*Expedience* founded on
Experience and particular Circumstances' (*TF* ii. 133).

In making his distinction between morality and politics,
Coleridge was no doubt thinking of that memorable passage
in the *Groundwork*, at the beginning of chapter 2, where Kant
insists on an account of morality which is entirely independent
of experience, taking its source solely in pure practical

Reason; for the inevitable result of attending to our experience of human conduct is, Kant writes, that 'we meet frequent and—as we ourselves admit—justified complaints that we can adduce no certain examples of the spirit which acts out of pure duty, and that, although much may be done *in accordance with* the commands of *duty*, it remains doubtful whether it really is done *for the sake of duty* and so has a moral value' (*Groundwork*, p. 71). In actual fact, so hidden and secret are our impulses to action that it is absolutely impossible to establish from experience 'a single case in which the maxim of an action in other respects right has rested solely on moral grounds and on the thought of one's duty' (*Groundwork*, p. 71). Out of love for humanity, Kant is 'willing to allow that most of our actions may accord with duty'; but if we look more closely at what he calls our 'scheming and striving, we everywhere come across the dear self, which is always turning up'. So subject are we to chance desires and inclinations that, at certain moments, and especially as one grows older and is made 'shrewder by experience', it is hard not 'to become doubtful whether any genuine virtue is actually to be encountered in the world' (*Groundwork*, p. 72). This sobering admission—that in talking of actions performed purely from a sense of duty, we are talking of actions 'of which the world has perhaps hitherto given no example'—leaves Kant no alternative but to vindicate his supreme moral principle in the realm of what ought to be, rather than what is in fact. Once the weakness of man's nature has been conceded, the only safeguard against a complete falling away from our 'Ideas of duty' is 'the clear conviction that even if there never have been actions springing from such pure sources, the question at issue here is not whether this or that has happened; that, on the contrary, reason by itself and independently of all appearances commands *what ought to happen*' (*Groundwork*, p. 72; my emphasis). In the same way that Kant endorses only abstract versions of Rousseau's political concepts, arguing that they are valid only as rational ideals, so too does he move his categorical imperative away from man as he is to man as he ought to be: a perfectly rational agent, worthy of being a legislating member of a Kingdom of Ends.

Thus, when Coleridge claims of Kant's supreme moral principle that it cannot help us to establish 'a rightful Government' (*TF* ii. 128), he is echoing Kant's own acknowledgement of the formal nature of his moral philosophy, the fact that it is confined to the enunciation of an ideal only, independent of what is known from experience. Kant's Reason 'gives no law for actions but only a law for the maxims of actions' (*Doctrine of Virtue*, p. 52), and it is this feature which, in Coleridge's eyes, disqualifies it as the sole guide to political action. Reason is the 'Calm and incorruptible Legislator of the Soul' (*TF* ii. 125), but in order to legislate for society as well, Reason needs the aid of 'positive and conventional Laws in the formation of which the Understanding must be our Guide, and which become just because they happen to be expedient' (*TF* ii. 131).

In thinking of the individual man, rather than abstract Reason alone, as the sovereign and rightful Lawgiver, Rousseau and his followers appeared to Coleridge to confuse two very different things, a confusion which often led them into glaring inconsistencies. In illustration of this, Coleridge cites the Assembly's exclusion of various groups from the franchise. Children, for instance, were denied the vote on the grounds that in them Reason was 'not yet adequately developed'. Women too were excluded because they were thought to be 'in a state of *dependence*', and therefore unable to exercise their Reason with freedom (*TF* ii. 129). The inconsistency of these qualifications with the revolutionaries' claim that all men were strictly equal had not escaped Burke either; with great scorn he noted that their 'metaphysic principle' of the equality of all men, 'to which law, custom, usage, policy, reason, were to yield, is to yield itself to their pleasure' (*Reflections*, p. 287). But whereas Burke ended his argument here, with this statement of a simple inconsistency, Coleridge moved beyond this point to demonstrate a profound contradiction within the system itself; for while the revolutionaries conceded by their actions that human beings necessarily differed from each other in degree, their whole system rested on the principle that Reason was 'not susceptible of degree' (*TF* ii. 129).

In thinking of this issue of universal suffrage, it is possible that Coleridge had in mind the kind of difficulty which confronted Kant as he tried to reconcile his belief that legislative power can belong only to the united will of the people[33] with his equally strong conviction that 'all are not equally qualified . . . to possess the right to vote, i.e. to be citizens and not just subjects among other subjects' (Reiss, p. 140). Distinguishing between 'active' citizens who are fit to vote, and 'passive' citizens who, because they are obliged to depend on others for their living, do not possess this right, Kant is forced to admit that this concept of 'passive' citizen seems to 'contradict the definition of the concept of a citizen altogether'. Nevertheless, he attempts to escape the dilemma by arguing that this 'dependence upon the will of others and consequent inequality does not . . . in any way conflict with the freedom and equality of all men as *human beings*' (Reiss, p. 140).[34]

Kant's double perspective on man, which he shares with Hooker and Burke,[35] provided Coleridge with a major clue as to where Rousseau and his followers had gone astray; we read in *The Friend* that their error lay in identifying 'the foundations of Government in the concrete with those of religion and morality in the abstract' (*TF* ii. 135). Years later, in his *Table Talk*, Coleridge elaborated on this idea in a warning against the dangers of confounding Church with State. Whereas a State 'must be based on classes and interests and unequal property', a Church is 'founded on the person, and has no qualification but personal merit' (*TT*, 10 April 1833). In fact, the Church represented for Coleridge 'the only pure democracy, because in it persons are alone considered, and one person a priori is equal to another' (*TT*, 28 Dec. 1831). George Fox and his Quakers had achieved an 'ideal democracy' of this kind—a

---

[33] 'only the unanimous and combined will of everyone whereby each decides the same for all and all decide the same for each—in other words, the general united will of the people—can legislate' (Reiss, p. 139).

[34] Similarly, Kant claimed that the 'uniform equality of human beings as subjects' was 'perfectly consistent with the utmost inequality of the mass in the degree of its possessions' (Reiss, p. 75).

[35] It is possible that Kant's own formulation derived from Burke; *Reflections* was translated into German in 1793 (see Reiss, p. 193).

community 'founded on the person'—but it was impossible
that a nation could ever do the same (*TT*, 23 April 1832; 10
April 1833). Of the two possible modes of unity in the State, a
hierarchy or a consensus of equals, the latter could never be
maintained 'without slavery as its condition and accompaniment' (*TT*, 10 April 1833).

Appropriately, Coleridge ends Number 9 with a defence of
property as the unequal and non-rational distribution of
goods upon which society is based. Following Burke's lead in
his famous defence of property in *Reflections*, Coleridge argues
that it is of the very essence of property to be unequal—'there
must be inequality of Property: the nature of the Earth and
the nature of the Mind unite to make the contrary impossible'
(*TF* ii. 132).[36] As he is later to make clear in Number 11,
Coleridge does not follow Burke beyond this point; for
whereas Burke defended heredity,[37] and the concentration of
property in the hands of the very few,[38] Coleridge disapproved
of 'the tendency of Wealth to accumulate in abiding Masses'.
In direct opposition to Burke, he believed (like Kant)[39] that
scope should be given to those with talent and ability: that
property should circulate freely, unimpeded 'by any positive
Laws or Customs' (*TF* ii. 146).

Coleridge's assertion that 'it is impossible to deduce the
Right of Property from pure Reason', and his claim that
Rousseau himself admits this (*TF* ii. 132), are in keeping with
the spirit of the rest of his essay. And it is difficult not to feel
that in his final thrust at Rousseau's political philosophy—his
disparagement of it as a form of Geometry which 'holds forth
an *Ideal*' only—he is once again thinking of Kant's moral
philosophy. Just as Kant's moral law could only provide us
with an ideal of moral action, the utmost which Reason could
give 'would be a property in the *forms* of things . . . In the

[36] Burke had written: 'The characteristic essence of property, formed out of the
combined principles of its acquisition and conservation, is to be *unequal*' (*Reflections*,
p. 140).

[37] 'The power of perpetuating our property in our families . . . tends the most to
the perpetuation of society itself' (*Reflections*, p. 140).

[38] Property must be represented 'in great masses of accumulation, or it is not
rightly protected' (*Reflections*, p. 140).

[39] For Kant's views on property, see Reiss, pp. 76–8.

matter it could give no Property' (*TF* ii. 132). Universal principles (and with this point Coleridge ends his essay) 'necessarily suppose uniform and perfect Subjects, which are to be found in the *Ideas* of pure Geometry and (I trust) in the *Realities* of Heaven, but never, never, in Creatures of Flesh and Blood' (*TF* ii. 133).

8
Religion and Politics:
The Gordian Knot

Consistency, energy, and unanimity in national wickedness must be counterbalanced by consistency and
undistracted Energy in national Virtue, which fully
exerted bring with them, from the recesses of their own
nature, a greater consistency, a more enduring Energy.
The atrocious Contempt of all moral must be met by an
heroic Contempt of all physical Consequences, and
Justice must act to the full stretch of it's Rights, where
Wickedness admits no other Limit than that of it's
Power.

Coleridge to Sir George Beaumont, December 1808

JOHN COLMER has remarked of *The Friend* that it reveals
'perhaps the most important change of all in Coleridge's
thought, the change from a loose equation of religious and
social morality to a formal distinction between the two'.[1]
While it is true that Coleridge distinguishes in *The Friend*
between religious and social codes of behaviour, it is not a
distinction with which he is entirely at ease. Furthermore, the
distinction does not carry over into a formal separation
between religion and politics; on the contrary, it is one of
Coleridge's explicit aims in *The Friend* to demonstrate the
supreme importance and centrality of private, religious values
in the public, political realm.[2] At no point in England's
history did this union of morality and politics, of private and
national life, seem more urgent than in the years 1809–10, a

---

[1] 'Coleridge and Politics', *Writers and their Background: S. T. Coleridge*, ed. R. L.
Brett (London, 1971), 251.
[2] Colmer adds that Coleridge believed politics should 'always be founded on
moral principles', but he does not weigh this claim against his account of Coleridge's
distinction between the different ends of religion and politics.

point which is made with great feeling and urgency in Number 22 of *The Friend*:

If ever there were a time when the formation of just *public* Principles becomes a duty of *private* Morality; when the principles of *Morality in general* ought to be made bear on our public suffrages, and to effect every great national determination; when, in short, his COUNTRY should have a place by every Englishman's Fire-side; and when the feelings and truths, which give dignity to the Fire-side and tranquillity to the Death-bed, ought to be present and influencive in the Cabinet and the Senate—that time is now with us.

(*TF* ii. 299–300.)

The 'close connection between private libertinism and national subversion' was a truth entailed upon his generation by the recent upheavals of the political world (*TF* ii. 30).

There are, however, a number of places in *The Friend* where the claims of private and public codes of morality, of Christianity and nationalism, pull against each other, and even threaten to spring apart into open opposition. Coleridge's position is a difficult one to maintain. In his anxiety to assert the essential harmony of a vigorous nationalism with private, Christian life, he stresses again and again that individuals and nations are subject to the same moral laws; against this claim, he must, however, make allowance for his belief that the duties pertaining to private and national life involve significant 'moral differences' (*TF* ii. 306).

These 'moral differences' emerge most conspicuously at times of national crisis. The law of nations is, in fact, completely unlike the law governing individuals, for 'in extraordinary cases', the conduct of states 'neither will, nor in the nature of things can be determined by any other consideration, but that of the imperious circumstances, which render a particular measure advisable' (*TF* ii. 328). This bald statement sounds very much like secular *Realpolitik*, but at no point in *The Friend* is Coleridge prepared to surrender his rapturous view of the State as a mystic, sacred entity embodying a principle higher than the self, and one which, in times of danger, must hold sway over personal, individual claims. Coleridge's fascination with moments of mystic unity and with the tremendous power generated by them, is illustrated early in *The Friend*, in an incident taken from his observation of the natural world:

On some wide Common or open Heath, peopled with Ant-hills, during some one of the grey cloudy days of late Autumn, many of my Readers may have noticed the effect of a sudden and momentary flash of Sunshine on all the countless little animals within his view, aware too that the self-same influence was darted co-instantaneously over all their swarming cities as far as his eye could reach; may have observed, with what a kindly force the Gleam stirs and quickens them all! and will have experienced no unpleasurable shock of Feeling in seeing myriads of myriads of living and sentient Beings united at the same moment in one gay sensation, one joyous activity!

(*TF* ii. 31.)

Transferred to the world of men, the same phenomenon was truly awe-inspiring. Recalling a visit to Göttingen by the Queen of Prussia, Coleridge wrote:

The spacious Outer Court of the Palace was crowded with men and women, a sea of Heads, with a number of children rising out of it from their Father's shoulders. After a Buz of two hours' expectation, the avant-courier rode at full speed into the Court. At the trampling of the Horses' Hoofs, and the loud cracks of his long whip, the universal Shock and Thrill of Emotion—I have not language to convey it—expressed as it was in such manifold looks, gestures, and attitudes, yet one and the same feeling in the eyes of all! Recovering from the first inevitable contagion of Sympathy, I involuntarily exclaimed, though in a language to myself alone intelligible, 'O Man! ever nobler than thy circumstances! Spread but the mist of obscure feeling over any form, and even a woman, incapable of blessing or of injury to thee, shall be welcomed with an intensity of emotion adequate to the reception of the Redeemer of the World!'

(*TF* ii. 31–2.)[3]

It was precisely this vision of a people united by feelings of awe and reverence that inspired Coleridge's cry for national unanimity. Concerned at the way in which human passions

---

[3] De Quincey displays a similar intoxication with power and images of unity in his essay, 'The English Mail-Coach'. In fulfilling its 'awful *political* mission' of diffusing war news throughout the Kingdom, the mail coach is the symbol of a 'central intellect', drawing together a scattered people 'into one steady co-operation to a national result' (*The Collected Writings of Thomas De Quincey*, ed. David Masson (14 vols.; Edinburgh, 1889–90), xiii. 272).

were so frequently squandered upon objects unworthy of them, he considered it 'the most imperious Duty and the noblest Task of Genius' to restore such powerful feelings to their 'rightful Claimants' (*TF* ii. 31),[4] the most needy of which was England, an innocent nation compelled by French imperialism to struggle for its safety and survival (*TF* ii. 328). That Genius was Coleridge himself, for as he admitted privately, while the people were 'stirring & heaving with an unwonted Sense of Right and Wrong', there was not a single politician 'to form a Channel for their Feelings—no one to retain, steady, and direct them' (*CL* iii. 132). By raising the tone of political debate, and directing his teachings to those who 'by Rank, or Fortune, or official Situation . . . are to *influence* the Multitude' (*CL* iii. 143), he would indirectly achieve his goal of tapping and channelling the nation's energies.

To this end, conflicting strains must be subsumed in an affirmation of the paramountcy of England's national interest. The form that this enterprise takes in *The Friend* is seen in the religious rapture of Coleridge's nationalistic rhetoric as it struggles to rise above the tension in his thought between the very different claims of religion and politics. In an essay on Machiavelli, Isaiah Berlin has described this tension as one which arises from 'a differentiation between two incompatible ideals of life, and therefore two moralities':

One is the morality of the pagan world: its values are courage, vigour, fortitude in adversity, public achievement, order, discipline, happiness, strength, justice, above all assertion of one's proper claims and the knowledge and power needed to secure their satisfaction . . . Against this moral universe (moral or ethical . . . in the traditional sense, that is, embodying ultimate human ends however these are conceived) stands in the first and foremost place, Christian morality. The ideals of Christianity are charity, mercy, sacrifice, love of God, forgiveness of enemies, contempt for the goods of this world, faith in the life hereafter, belief in the salvation of the individual soul as being of incomparable value—higher than, indeed

---

[4] One of the principal objects of *The Friend* was to 'refer men's opinions to their absolute Principles, and thence their Feelings to the appropriate Objects, and in their due degrees' (*TF* ii. 276).

wholly incommensurable with, any social or political or other terrestrial goal, any economic or military or aesthetic consideration.[5]

For Berlin, the originality of Machiavelli's political thought lies in his frank and unsqueamish admission that Christian values are insuperable obstacles to the building of a strong, secure, and satisfying human society.

The clash between these two moralities occurs at those points in *The Friend* where, as a realist and pragmatist, Coleridge urges the primacy of national survival, and the necessary dependence of England's success upon political strength and effectiveness. The dilemma which this kind of realism customarily presents to the Christian is partially obscured in Coleridge's case by his denunciation of those who argue that state policy cannot always take morality into account, and his passionate emphasis upon national virtue; but the call for national virtue co-exists, as we shall see, with the invocation of a Justice acting, not just 'to the full stretch of it's Rights' (*CL* iii. 147), but even beyond these.

Throughout the Napoleonic wars, the relationship between politics and morality was much debated in books and periodicals. Coleridge's thoughts on this issue constitute a response to two very different points of view current at this time, each representative of two quite distinct traditions. The first view was associated with the Quakers and other Dissenting groups, all of whom opposed the war either because they were pacifists or because they disagreed with the principles on which the war was being fought. The Dissenters' contribution to the debate was summed up by Clarkson in his *Portraiture of Quakerism*, when he denounced as 'infamous' the system which distinguished between 'political expediency and moral right' (iii. 198); if a conflict arose between political expediency and the requirements of morality, then the latter should automatically take precedence, for it was a cherished maxim amongst Dissenters that men ought not to do evil that good may come (iii. 201). The second of these views was the

---

[5] 'The Originality of Machiavelli', *Against the Current: Essays in the History of Ideas* (Oxford, 1981), 45.

popular one of 'might is right', vociferously championed by
Cobbett in his *Political Register*. Those who held to this slogan
placed political expedience above every other consideration; if
a situation arose in which the interests of a large nation like
Britain could be furthered by unjust actions against smaller,
less important countries, then it was a duty for British
politicians to lay aside moral questions and pursue the
nation's advantage.

As we have already seen, Coleridge detested Cobbett, but
the distinctions drawn up in *The Friend* between the private
individual and the individual as citizen, between the layman
and the statesman, placed him closer to his enemy than to
those, like Clarkson and the Quakers, who repudiated such
distinctions. It is even possible that Coleridge's arguments in
The Friend were intended as a deliberate challenge to Clarkson's
approval in his *Portraiture* of the Quakers' adherence to a
single, undifferentiated code of morality, regardless of the
exigencies of political life.

Clarkson opens his work with a brief résumé of his principal
reasons for admiring the Quakers. He writes of his great
regard

for men, of whom it is a just feature in their character, that whenever
they can be brought to argue upon political subjects, they reason
upon principle and not upon consequences; for if this mode of
reasoning had been adopted by others, but particularly by men in
exalted stations, policy had given way to moral justice, and there
had been but little public wickedness in the world. (vol. i, pp. vi–vii.)

The elevation of Principle in contradistinction to a calculating
and prudential attention to consequences is already familiar
to us from Coleridge's letters advertising *The Friend*. But
whereas Coleridge took care to leave himself an escape route
from a hard and fast distinction between Principle and
Prudence, Clarkson makes it clear that the Quakers hold
firmly to a single code of morality: whatever the problems of
practical, political life, Quakers believed that all essential
political truths were to be deduced from scripture. Preaching
the primacy of religious principle in all worldly affairs, they
did not see political morality as a separate issue: a politician's

actions were held to be subject to the same constraints as those of any Christian individual. Clarkson devoted an entire chapter of his *Portraiture* to this subject, and he underscored the importance of the Quakers' stance upon Principle by remarking: 'I do not know any trait which ever impressed me more than this in all my intercourse with the members of this Society. It was one of those which obtruded itself to my notice on my first acquaintance with them, and it has continued equally conspicuous to the present time' (iii. 199–200). Religious principles were never to be laid aside for political advantage, and nothing was considered to be more dangerous than the setting up of a special morality of the state.

Clarkson's endorsement of this single code of morality led inevitably to a quietist acceptance of an irreconcilable conflict between the ways of the world and the ways of the spirit. In order to preserve their Christian character intact, the Quakers were obliged to turn their backs on all that did not conform to Christ's law; for nothing is more true, writes Clarkson, 'than that a Christian is expected to be singular with respect to the corruptions of the world' (*Portraiture*, iii. 198).

Coleridge makes it clear in *The Friend* that he does not think much of those who piously renounce the world because they are unable to square the necessities of political life with the dictates of their consciences, orientated as these are towards individual duties. At best it seemed to Coleridge to be extremely impractical to deny that there is a difference between how one acts as an individual, and how one acts as a citizen; at worst, in a country at war with Napoleonic France, it was unthinking and unpatriotic. In Number 22, in his essay defending British policy in Malta, Coleridge writes,

he who cannot perceive the moral differences of national and individual duties, comprehends neither the one or the other, and is not a whit the better Christian for being a bad Patriot.   (*TF* ii. 306.)

In this very clever remark, what begins as an assertion of difference, ends in a confirmation of the essential unity of the roles of Christian and patriot. Those who hold as binding only those duties which pertain to Christians as private individuals are deaf to the higher harmony of Christian and patriotic life.

One of Coleridge's favourite books at the time was the Revd Walter Harte's *Life* of Gustavus Adolphus, a handbook of religious and moral instruction for military men.[6] Just as *The Friend* argued that Christianity is allied to patriotism, Harte identified true religious feeling with the martial spirit, claiming that 'the religious and good man . . . stands the best chance to be the bravest too' (vol. i, p. xii).

Because Coleridge maintained that the spirit of Christian morality governing national politics was one and the same with that which governed our private lives, he would not admit that a situation might arise in which one's Christianity was at odds with political duty. On Coleridge's account, the man whose conscience causes him to turn his back on political life fails to see that the circumstances attending political action are simply different from those which attend private action, and of course that the same moral principles can issue in different obligations when the circumstances are different:

As the circumstances then, under which men act as Statesmen, are different from those under which they act as Individuals, a proportionate difference must be expected in the practical rules by which their public conduct is to be determined.   (*TF* ii. 322.)

Fearing that this statement might be taken to imply a special exemption for statesmen from the claims of morality, Coleridge immediately adds:

Let me not be misunderstood: I speak of a difference in the practical rules not in the moral law itself which these rules point out the means of administering in particular cases, and under given circumstances. The spirit continues one and the same, though it may vary its' form according to the element into which it is transported.   (*TF* ii. 322.)

That this unvarying moral law offered only an illusory security can be seen whenever Coleridge speaks of the different practical rules governing individuals and nations. In Number 22, for example, in a discussion of the Treaty of Amiens, Coleridge writes that 'a spirit of diffidence and

---

[6] *The History of Gustavus Adolphus . . . to which is Prefixed an Essay on the Military State of Europe*, 3rd edn. (2 vols.; London, 1807). For Coleridge's recommendations of this work to friends, see *CL* iii. 200, 225–6, 241.

toleration' is 'amiable' in an individual, 'yet in a Nation, and above all in an opulent and luxurious Nation, is always too nearly akin to apathy and selfish indulgence' (*TF* ii. 300). In this particular instance, the distinction between nations and individuals leads Coleridge perilously close to an admission that nationalistic feeling is exclusive of Christian virtues, such as meekness and forgiveness. Later in the same number, Coleridge runs into even deeper trouble, in an eloquent passage alluding to Samuel Johnson's denunciation of the belligerent 'hypocrites of patriotism' who raised the war-cry over the Falkland Islands, 'a bleak and barren spot in the Magellanic ocean, of which no use could be made'. Let it not be forgotten, Johnson had urged,

that by the howling violence of patriotic rage, the nation was for a time exasperated to such madness, that for a barren rock under a stormy sky, we might have now been fighting and dying, had not our competitors been wiser than ourselves; and those who are now courting the favour of the people by noisy professions of public spirit would, while they were counting the profits of their artifice, have enjoyed the patriotic pleasure of hearing sometimes, that thousands had been slaughtered in a battle, and sometimes that a navy had been dispeopled by poisoned air and corrupted food.[7]

With Johnson's pragmatic and utilitarian attitude to these Islands in mind, Coleridge writes:

There is no feeling more honourable to our nature . . . than the jealousy concerning a positive Right independent of an immediate Interest. To surrender, in our national character, the merest Trifle, that is strictly our Right, the merest Rock on which the waves will scarcely permit the Sea-fowl to lay its' Eggs, at the demand of an insolent and powerful Rival, on a shop-keeper's calculation of Loss and Gain, is in its' final, and assuredly not very distant consequences, a Loss of every thing—of national Spirit, of national Independence, and with these of the very wealth, for which the low calculation was made. This feeling in individuals, indeed and in private life, is to be sacrificed to Religion.   (*TF* ii. 305.)

For a brief moment here, Coleridge's enthusiasm carries him over into the morality of the pagan world, the world which,

[7] From 'The Patriot' (1774), *The Yale Edition of the Works of Samuel Johnson*, ed. A. T. Hazen (New Haven, 1977), x. 396.

according to Isaiah Berlin, values above all else the 'assertion of one's proper claims and the knowledge and power needed to secure their satisfaction'. Conscious that his rhetoric has betrayed him, and that he runs the risk of appearing antagonistic to Christian values, Coleridge cautiously reins his words back in and adds,

Say rather, that by Religion it [nationalistic feeling] is transmuted into a higher Virtue, growing on an higher and engrafted Branch, yet nourished from the same root; that it remains in its' essence the same Spirit, but
    Made pure by Thought, and naturaliz'd in Heaven;
                                                        (*TF* ii. 305–6.)

This sudden turnabout is not very convincing, and as a way of countering the difficulties generated by his enthusiastic nationalism, he draws an important distinction between the spirit and the letter of the Law of Morality. This is the pivot on which all of Coleridge's distinctions turn; it is also the pivot which he hoped would give him sufficient flexibility to hold steady his claim that religious and nationalistic feelings flourish together under one universal and unchanging spirit.

At the beginning of his essay 'On the Law of Nations', Coleridge writes:

It were absurd to suppose, that Individuals should be under a law of moral obligation, and yet that a million of the same individuals, acting collectively or through representatives, should be exempt from all law: for Morality is no accident of human nature, but its' essential characteristic.   (*TF* ii. 321.)

For this reason, men who have written wisely on the Law of Nations 'have always considered the several States of the civilized world, as so many Individuals, and equally with the latter under a moral obligation to exercise their free agency within such bounds, as render it compatible with the existence of free agency in others' (*TF* ii. 321).[8] 'But'—and this is where

---

[8] In the 1818 *Friend*, Coleridge reinforces this point by prefacing his essay 'On the Law of Nations' with the following motto from Plato's *Laws*: 'For all things that regard the well-being and justice of a State are pre-ordained and established in the nature of the individual' (*TF* i. 289).

the analogy between individuals and nations begins to break down—

> in all Morality, though the principle, which is the abiding *spirit* of the Law, remains perpetual and unaltered, even as that supreme Reason in whom and from whom it has its' being, yet the *Letter* of the Law, that is, the application of it to particular instances and the mode of realizing it in actual practice, must be modified by the existing circumstances. *What* we should desire to do, the conscience alone will inform us; but *how* and *when* we are to make the attempt, and to what extent it is in our power to accomplish it, are questions for the judgement, and require an acquaintance with facts and their bearings on each other.   (*TF* ii. 321.)

By the 'Letter' of the Law, Coleridge means positive law, a body of legislation enforceable by authority; the 'spirit', on the other hand, stands for the requirements of morality. The distinction in this passage between the letter and the spirit is paralleled by a further distinction between the realms of conscience and practicability. In emphasizing the need for attending to the particular circumstances and facts of a given case—the 'how' and the 'when' of our actions—Coleridge suggests that it is not enough for the dictates of conscience to be in harmony with a 'perpetual and unaltered' law; they must also be practical and flexible enough to take into account the whole circumstances of a particular case.

Having set forth what he sees to be the difference in 'the practical rules' governing the actions of individuals and nations, Coleridge proceeds to a discussion of the main subject of this number, the Law of Nations. Articles on international law appeared regularly in newspapers and journals throughout the war, and Coleridge no doubt welcomed the opportunity of voicing his views. But he also had a particular purpose in mind—namely, to provide a defence of Britain's violation of Denmark's neutrality in 1807.

At no time did the debate on international law and morality rage more fiercely than in the wake of Britain's simultaneous seizure of the neutral Danish fleet and bombardment of Copenhagen. Public opinion was divided between those who argued that the measure was justifiable on the grounds of national self-defence, and those who held that Britain's attack was an act of ruthless expediency, in open defiance of international law and morality. The first view was espoused by the man responsible for Britain's attack, the Foreign Secretary and subscriber to *The Friend*, George Canning (*TF* ii. 419). The second view was held by Liberals, such as William Roscoe. Roscoe was a leading Dissenter, an old friend of Coleridge[9] and, like Canning, a subscriber to his periodical (*TF* ii. 454). He was also one of the most eloquent spokesmen for the Opposition in the period 1807–9,[10] and it was his denunciation of the Copenhagen affair which initially polarized public opinion.

At the time of the controversy, Coleridge found himself out of sympathy with both sides of the debate. Unlike Roscoe, he believed that Britain was right to seize the fleet, and early in 1808 he claimed he had written all but the concluding paragraph 'to a moral & political Defence of the Copenhagen Business' (*CL* iii. 75). At the same time, however, he was, like many of his friends, disgusted with the language of brute expedience enlisted by Canning and his apologist in the press, William Cobbett. The principles on which the Danish expedition was defended appeared disgraceful to him, a view shared by Wordsworth who referred to the Ministers' language as 'horrible' (*MY* i. 267). To Stuart's high opinion of Canning at this time, Coleridge replied: 'I never can think that statesman a great man, who to defend a measure will assert—not once but repeatedly—that state-policy can not and ought not to be always regulated by morality.' (*CL* iii. 195.) This view is aired in *The Friend*, but it is phrased more mildly and Canning is not named. The assertion that '*national policy* cannot in all cases be subordinated to the Laws of Morality . . . was hazarded (I record it with unfeigned regret) by a Minister of State, on the affair of Copenhagen.

[9] See Roscoe's letter to Revd Mr Edwards of Birmingham, quoted by Henry Roscoe in his biography of his father, *The Life of William Roscoe* (2 vols.; London, 1833), i. 231–3.

[10] In 1808 Roscoe published two substantial anti-ministerial tracts. For a collection of his political writings from 1793 to 1810, see his *Occasional Tracts Relative to the War between Great Britain and France Written and Published at Different Periods from the year 1793* (London, 1810).

Tremendous assertion!' (*TF* ii. 308). Despite this castigation, however, Coleridge is to emerge as Canning's defender by arguing that, despite the Foreign Secretary's own statements to the contrary, the Copenhagen affair was (as he had held from the beginning) 'strictly moral & in the true spirit of the Law of Nations' (*CL* iii. 195).

A more sophisticated government apologist than Cobbett, Coleridge argues that if men like Canning sound immoral and cynical when they justify their actions as statesmen, this is due not to the fact that they, or their actions, *are* immoral, but simply to the fact that they do not know how to resolve their troubled realization that it is sometimes impracticable to apply the same moral criteria to nations as to individuals. The recognition of this impracticability causes 'a perplexity in the moral feelings', a perplexity which often leads to 'extensively injurious' consequences:

For men hearing the duties, which would be binding on two individuals living under the same Laws, insisted on as equally obligatory on two independent states, in extreme cases, where they see clearly the impracticability of realizing such a notion; and having at the same time a dim half-consciousness, that two States can never be placed exactly on the same ground as two Individuals; relieve themselves from their perplexity by cutting what they cannot untie, and assert . . . that a Government may act with injustice, and yet remain blameless.   (*TF* ii. 307–8.)

This passage marks the first stage in Coleridge's substitution of moral arguments for those of ruthless expediency. Allowing the disjunction between an individual and a nation, he denies the wisdom and necessity of arguing from this position for an exemption of national policy from all moral criteria. In Coleridge's eyes, the man is rash and unthinking who, when faced with the inappropriateness of certain codes of Christian behaviour in the world of politics, rudely asserts that the two spheres are utterly incompatible. Such a disjunction presented itself as a hopeless impasse, and one which he was determined to avoid. Unlike Canning who, in his perplexity, cut the knot between religion and politics, Coleridge believed he had sufficient art and eloquence to untie the cords which held

Britain back from emerging with its honour unsullied. If ministers recklessly asserted the necessity of brute expedience in government policy, the onus was on Coleridge to make that political expediency look like virtue.

The theoretical underpinning of his defence of the ministry's action is to be found in the distinction, outlined above, between the letter and the spirit of the Law. Whereas relations between individuals 'are and must be under positive Laws', relations between states or nations 'neither are, nor can be' under such laws (*TF* ii. 328); the Law of Nations is not 'fixed or positive in itself, nor supplied with any regular means of being enforced' (*TF* ii. 322). In fact, the 'only fixed part of the Law of Nations is the spirit: the Letter of the Law consists wholly in the circumstances, to which the Spirit of the Law is applied' (*TF* ii. 328). Thus, in determining what is morally right in international relations, we must look at the whole of the circumstances governing the case, and not merely to the sorts of general moral maxims which one might well look to in formulating a body of positive law. In general terms it might be considered a moral wrong to violate a country's neutrality, but since there exists no body of positive law, the 'Law of Nations' can only appeal to the particular circumstances of the case, and 'to the conscience and prudence of the Parties concerned' (*TF* ii. 322).

Given the public furore sparked off by the attack on Denmark, Coleridge was not exaggerating when he said his defence would 'disgust many friends' (*CL* iii. 75). Southey, for one, was outraged by the incident. Although he shared Coleridge's belief that the war should be pursued as vigorously as possible, he found it impossible to take the government's side:

God help us! that the main principle, the foundation and main spring of all public and all private morality, should still openly be set at defiance, and laughed to scorn! . . . Woe be to the nation, and to the individual who believes that anything which is wrong can ever be expedient! (Warter, ii. 26.)

Incensed by the Government's open adoption of the 'damnable doctrine of expediency' (Curry, i. 458), he did not, like

Coleridge, divorce ministerial language from ministerial action. Echoing the arguments of the Opposition, he believed that 'with the best cause in the world, we have contrived to put ourselves in the wrong, and to make ourselves more detested, and even with more justice, than Bonaparte' (Curry, i. 462). It was this forfeiture of England's moral superiority which disturbed Southey most. Now that ministers had lowered themselves to a level with Bonaparte, 'and voluntarily chosen to fight him with his own weapons of cruelty, and tyranny, and injustice' (Warter, ii. 25–6), they could no longer claim credit for waging war against an oppressor. The charge that Britain had behaved no better than her enemy was repeatedly voiced by those repelled by Britain's pre-emptive strike, and it was a claim which Coleridge found even more reprehensible than the one of expediency put forward in Britain's defence.

William Roscoe was a vociferous proponent of Southey's view; so too was Richard Sharp, another of Coleridge's subscribers. In a stirring address delivered before the House of Commons in March 1808, Sharp denounced the Government for its adoption of Napoleonic tactics.[11] Many other subscribers of liberal persuasion no doubt felt the same—men like Josiah Wedgwood, William Strutt, and his brothers, Peter Crompton and Samuel Galton; they were all friends of Roscoe (and of Coleridge too, for that matter) and strongly opposed to the war.[12]

In January 1808, when the Copenhagen affair was being debated in Parliament, Roscoe published an influential and controversial tract denouncing Britain's conduct since the Treaty of Amiens. Entitled *Considerations on the Causes, Objects and Consequences of the Present War, and on the Expediency, or the Danger of Peace with France*, the pamphlet quickly achieved a large circulation and a certain notoriety. Within less than a month it had reached a fourth edition,[13] and for four successive weeks its arguments were the subject of Cobbett's

---

[11] *The Parliamentary Debates from the year 1803 to the present time: Debates in the House of Commons, Hansard x* (21 Jan. to 8 Apr. 1808) (London, 1812), 1211.

[12] See J. E. Cookson, *The Friends of Peace: Anti-War Liberalism in England, 1793–1815* (Cambridge, 1982).   [13] H. Roscoe, *Life of William Roscoe*, i. 425.

scorn and abuse.[14] Coleridge, too, had nothing but contempt for the arguments of 'peace men' like Roscoe, and he referred slightingly to this tract as a 'whimpering Scotch Review Pamphlet' (*CL* iii. 58).

In the Advertisement to his *Considerations*, Roscoe included as one of the aims of his pamphlet the awakening of the people 'to a just sense of the importance of the great cause of political morality' (p. iv). For Roscoe, and other Dissenters, morality was grounded on eternal principles of right and justice, a belief which invalidated all distinctions between laymen and politicians, individuals and nations. Appealing to the authority of scripture Roscoe asks: 'Are not nations uniformly spoken of in the sacred writings, as accountable, collectively, for their moral conduct? as being just or unjust; oppressors, or oppressed? and are they not, as such, punished or rewarded?' (*Considerations*, p. 75.) The biblical precepts, 'to do justice', 'to love mercy' and 'to walk humbly with God' were 'equally applicable to nations as to individuals' (*Considerations*, pp. 76–7), and the model politician was one who could unite 'the speculative virtues of the closet with the public conduct of the statesman, and exhibit to the world a noble proof, that amidst the rage of national and individual animosity, the eternal laws of justice and of virtue were neither overthrown nor shaken' (*Considerations*, p. 44). This passage forms part of a tribute to Charles James Fox, the man who Roscoe put forward as an infallible model for the conduct of politicians. By warning Talleyrand in 1806 of a plan to assassinate Napoleon, Fox exhibited, 'one of the most important maxims of morality—*that it is never expedient to do evil in the hope of producing an eventual good*' (*Considerations*, p. 44).

Like Coleridge and Southey, and so many others, Roscoe was particularly repelled by the Government's language of self-justification. Quoting the King's official statement as to the 'cruel necessity' which drove England to attack Denmark, he claimed that, 'upon this excuse, every crime and every atrocity may be equally justified'; he then added: 'That such

[14] See Cobbett's four 'Letters to William Roscoe', *PR* xiii. 225–41, 257–68, 322–33, 353–65 (13, 20, 27 Feb., 5 Mar.).

doctrines have of late been asserted in this country, in the most open and profligate manner, is a dreadful symptom of that moral and intellectual depravity which precedes the fall of nations. To read the daily effusions of some of our popular writers, one would suppose that the human race was not the offspring of one common parent.' (*Considerations*, p. 73.)

Sharp made the same point in his speech before the House: 'There seems to have grown up of late a disposition to consider all political morality as an incumbrance in real affairs, and we have recently heard them ridiculed in this house, as fit only for the schools, but unfit for the guidance of parliaments, and of ministers.' (*Hansard* x. 1200.)[15] Both men blamed Cobbett for this new mood of cynicism and immorality. It was the *Political Register* which had 'dared to insult the common feelings, and the common sense of mankind, by asserting, that *might constitutes right*' (*Considerations*, p. 74).[16]

Cobbett's name had come to be associated with certain political doctrines, many of which have a bearing on Coleridge's arguments in *The Friend*. First, and most importantly, Cobbett held that the Law of Nations was a chimera, a mere 'creature of the imagination':

It is very true, that a Dutchman, named Grotius; another Dutchman, high or low, named Puffendorff; another, named Binkershoech; and a Frenchman, named Vattel; have written books upon what has been called, for want of a better name, the law of nations. But, besides that of these writers, there are no three who agree with each other upon scarcely any one point of great and general importance; their books contain merely the history of what such and such nations have done in such and such cases, together with the *opinions* of the writers respectively as to what *ought* to be the rules for the conduct of nations towards each other; each writer observing, however, that, unhappily, these rules are frequently set at nought.   (*PR* xii. 390–1.)

In his writings on war, and on the balance of power in Europe, the only thing which seemed to Cobbett to be of any

---

[15] In the first six months of 1808, 'Whig speeches were liberally sprinkled with sarcasms on the "new morality"' (Michael Roberts, *The Whig Party 1807–1812* (London, 1939), 113).

[16] Cobbett responded indignantly to this passage in his third 'Letter to William Roscoe' (*PR* xiii. 325).

importance was the relative strength of the two warring powers, England and France. Since there was no such thing as a Law of Nations, force alone 'confers right in affairs wherein nations are concerned' (*PR* xii. 429),[17] and the belief that might is right went hand in hand with the plea that ministers be vigorous in upholding 'the ancient rights and practices of England upon the seas' (*PR* xii. 426). If abuse of power was held in check by any single circumstance, it was due—not to an internationally accepted code of laws—but to 'the rivalship of the strong, their mutual jealousies, their quarrels with one another, and the necessity, which, for their own sakes, they have, at various times, been under, of affording protection, and even of granting favours, to nations incapable of self-defence.' (*PR* xii. 392.)

A vociferous champion of the view that Britain's survival depended upon her imitation of Napoleon's example, Cobbett applauded the attack upon Copenhagen, and in a mock address to the ruler of France he taunted: 'if you will be the sole sovereign of all the land, we will be the sole sovereign of all the sea. You make power the standard of right, and so must we.' (*PR* xii. 395.) Furthermore, just as the law of nations seemed a chimera to Cobbett, the notion of any equality amongst nations existed 'in imagination only': 'The proposition, that all nations are upon a footing of perfect equality, as to their rights upon the seas, is what I deny ... it is a proposition, not only unnecessary to be declared, but a proposition containing an abandonment of the ancient claims of our country.' (*PR* xii. 519.) In open contempt of Denmark's neutrality, Cobbett argued that 'little nations must be made instruments in the hands of great nations' (*PR* xiii. 164), and with great belligerence he denied that England was in any way bound to respect the independence of other European powers, 'especially those within the reach of

---

[17] 'I ... assert, that there is no law, to which nations implicitly bow; that there is no common tribunal amongst them; that there is no where any judge to decide between them and no where any power to enforce obedience to any decision; and that, therefore, it is, after all, amongst nations, might which constitutes right, and must constitute right in all cases, where the sword is the judge' ('Letter III, To William Roscoe', *PR* xiii. 325).

France'. It was aggressive, John Bullish rhetoric of this kind which drew forth from the House of Lords the powerful declaration that,

> to justify the attack and plunder of a weak unoffending power, upon . the assumption that a stronger belligerent might otherwise attack and plunder her, would be to erect a new public law upon the foundations of dishonour and violence, making the tyranny of one nation a warrant for substituting the dominion of oppression for the sacred obligations of morality, humanity, and justice.
>
> (*Hansard* x. 35.)

The single most important theme running through Cobbett's defence of the Ministry was the extremity of the circumstances in which it found itself in 1807. Because France had swallowed up almost every other country in Europe, it seemed clear to Cobbett that, even if one believed in the existence of a law of nations, or an internationally recognized code of conduct, this code was effectively annulled by the new circumstances of Europe. No state could be called to account, he argued, for failing to act upon a superseded code: 'In short, the expedition against Copenhagen is to be tried by no settled rules relating to the practices of nations: the circumstances, under which it was resolved on, were entirely without example: and our justification rests solely upon the seizure of the fleet being necessary to our safety.' (*PR* xiii. 165.) Even Cobbett's *bête noire*, the editor of the *Morning Chronicle*, had been 'so condescending as to allow', in his arguments for the existence of a 'code of public laws',

> that, if there be a nation which sets this code at defiance its enemy may also set it at defiance, *with respect to it*; because the latter 'cannot be bound to submit to a rule of restraint upon his force, from which his adversary takes the advantage of being exempted. Therefore, *with respect to France*, we have, undoubtedly, *a right of exercising the law which she practices*'. More than this we need not ask in support of the seizure upon the Danish fleet and naval arsenals; for the *law* . . . which [France] practices, is, to suffer no nation to remain neutral with regard to England, if that nation be placed within the reach of her power. (*PR* xii. 392.)

Because France's violation of international law radically altered the balance of power in Europe, the circumstances which had originally given rise to the law were, as a consequence, no longer in existence. For Cobbett, and also for Coleridge, once a particular set of circumstances had passed, the laws which sprang from it were effectively annulled. But whereas Cobbett used this argument to demonstrate that Britain was free to behave in exactly the same way as France, Coleridge harnessed the same argument to a very different conclusion—namely, that changed circumstances made it impossible for England to imitate France. It was, in his view, absurd for Cobbett to relish the thought of England released from all bonds and free to break the *same* law as Napoleon. Similarly, it was 'mere puerile declamation' for the critics of the Ministry

to rail against a Country, as having imitated the very measures for which it had most blamed its' ambitious Enemy, if that Enemy have previously changed all the relative circumstances which *had* existed for *him*, and therefore rendered *his* conduct iniquitous; but which, having been removed, however iniquitously, cannot without absurdity be supposed any longer to control the measures of an innocent Nation, necessitated to struggle for its' own safety, especially when the measures in question were adopted for the very purpose of *restoring* those circumstances.   (*TF* ii. 328.)

It would be difficult to decide which of the two offended Coleridge more—the accusation of Opposition ministers that England had begun to imitate Napoleon, or the delight with which Cobbett greeted this very charge in the columns of his *Political Register*. Certainly Coleridge goes to great lengths in *The Friend* to repudiate Cobbett's claim that Britain's success lay in fighting Napoleon with his own weapons (*PR* iii. 163). The cry that injustice be met with injustice would surely lead to disaster, he argued, for nothing but Virtue could overcome Evil:

where Ambition admits no boundary but that of its' own power, and all the *Vices* are allied and systematized against us; there can be no hope of successful resistance, but in an equal union of all the *Virtues* of the human character . . . If the present Empire of France be rightly considered as one bad great Man wielding the strength and weaponry of millions, in all just proportion the Kingdom, that is to resist him, and which must perish if it does not resist him adequately, ought to be (as Milton with his accustomed grandeur hath expressed it) 'but as one vast Personage, one mighty growth and stature of an honest Man, as big and compact in virtue as in body.' Scarcely can that be too often enforced, the practice of which is both necessary and inexhaustible: and the principle of Evil fights his battles cheap, if he may still use the same Sword, and good Men not employ the same Buckler.   (*TF* ii. 300.)

The thinly veiled allegory of the seizure of the Danish fleet (*TF* ii. 328–33) is Coleridge's attempt to prove that England did not exchange its buckler for a sword of Napoleon's own making: that it did not, as Southey claimed, voluntarily choose to fight Napoleon 'with his own weapons of cruelty, and tyranny and injustice'. Within the terms in which Coleridge has himself defined a Law of Nations, his allegory must prove 'the identity of international Law and the Law of Morality in *spirit*, and the reasons of their difference in *practice*, in those extreme cases in which alone they have been allowed to differ' (*TF* ii. 333).

Coleridge's allegory attempts to portray both the Law of Nations and the balance of power among the European states by describing a colony consisting of 'from twenty to thirty Households, or separate Establishments'. Each Household differs greatly in the number of retainers and extent of possessions, but it is the unwritten law of the colony that each 'possesses its' own domain, the least not less than the greatest, in full right' (*TF* ii. 329). Thus, by implication, Coleridge concedes the right of independence to small countries such as Denmark, but he quickly makes it clear that this right carries with it certain communal duties. Chief of the 'virtual Laws' governing these Households is the following:

that as no man ought to interfere in the affairs of another against his will, so if any Master of a household, instead of employing himself in the improvement of his own fields and flocks, or in the better regulation of his own Establishment, should be foolish and wicked enough to employ his children and servants in breaking down the

fences and taking possession of the lands and property of a Fellow-
colonist . . . then that it became the duty and interest of the other
Colonists to join against the Aggressor, and to do all in their power to
prevent him from accomplishing his bad purposes, or to compel him
to make restitution and compensation.   (*TF* ii. 329.)

The aggressor in the tale is called Misetes, 'Hater' (Napoleon),
a man who fears 'neither God nor his own Conscience' (*TF*
ii. 330). His main rival is Pamphilus, 'Friend to all, beloved of
all' (England), a good man who has the interests of the Colony
at heart:

throughout the whole Colony there was not a single Establishment,
which did not owe some of its' best buildings, the encreased produce
of its' fields, its' improved implements of industry, and the general
more decent appearance of its' Members, to the information given
and the encouragements afforded by Pamphilus and those of his
household. Whoever raised more than they wanted for their own
establishment, were sure to find a ready purchaser in Pamphilus,
and oftentimes for articles which they had themselves been before
accustomed to regard as worthless, or even as nuisances: and they
received in return things necessary or agreeable, and always in one
respect at least useful, that they roused the Purchasers to industry
and its' accompanying virtues. In this intercommunion all were
benefited: for the wealth of Pamphilus was increased by the
increasing Industry of his Fellow-colonists, and their Industry
needed the support and encouraging Influences of Pamphilus's
Capital.   (*TF* ii. 330.)

The third character in the tale is the independent Proprietor
Lathrodacnus, 'One who bites secretly' (Denmark), a kinsman
of Pamphilus but a man of no influence in the colony.[18]
Furthermore, in a statement which effectively undermines the
earlier claim that each household possesses its own domain 'in
full right', Lathrodacnus is described as owing 'his
independence and prosperity' to the power and protection of
Pamphilus:

the very existence of Lathrodacnus, as an independent Colonist, had
no solid ground, but in the strength and prosperity of Pamphilus;

---

[18] All three names used by Coleridge are transliterations of Greek words:
μισητης, παμφιλος, λαθροδακνης.

and as the interests of the one in no respect interfered with those of the other; Pamphilus for a considerable time remained without any anxiety, and looked on the river-craft of Lathrodacnus with as little alarm, as on those of his own Establishment.   (*TF* ii. 331.)

The river-craft are of extreme importance because Pamphilus' main property is divided from Misetes and the rest of the Colony by a wide and dangerous river. The means of crossing this river are possessed exclusively by Pamphilus and his kinsman, so there is cause for some alarm when Pamphilus discovers that Lathrodacnus is building and collecting 'a very unusual number' of boats. Pamphilus contents himself at first with urgent yet friendly remonstrances, but these only elicit from Lathrodacnus the following response:

that by the Law of the Colony, which Pamphilus had made so many professions of revering, every Proprietor was an independent Sovereign within his own boundaries; that the Boats were his own, and the opposite shore, to which they were fastened, part of a field which belonged to him; and, in short, that Pamphilus had no right to interfere with the management of his Property, which, trifling as it might be compared with that of Pamphilus, was no less sacred by the Law of the Colony.   (*TF* ii. 331.)

Pamphilus replies to this by claiming that the Law of the Colony, to which Lathrodacnus appeals, 'had been effectually annulled by the unexampled tyranny and success of Misetes, together with the circumstances which had given occasion to the law, and made it wise and practicable' (*TF* ii. 331). In addition to this appeal to the extreme circumstances of the case, Pamphilus urges two further claims: first, that the Law of the Colony

was not made for the benefit of any one Man, but for the common safety and advantage of all: that it was absurd to suppose that either he (Pamphilus) or that Lathrodacnus himself, or any other Proprietor, ever did or could acknowledge this law in the sense, that it was to survive the very circumstances which made it just and proper, much less could they have even tacitly assented to it, if they had ever understood it as authorizing one Neighbour to endanger the absolute ruin of another, who had perhaps fifty times the property to lose, and perhaps ten times the number of souls to answer for, and yet forbidding the injured person to take any steps in his own defence: and, lastly, that this Law gave no right without imposing a corresponding duty, and therefore if Lathrodacnus insisted on the *rights* given him by the law, he ought at the same time to perform the *duties* which it required, and join heart and hand with Pamphilus in his endeavours to defend his independence, to restore the former state of the Colony, and with this to re-enforce the old Law, in opposition to Misetes, who had enslaved the one and set at nought the other.   (*TF* ii. 331–2.)

In appealing to the special and unprecedented situation created by Misetes' tyranny, Pamphilus echoes the arguments of both Cobbett and Coleridge. Similarly, when Coleridge describes Pamphilus' seizure of Lathrodacnus' boats as an act of obedience to 'the dictates of self-preservation' (*TF* ii. 332), he is concurring with Cobbett's claim that national self-defence must always be treated as an overriding consideration. The difference between the two writers only emerges when Coleridge's higher moral language comes into play. Whereas Cobbett rejoiced at the thought that Napoleon's disregard for international law freed Britain from all former restraints, Coleridge lays great emphasis upon Pamphilus' profound attachment to the Law:

So ardently was Pamphilus attached to the Law, that excepting his own safety and independence, there was no price which he would not pay, no sacrifice which he would not make for its' restoration. His reverence for the very memory of the law was such, that the mere appearance of transgressing it would be a heavy affliction to him.   (*TF* ii. 332.)

Nevertheless, the dictates of self-preservation drive him to violate Lathrodacnus' rights as an independent Proprietor by taking possession of his boats by force. Instantly, 'a great outcry was raised against Pamphilus, who was charged in the bitterest terms with having first abused Misetes, and then imitated him in his worst acts of violence' (*TF* ii. 332).

Pamphilus' response, made in the 'calmness of a good conscience', is to impugn the integrity of Lathrodacnus' neutrality. To this end, Coleridge invents his analogy of the Quaker on a shooting party, a story which, as we saw in chapter 5, (p. 106), succinctly conveys his contempt for pacifism. As part of an essay on 'The Law of Nations', however, the story does more than this: it neatly illustrates the way in which principle comes to be overruled by extremity, and through the use of personification, reinforces Coleridge's point that the 'morality' governing nations is identical in spirit to that which governs individuals.

When taken to task by a 'valued Correspondent' for his allegory, Coleridge made public the complaint, and conceded the existence of 'many reasons' against the Copenhagen affair, as well as many for it; but of the reasons against, he adduced only one, and that was the quite cynical one that, when Britain took the ships, she left Napoleon the Danish sailors (*TF* ii. 357); the half-heartedness of this attempt to see the other side of the question only strengthens the impression of Coleridge's bias. And to his Correspondent's hard-hitting observation that he used the allegory as a cover for his political opinions, Coleridge replied with the extraordinary claim that he was 'neither defending or attacking the measure itself':

my arguments were confined to the *grounds*, which had been taken both in the arraigning of that measure, and in its' defence, because I thought both equally untenable. I was not enough master of facts to form a decisive opinion on the enterprize, even for my own mind; but I had no hesitation in affirming, that the *principles*, on which it was *defended* in the legislature, appeared to me fitter objects of indignant reprobation, than the act itself.   (*TF* ii. 356–7.)

There is inexcusable sophistry here in Coleridge's attempt to separate the grounds or principles of the controversy from the facts upon which this controversy necessarily drew fire; and the claim that he had no 'decisive opinion' concerning these facts is, of course, plainly false, for the internal cogency of the allegory depends upon a strong and very one-sided reading of the events in question. It is, indeed, a relatively easy task to show that instead of placing his arguments on a high plane of disinterestedness, Coleridge in fact distorts certain features of the case in order to produce a watertight justification for the Government's action.

For instance, whereas the question of Denmark's disposition towards Britain had been the subject of much dispute, Coleridge quite simply claims that Pamphilus received 'certain intelligence' of Lathrodacnus' hostile intentions towards him.[19] It is significant that in the official statement published shortly after the bombing of Copenhagen, the King revealed himself to be relatively uninterested in the question of Denmark's disposition towards Britain. Much more weight was given to the claim that Britain had received 'the most positive information' concerning the intentions of France. According to the King, Napoleon was determined

to occupy, with a military force, the territory of Holstein, for the purpose of excluding Great Britain from all her accustomed channels of communication with the continent; of inducing or compelling the court of Denmark to close the passage of the Sound against the British commerce, and navigation; and of availing himself of the aid of the Danish marine for the invasion of Great Britain and Ireland.[20]

It was precisely because the entire burden of the King's self-justification lay not, as one might expect, with the hostile intentions of Denmark, but with the hostile intentions of France, that his public statement gave rise to grave speculation concerning Britain's motive for seizing the fleet. Were the ships seized because Denmark was known to be on the point of going over to Napoleon? or were they seized because of her inability to withstand a French invasion? The suspicion that the latter was so, and that Britain's motive was the simple one of grabbing Denmark's navy before Napoleon did, was strengthened by the King's reference to Denmark's 'avowed inability to resist the operation of external influence, and the threats of a formidable neighbouring power' (*PR* xii. 544).[21]

[19] Coleridge made the same claim two years later in *The Courier*: 'We had a perfect conviction that the force of Denmark was to be employed against us—that it was to be an engine in the hands of Buonaparte' (*EOT* ii. 208–9); cf. *S. Life* iii. 141.

[20] 'Declaration of the King of Great Britain, relative to the War with Denmark, dated Westminster, Sept. 25, 1807', quoted in Cobbett (*PR* xii. 543–4).

[21] Roscoe capitalized on this reference to Denmark's vulnerability: 'If it had happened that Denmark had, of her own accord, thrown off her pacific connections with Great Britain, and intentionally entered into the views of France, this would indeed have afforded a better apology for the conduct of the British Ministry . . . But no such pretext is even alluded to in the justification' (*Considerations*, pp. 80–1).

In Parliament, Canning tried to mitigate the effects of the King's gaffe by promising his critics 'positive proof' of Denmark's hostile intentions, but the evidence was never produced, and the Government lost a good deal of its credibility (see *ER* xiii. 494–5).

Cobbett saw Canning's promise of proof as foolhardy, believing that the Government need do no more than rest its justification upon 'the notorious circumstances of the case' (*PR* xiii. 274). Coleridge must also have felt that Canning exceeded his brief in this matter. Distinguishing in *The Friend* between the duties of a Juror and a Senator, he claims that while the former 'lays aside his private knowledge and his private connections, and judges exclusively according to the evidence adduced in the Court', the Senator 'acts upon his own internal convictions, and oftentimes upon private inform-ation which it would be imprudent or criminal to disclose. Though his ostensible Reason ought to be a true and just one, it is by no means necessary, that it should be his sole or even his chief reason' (*TF* ii. 304). In other words, while the ostensible pretext for aggression against Denmark was that her neutrality cloaked hostility to Britain, there might be other factors, more decisive yet not so palatable, which were too damaging to mention.

Another issue which was much discussed at the time, and which had a bearing on Denmark's status as a neutral country, concerned the newness of her fleet and its readiness for war. Of the thirty-nine ships and vessels surrendered by Denmark, only eleven were built after 1800 (*PR* xii. 480); and according to one English observer resident in Copenhagen at this time, 'the fleet of Denmark, with the exception of one ship of the line, was laid up in ordinary' (*ER* xiii. 497).[22] These facts are simply ignored by Coleridge, who in his allegory claims that Lathrodacnus was employed in 'building and collecting a very unusual number of . . . Boats' (*TF* ii. 331). Coleridge also presents Pamphilus' seizure of the fleet as the

---

[22] Roscoe claimed of the Danish navy that 'not a ship was rigged, and the crews were absent' (*Considerations*, p. 69). Similarly, Sharp argued that the fleet continued 'just in the same state of preparation in which it had been for nearly half a century, nor could it have been ready for sea, in less than six or eight weeks' (*Hansard* x. 1193).

only injury committed against Lathrodacnus. No reference is made to the fact that Britain bombarded Copenhagen for three days and nights, and only ceased its aggression when the city surrendered to its terms (*PR* xii. 473–80; *ER* xiii. 492).[23] But perhaps the most objectionable part of Coleridge's allegory is the insinuation that Denmark was never really on an equal footing with Britain. Lathrodacnus owes his independence and prosperity to Pamphilus, who in turn considers that he has special claims on his 'kinsman'. Thus does Coleridge fudge the crucial issue of Denmark's rights as a neutral and independent nation. It would seem that Coleridge shared Cobbett's belief that small European countries like Denmark were pawns in the hands of greater nations like France and England. It was not a view with which he would like to be associated, but it is surely there in the allegory— in the sense of Lathrodacnus owing his independence to Pamphilus, and in the grounds of the latter's appeal to his smaller neighbour: that in any contest between them, he (Pamphilus) 'had perhaps fifty times the property to lose, and perhaps ten times the number of souls to answer for' (*TF* ii. 332).

From this brief sketch we can summarize Coleridge's method in the following way: beginning with the principle that the circumstances of a given case must always determine the conduct of nations, he gives his own biased version of these circumstances, and then fends off criticism by claiming that he is not concerned with externals at all, but only with principles. But even if, contrary to the evidence, we grant his reading of the episode, and concede that Denmark's navy posed a serious threat to Britain's security, at no point does he consider the issue which perturbed so many: the harshness with which the affair was conducted. The King himself expressed regret that his Government had been forced to resort to such violent and extreme measures of self-preservation:

---

[23] The bombing of Copenhagen was an event which Coleridge continued to ignore in all his accounts of the Danish expedition. Two years after the publication of *The Friend* he wrote in *The Courier*, 'we did, what by the Law of Nations, of self-defence, and of self-preservation, we had a right to do—we deprived [Buonaparte] of that engine, we took the Danish fleet, and then retired from the island' (*EOT* ii. 209).

'That the state and circumstances of the world are such as to have required and justified the measures of self-preservation, to which his Majesty has found himself under the necessity of resorting, is a truth which his Majesty deeply deplores . . .' (*PR* xii. 576).

There is no reason to doubt Coleridge's sincerity when he claimed to be shocked and disturbed by the flagrant disregard of moral considerations exhibited in the public speeches and writings of politicians like Canning. The problem is that he considered this indifference to moral argument as the only unsavoury aspect of the Danish expedition. Even worse, he staunchly maintained that, unbeknown to itself, and in direct contradiction of all public pronouncements, the British Government had behaved in a manner consonant with the highest dictates of morality; for self-defence, whether national or individual, is an overriding moral imperative. But even if we think that Coleridge is right about the sort of situation he describes in his allegory, this demonstrates neither that self-preservation *always* constitutes an overriding justification, nor—thanks to his partial interpretation of the facts—that it justified Britain's actions in this particular case.

When Coleridge first interested himself in the task of defending the Government on this issue, he claimed that he was acting from conscience (*CL* iii. 75), but in a bitter and complaining letter written four years after *The Friend*, he referred to the allegory as one of the many labours for which he had never been thanked by 'those in power'. For all his writings 'against Weakness, and Despondency and Faction and factious *Goodiness* at home' (that is, the Dissenters), he was 'Unthanked and left worse than defenceless by the Friends of the Government and the Establishment, to be undermined or outraged by all the malice, hatred, & calumny of it's Enemies' (*CL* iii. 532). When Peter Crompton wrote to Coleridge to renew his subscription, he let it be known that he was by no means 'a convert' to all that *The Friend* preached. It is in this letter, too, written three weeks before the allegory appeared, that he reported what must have been so painful for Coleridge to hear: that certain people thought he was writing in *The Friend* to please those in power and 'get a good berth' for

himself (WL MS A/Crompton/1). Perhaps it was the knowledge that his motives were already under suspicion which
provoked him to be more openly pro-Government; certainly,
in justifying such an unpopular measure, he ran the risk of
alienating a large proportion of his subscribers and supporters.

If Coleridge had not, in this one particular incident, been so
determined to exonerate Britain from all blame and suspicion,
he might have enlisted in his country's defence an excep-
tionally honest and moving passage from an earlier number.
In this passage, Coleridge laments the unavoidable cost to
Britain of its fight for survival against an enemy bent on its
destruction:

> it is a mournful Truth, that as Devastation is incomparably an easier
> Work than Production, so all its means and instruments may be
> more easily arranged into a scheme and System. Even as in a Siege
> every Building and Garden which the faithful Governor must
> destroy as impeding the defensive means of the Garrison, or
> furnishing means of Offence to the Besieger, occasions a Wound in
> feelings which Virtue herself has fostered: and Virtue, because it is
> Virtue, loses perforce part of her energy in the reluctance, with
> which she proceeds to a business so repugnant to her wishes, as a
> choice of Evils.   (*TF* ii. 84.)

A compromised virtue, a wound inflicted on feelings which
virtue herself has fostered—these are the high prices which
must be paid for national self-preservation.

Conclusion

COLERIDGE'S half-hearted defence of the allegory occurs in the second last number of *The Friend*. Six weeks later, with Sara gone, he reverted to the state in which the Wordsworths first found him upon his return from Malta. Lying in bed until late in the afternoon, and only appearing for meals, he seemed to want nothing more than to be left to his solitude. Writing to her close friend Catherine Clarkson, whom she begged twice to burn the letter, Dorothy confided that there were times when 'he does not speak a word, and when he does talk it is always very much and upon subjects as far aloof from himself or his friends as possible . . . He speaks of *The Friend* always as if it were going on, and would go on'. For all their efforts, he remained 'just as much the slave of stimulants as ever', and his whole time and thoughts were spent in 'deceiving himself, and seeking to deceive others', a habit which brought 'new hollowness and emptiness' to all his words and actions (*MY* i. 399).

From Allan Bank, Coleridge went to Keswick to rejoin his wife and family. Here, as we learn from Mrs Coleridge, the same pattern of behaviour was repeated: 'The last No. of the 'Friend' lies on his Desk, the sight of which fills my heart with grief, and my Eyes with tears . . . he has not *appeared* to be employed in composition, although he has repeatedly assured me he was.'[1]

Although wanting to deceive others, Coleridge was not self-deceived. He was simply embodying the idea of conscience sketched in Number 1: a conscience stupefied but not deluded, suspended but not annihilated. To Lady Beaumont he frankly confessed that he was in search of '*forgetfulness*, a sort of counterfeit of that true substantial tranquillity, which a satisfied Conscience alone can procure for us' (*CL* iii. 287).

[1] *Minnow Among Tritons: Mrs S. T. Coleridge's Letters to Thomas Poole, 1799–1834*, ed. Stephen Potter (London, 1934), 11.

Appendix of Subscribers[1]

Quaker Subscribers

William Allen, Plough Court, Lombard Street, London.
Jonathan Backhouse, Darlington.
David Barclay, Walthamstow, nr. London.
Robert Barclay, 56 Lombard Street, London.
Daniel Bell, Jun., 6 Freemans Court, Cornhill.
Morris Birkbeck, Jun., Wanborough, nr. Guildford, Surrey.
George Braithwaite, Stricklandgate, Kendal.
Isaac Braithwaite, Kendal.
William Calvert, Keswick.
David Carrick, Jun., Carlisle.
John Corbyn, 300 Holborn, London.
Thomas Furly Forster, Five Houses, Clapton, nr. London.
Joseph Foster, Bromley, nr. Bow, Middlesex.
Samuel Galton, Birmingham.
Sampson Hanbury, London.
R. P. Harris, 147 Fenchurch Street, London.
Luke Howard, Plough Court, Lombard Street, London.
John Hull, Uxbridge, Middlesex.
Samuel Hull, Uxbridge, Middlesex.
Mrs Hustler, Ulverstone.
Halsey Janson, Bull Head Passage, Wood Street, London.
William Knight, Chelmsford, Essex.
William Knight, Jun., Chelmsford, Essex.
Dr William Lewis, Ross, Herefordshire.
[?] Lloyd, Hawkshead Field, Kendal.
Charles Lloyd, Sen., Birmingham.
Charles Lloyd, Jun., Old Brathay, Cumbria.

[1] Several sources have been helpful in compiling this Appendix: The Dictionary of Quaker Biography, Library of the Society of Friends, Friends' House, London; Appendix E of *The Friend* (*TF* ii. 407–67); *The House of Commons 1790–1820* (5 vols., London, 1986), ed. R. G. Thorne; and the *Dictionary of National Biography*, ed. Leslie Stephen and Sidney Lee (63 vols., London, 1885–1900).

Robert Lloyd, Birmingham (Banker).
Robert Lloyd, Birmingham (Bookseller).
Samuel Lloyd, Birmingham.
Samuel Edward Lloyd, Bristol.
James Losh, Jesmond, Newcastle.
William Lucas, Jun., Hitchin, Hertfordshire.
Mr Maude, Sunnyside, Sunderland, Durham.
Pim Nevins, Leeds.
Josiah Newman, Ross, Herefordshire.
Richard Phillips, 32 East Street, Red Lion Square, London.
James Powles, Ross, Herefordshire.
Thomas Prichard, Brook End, Ross, Herefordshire.
Jonathan Priestman, Malton, Yorkshire.
F. Smith, 29 Haymarket, London.
F. Smith, Jun., 29 Haymarket, London.
John Smith, Thirsk.
Thomas Smith, at the Bank, Uxbridge.
Thomas Woodruffe Smith, Stockwell Park, Surrey.
Samuel Tuke, Cumbria.
Thomas Westfalling, Reed Hall, nr. Ross, Herefordshire.
Thomas Wilkinson, Yanwath, Penrith.
W. Woodcock, Coventry.
(25 copies of *The Friend* were sent to the Quaker firm of Knott and
Lloyd, Booksellers, Birmingham.)

Possible Quaker Subscribers

Samuel Ash, King's Square, Bristol.
Miss Brown, Meeting House Lane, Peckham.
Mr Elam, Leeds.
Alexander Henderson, 22 Princes Street, Edinburgh.
James Lean, Bristol.
Henry Revell Reynolds, Bedford Row, London.
J. R. Rowntree, Stockton.
Henry Schimmelpenninck, Bristol.
Miss Schimmelpenninck, Bristol.
Emmot Skidmore, Rickmansworth, Hertfordshire.
James Taylor, Birmingham.
Thomas Vipan, Thetford, Norfolk.

Establishment Figures

Earl of Altamont, 10 Grafton Street, London.
Sir George Armytage, Kirklees, nr. Leeds.
Bishop of Bath and Wells
Lady Susan Bathurst, Cadogan Place No. 3, London.
Sir George and Lady Beaumont, Grosvenor Square, London.
Countess of Beverley, Portman Square, London.
Marquis of Blandford, Grosvenor Square, London.
Sir George Cayley, Brompton, Yorkshire.
Earl of Cork, Hamilton Place, London.
Rt. Hon. Lady Craven, Lower Grosvenor Street, London.
Bishop of Durham
Marchioness of Exeter, Whitehall, London.
Earl of Hardwicke, St James Square, London.
Viscount Hinchingbrooke, Grafton Street, Bond Street, London.
Lady Anne Hudson, Yorkshire.
Sir Robert Kingsmill, Sidmanton House, nr. Newbury, Berkshire.
Duke of Leeds
Richard Watson, Bishop of Llandaff, Calgarth.
Countess of Lonsdale, Charles Street, Berkeley Square, London.
Earl of Lonsdale, Charles Street, Berkeley Square, London.
Lady Anne Lowther, Charles Street, Berkeley Square, London.
Lady Elizabeth Lowther, Charles Street, Berkeley Square, London.
Lady Mary Lowther, Charles Street, Berkeley Square, London.
Duchess Dowager of Newcastle, Charles Street, Berkeley Square, London.
Sir Stafford Northcote, Pynes, Exeter.
Sir Samuel Romilly, Russell Square, London.
Viscountess St Asaph, Berkeley Square, London.
Lady Elizabeth Spencer, Wheatfield House, Tetsworth.
Sir John Swinburne, Capheaton, Newcastle.
Lady Harriet Townshend
Sir Francis Wood, Henworth, Pontefract, Yorkshire.

Members of Parliament 1790–1820

Sir George Beaumont (Bere Alston 1790–6). A supporter of
Government but temperamentally unsuited to political life. In

1806 he was mentioned as a possible candidate for Leicestershire but he did not stand.

Marquis of Blandford (Oxfordshire 1790–6, Tregony 1802–4). Generally regarded as a feckless dilettante, he began as a Pittite, swung round to Grenville in 1806, and in 1809 joined Brooks's Club, a Whig stronghold. He died a High Tory.

Samuel Boddington (Tralee 1807). Son of a wealthy West India merchant, he was described as 'a steady supporter of civil and religious liberty' and was a friend of many prominent Whigs. In 1809 he was in business with Richard Sharp and later with George Philips. His Whig connections were reinforced by the marriage of his daughter to Lord Holland's younger son in 1824.

William Sturges Bourne (Hastings 1798–1802, Christchurch 1802–12). A Pittite, and a close ally of Canning. At the time of *The Friend*, he was a member of Cabinet (Lord of the Treasury).

Charles Brandling (Newcastle-Upon-Tyne 1798–1812). An ardent Pittite, and ally of Canning in 1809.

George Canning (Newtown I.o.W. 1793–6, Wendover 1796–1802, Tralee 1802–6, Newtown I.o.W. 1806–7, Hastings 1807–12, Liverpool 1812–22). Secretary of State for Foreign Affairs 1807–9, he was the architect of the Copenhagen expedition. A fanatical disciple of Pitt, who considered him his political heir, Canning was generally believed to be the most talented member of the House of Commons of his generation. He was one of the founders of the *Antijacobin* (1797–8).

John Christian Curwen (Carlisle 1786–90, 1791–1812, 1816–20). A Foxite Whig, opposed to the war and to any suspension of civil liberties. Describing himself as 'a friend to the democratic part of the constitution' he stood against corruption and the excessive power of the Crown. In May 1809 he introduced a parliamentary reform bill which was supported by the moderate Whigs but opposed by the radical wing led by Sir Francis Burdett.

Thomas Estcourt (Cricklade 1790–1806). Voted with Government until 1804, then became a warm supporter of Addington's ministry.

Thomas Grimston Estcourt (Devizes 1805–26). Like his father, Thomas Estcourt, he was a follower of Addington, who was his wife's uncle. He opposed the Copenhagen expedition.

William Fawkes (Yorkshire 1806–7). Joined the Whig Club in 1798 and Brooks's Club in 1807. By 1808 he had attached himself to his old schoolfellow Sir Francis Burdett and his band of radical reformers.

Earl of Hardwicke (Cambridgeshire 1780–90). In politics he initially followed Fox but rallied to the Government in 1794. He was Lord Lieutenant of Ireland under both Addington and Pitt.

George Hibbert (Seaford 1806–12). A leading figure in the London commercial world, he was an old fashioned Whig who disassociated himself from the Foxites. He supported the 'Talents' Ministry but was opposed to the abolition of the slave trade on practical grounds. He advocated peace with Napoleon in 1808 and was an active supporter of the campaign for economic reform from 1809 onwards.

Viscount Hinchingbrooke (Huntingdonshire 1794–1814). Supported successive administrations until 1806, when the Grenville ministry deprived his father of his place. His father being restored to office in 1807, he again supported Government.

Benjamin Hobhouse (Bletchingley 1797–1802), Grampound 1802–6, Hindon 1806–18). A champion of Joseph Priestley, he was attracted to Unitarianism and, according to Lady Holland, was 'a leading man among the dissenters'. The son of a Bristol merchant, he argued for peace with Napoleon until 1803, when he vindicated Addington on the resumption of hostilities with France. In 1809 he spoke out against ministerial corruption and the conduct of military affairs.

Henry Holland (Oakhampton 1802–6). During 1805 he voted regularly with the opposition against Pitt's ministry. A follower of Windham, Fox, and Grenville, he was recommended by his father, the famous architect, for employment in the 'Talents' ministry. Nothing came of these overtures.

Samuel Horrocks (Preston 1804–26). A waverer in politics, he was initially classed as 'doubtful' and then under 'Pitt' in 1804; in 1805 he was described 'doubtful Pitt'. He supported the Grenville Ministry, then the Portland Government.

William Jacob (Westbury 1806–7, Rye 1808–12). A merchant who supported the abolition of the slave trade on the grounds that its continuance would lead to over-production. He contested Great Yarmouth in 1807 with the support of the Portland Government and the Townshend interest. Although he claimed to be independent of 'a court faction', he was classed 'Government' by the Whigs in 1810.

R. Knight (Wootton Bassett 1806–7, 1811–12). Wrongly identified by Rooke as 'H. Knight, an army officer'. A friend of Sir Francis Burdett, and steward for his election for Middlesex in 1804, Knight was an advanced Whig and had a reputation as a Bonapartist.

Earl of Lonsdale (Rutland 1796–1802). An adherent of Pitt who welcomed his return to power in 1804 but was disillusioned by his reconciliation with Addington in January 1805. He opposed Grenville's ministry when Pitt's friends were excluded and Fox's given preference, and he rallied to the Portland administration in 1807.

Lord Lowther (Cockermouth 1808–13, Westmorland 1813–31). Son of the Earl of Lonsdale, and Lord of the Admiralty, 1809–10. He supported Perceval and opposed parliamentary reform in 1810.

Matthew Montagu (Tregorny 1786–90, St Germans 1806–12). A staunch Pittite throughout the 1790s. He deplored the peace negotiations of the Grenville ministry in 1807 and supported Portland and Perceval. He defended foreign policy in 1808 and opposed reform of any kind at home.

George Philips (Ilchester 1812–18, Steyning 1818–20). A wealthy cotton manufacturer who frequented the Lake District. He was a friend of Wordsworth, and was closely associated with intellectual Whigs such as Richard Sharp and William Smith. He joined Brooks's Club in 1812 and voted with opposition consistently and regularly.

Sir Samuel Romilly (Queenborough 1806–7, Horsham 1807–8, Wareham 1808–12, Arundel 1812–18, Westminster 1818). Solicitor-General 1806–7 under Fox, and friend of Sir Francis Burdett. A philanthropist and a sturdy independent in politics, he was committed to reforming the penal code and, in a letter to Cartwright of 1809, endorsed public agitation for parliamentary reform.

William Roscoe (Liverpool 1806–7). A publicist of humble origins, he opposed the slave trade on which the prosperity of Liverpool was based. He sympathized with the French Revolution, attacked Burke in a pamphlet of 1796, and detested Pitt's alarmist and repressive legislation in the 1790s. He opposed the war with

France, believing that it was 'not a war against the French but a war of the English aristocracy against the friends of reform in this country' (1798). In 1806, after he was elected for Liverpool, he explained that his principles were peace and retrenchment, parliamentary reform and the abolition of the slave trade.

William Rose (Christchurch 1796–1800). A Pittite like his father, he went out of the House of Commons when appointed as reading clerk to the House of Lords (1800–24). He, and his friend Canning, subscribed to *The Friend* through Sturges Bourne.

Humphrey Senhouse (Cumberland 1790–6). His family had long been active in Cumbrian politics, and owed much to the patronage of the Lowthers. He cast no vote against Pitt's administration while MP.

Richard 'Conversation' Sharp (Castle Rising 1806–12), Portalington 1816–19). A hatter by trade, he went into business with Samuel Boddington and George Philips, and later became a well-known figure in the intellectual and literary life of London. He started out in politics as a dissenting radical and in 1806 was considered a 'very stout Whig'. In 1808 he passed a motion of censure on ministers for the Copenhagen expedition.

William Smith (Camelford 1791–6, Sudbury 1796–1802, Norwich 1802–6, 1807–30). Son of a well-to-do dissenting merchant, he started out as a Pittite but went over to Fox because of his concern for parliamentary reform, emancipation of religious dissenters from civil disabilities, and the abolition of the slave trade. He emerged as a pacifist in 1793 and advocated peace negotiations with Napoleon in Jan. 1808. Although he did not think the Copenhagen expedition totally unjustifiable, he opposed the vote of thanks for the confiscation of the Danish fleet. He was a supporter of Romilly's attempts to reform the penal code, and a critic of the Government's foreign policy in 1809.

Early Associates, Dissenters and Radicals

Charles Berry (Unitarian Minister).
Revd George Caldwell (old friend of Coleridge).
Michael Castle (old friend from *Watchman* days).
John Chubb (old friend of Coleridge).

Dr Edward Daniel Clarke (friend of the scholar and landscape theorist Richard Payne Knight whose poetry was described by Canning as 'full of democracy and infidelity').

Joseph Cottle (early friend of Coleridge, and publisher of his poetry).

John Coulson (friend from *Watchman* days).

Peter Crompton (Liverpool philanthropist and liberal; and old friend from early *Watchman* days).

Miss Crompton (Peter Crompton's sister).

Charles Danvers (friend from early Bristol days).

John Edwards (Unitarian minister and poet, and friend of the poet and radical James Montgomery).

John Prior (Unitarian minister, and old Bristol friend).

Mrs Evans (daughter of the inventor Jedediah Strutt).

Samuel Fox (married to Martha Strutt, another of Jedediah's daughters).

Miss Gales (sister of Joseph Gales, proprietor of the *Sheffield Register* who had to flee to America in 1794; she was a friend of James Montgomery).

T. L. Hawkes (early associate of Coleridge).

Revd Edward Higginson (Unitarian minister).

Mrs Hincks (wife of Unitarian William Hincks).

Benjamin Hobhouse (a leading dissenter with leanings towards Unitarianism).

Francis Jeffrey (one of the founding editors of the *Edinburgh Review* and a Whig MP in the 1830s).

Charles Lamb (essayist and life-long friend of Coleridge).

Capel Lofft (writer and reformer, staunch supporter of Napoleon).

Thomas Longman (publisher with predominantly Dissenting clientele; his younger brother George was Whig MP for Maidstone at the time of *The Friend*).

John Losh (brother of the Quaker James Losh, and friend of J. C. Curwen).

John Marshall (reformer of the Whig/Liberal persuasion).

Andrew Mitchell (writer and abolitionist).

Basil Montagu (lawyer and author).

James Montgomery (radical and poet, editor of the *Sheffield Iris*). Coleridge sent him a parcel of Prospectuses to distribute (*CL* iii. 138–9).

James Perry (editor of the *Morning Chronicle* and a friend of Leigh Hunt).

George Philips (a dissenter, like his friend William Smith).

Thomas Poole (old friend of Coleridge, a Whig in politics).

Samuel Purkis (a tanner and friend of Thomas Poole).

George Robinson (Dissenting bookseller).

Samuel Romilly (deist and law reformer).

William Roscoe (eminent Unitarian).

Richard 'Conversation' Sharp (dissenting radical and friend of John Horne Tooke).

Samuel Shore (William Shore's brother; Coleridge met him on his *Watchman* tour).

William Shore (wealthy Unitarian whose son married William Smith's daughter).

William Smith (staunch Unitarian).

Strutt family, Derby.

Wedgwood family, Etruria, Staffordshire.

Francis Wrangham (an old friend of Wordsworth and Coleridge, and a moderate Whig in politics).

Bibliography

1. Manuscript Material

(i) *Wordsworth Library, Grasmere*

Letters concerning *The Friend*, to be found in the Alphabetical
  Sequence (WL MS A)
Special Collections (WLL):
  Beaumont Letters
  Hutchinson Letters
  Monkhouse Letters

(ii) Friends' House Library, London

Three collections of Lloyd MSS
Papers relating to Thomas Wilkinson and Jos. Matthews
Birkbeck Misc. papers
Dictionary of Quaker Biography

2. Primary and Related Sources

The Annual Monitor; or, New Letter Case and Memorandum Book,
  nos. 1–30 (York, 1813–41).
BARRUEL, Abbé AUGUSTIN, *Memoirs, Illustrating the Antichristian
  Conspiracy: A Translation [by the Hon. Robert Clifford] from the French
  [of pt. 1 of 'Mémoires pour servir à l'histoire du Jacobinisme']* (Dublin:
  William Watson, 1798).
BRISSOT, JACQUES PIERRE, *New Travels in the United States of America
  Performed in 1788*, trans. [Joel Barlow] (London: J. S. Jordan,
  1792).
BURKE, EDMUND, *Reflections on the Revolution in France and on the
  Proceedings in Certain Societies in London Relative to that Event* (1790),
  ed., with an introduction, Conor Cruise O'Brien (Harmonds-
  worth: Penguin Books, 1969).
—— *The Works and Correspondence of the Right Honourable Edmund
  Burke*, ed. Charles William, Earl Fitzwilliam, and Sir Richard
  Bourke (8 vols.; London: Francis and John Rivington, 1852).
BUTLER, MARILYN (ed.), *Burke, Paine, Godwin and the Revolution*

Controversy (Cambridge: Cambridge University Press, 1984).

CLARKSON, THOMAS, *A Portraiture of Quakerism, as Taken from a View of the Moral Education, Discipline, Peculiar Customs, Religious Principles, Political and Civil Economy, and Character, of the Society of Friends* (3 vols.; London: Longman, 1806).

—— *The History of the Rise, Progress, and Accomplishment of the Abolition of the African Slave Trade by the British Parliament* (2 vols.; London: Longman, 1808).

—— *Memoirs of the Private and Public Life of William Penn* (2 vols.; London: Longman, 1813).

COBBETT, WILLIAM, *Cobbett's Political Register* (London: Cox and Baylis, 1802–18).

Denmark. Proclamation issued, 16 August, at Zealand by Admiral Gambier and Lord Cathcart (xii (1807), 377–9).

Proclamation of the Danish Government against England, 16 August (xii (1807) 379–80).

Summary of Politics. Danish War (xii (1807) 385–400, and *passim*).

Declaration published by the Court of Denmark against England (xii (1807) 409–11).

Summary of Politics. Dominion of the Seas (xii (1807) 418–22, 513–31).

Capitulation of Copenhagen and Surrender of the Danish Fleet. From the London Gazette Extraordinary, 16 September (xii (1807) 473–80).

Declaration of the King of Great Britain (xii (1807), 543–4, 575–6).

On the Danish War. From the Moniteur, 20 September (xii (1807) 634–7).

Letter from Lord Cathcart to the Commandant of Copenhagen, previous to the Siege of that city, 20 August (xii (1807) 735–6).

Summary of Politics. Parliamentary Proceedings. King's Speech (xiii (1808) 161–5, 274–7).

Letters to William Roscoe (xiii (1808) 225–41, 257–68, 322–33, 353–65).

COLE, G. D.H. (trans.) *The Social Contract* (London: Everyman's Library, repr. 1955).

COLERIDGE, SAMUEL TAYLOR, *Aids to Reflection*, ed. Derwent Coleridge (London: E. Moxon, 1854).

—— *Anima Poetae*, ed. E. H. Coleridge (London: Heinemann, 1895).

—— *The Complete Poetical Works of Samuel Taylor Coleridge*, ed. E. H. Coleridge (2 vols.; Oxford: Clarendon Press, 1912).

—— *Poems on Various Subjects* (London: J. Robinson and J. Cottle, 1796).

—— *The Notebooks of Samuel Taylor Coleridge*, ed. Kathleen Coburn (3 [of 6] vols.; London: Routledge and Kegan Paul, 1957–).

—— *The Complete Works of Samuel Taylor Coleridge*, ed. W. G. T. Shedd (7 vols.; New York: Harper Brothers, 1958).

—— *The Collected Works of Samuel Taylor Coleridge*, Bollingen Series lxxv (London and Princeton, NJ: Routledge and Kegan Paul and Princeton University Press):

  1. *Lectures 1795: On Politics and Religion*, ed. Lewis Patton and Peter Mann (1971).
  2. *The Watchman*, ed. Lewis Patton (1970).
  3. *Essays on His Times in the 'Morning Post and 'The Courier'*, ed. David V. Erdman (3 vols.; 1978).
  4. *The Friend*, ed. Barbara E. Rooke (2 vols.; 1969).
  6. *Lay Sermons* [being *The Statesman's Manual* and *A Lay Sermon*], ed. R. J. White (1972).
  7. *Biographia Literaria*, ed. James Engell and W. Jackson Bate (2 vols.; 1983).
  10. *On the Constitution of the Church and State*, ed. John Colmer (1976).
  12. *Marginalia*, ed. George Whalley (2 vols.; 1980–).
  13. *Logic*, ed. J. R. de J. Jackson (1981).

—— *Inquiring Spirit: A New Presentation of Coleridge from his Published and Unpublished Prose Writings*, ed. Kathleen Coburn (London: Routledge and Kegan Paul, 1951; rev. edn. Toronto: University of Toronto Press, 1979).

—— *Shakespearean Criticism*, ed. T. M. Raysor (2 vols.; London: Constable, 1930).

—— *Specimens of the Table Talk of the late Samuel Taylor Coleridge*, ed. H. N. Coleridge (2 vols.; London: John Murray, 1835).

—— *The Literary Remains of Samuel Taylor Coleridge*, ed. H. N. Coleridge (London: William Pickering, 1836–9).

DE QUINCEY, THOMAS, *The Collected Writings of Thomas De Quincey*, ed. David Masson (14 vols.; Edinburgh: Adam and Charles Black, 1889–90).

The Edinburgh Review, or Critical Journal (Edinburgh: Constable, 1803 [1802]–).

Belsham, William, 'History of Great Britain' (vi (July 1805), 421–8).

Clarkson, T., 'A Portraiture of Quakerism, as taken from a View of the Moral Education, Discipline, Peculiar Customs, Religious Principles, Political and Civil Economy, and Character, of the Society of Friends (x (April 1807), 85–102).

'Cobbett's *Political Register*' (x (July 1807), 386–421).

Alvarez Espriella, Don Manuel, 'Letters from England' (xi (January 1808), 370–90).

Clarkson, T., 'History of the Abolition of the Slave Trade' (xii (July 1808), 355–79).

Leckie, G. Francis, 'An Historical Survey of the Foreign Affairs of Great Britain, with a View to explain the Causes of the Disasters of the late and present Wars' (xiii (October 1808), 186–205).

Cevallos, Don Pedro, 'Exposition of the Practices and Machinations which led to the Usurpation of the Crown of Spain, and the Means adopted by the Emperor of the French to carry it into Execution'. Translated from the Original Spanish (xiii (October 1808), 215–34).

'An examination of the Causes which led to the late Expedition against Copenhagen'. By an Observer (xiii (January 1809), 488–99).

'Short Remarks on the State of Parties at the Close of the Year 1809' (xv (January, 1810), 504–21).

FREND, WILLIAM, *Patriotism; or, the Love of our Country: An Essay, Illustrated by Examples from Ancient and Modern History; Dedicated to the Volunteers of the United Kingdom* (London, 1804).

HARTE, WALTER, *The History of Gustavus Adolphus . . . To which is Prefixed an Essay on the Military State of Europe . . . The third edition, with . . . additions, etc.* (2 vols.; London: J. J. Stockdale, 1807).

HAZLITT, WILLIAM, *The Complete Works of William Hazlitt*, ed. P. P. Howe (21 vols.; London and Toronto: J. M. Dent, 1930–4).

HILL, W. SPEED, (ed.) *The Folger Library Edition of the Works of Richard Hooker* (vols 1– ; Cambridge, Mass.: Harvard University Press, 1977–).

HOOKER, RICHARD, *The Folger Library Edition of the Works of Richard Hooker*, General Editor W. Speed Hill, (vols. 1– ; Cambridge, Mass.: Harvard University Press, 1977–):
vol. i: *Of the Lawes of Ecclesiasticall Politie*, Preface, Books I–IV (1593), ed. Georges Edelen (1977).
vol. ii: *Of the Lawes of Ecclesiasticall Politie*, Book V (1597), ed. W. Speed Hill (1977).
vol. iii: *Of the Lawes of Ecclesiasticall Politie*, Books VI–VIII (1648 and 1662), ed. P. G. Stanwood (1981).
JOHNSON, SAMUEL, *The Yale Edition of the Works of Samuel Johnson*, General Editor A. T. Hazen (vols. i– , New Haven: Yale University Press, 1958–).
KANT, IMMANUEL, *Groundwork of the Metaphysic of Morals* (1785), trans. H. J. Paton as *The Moral Law* (London: Hutchinson University Library, 1976).
—— *Critique of Practical Reason* (1788), trans. L. W. Beck (New York: Liberal Arts Press, 1956).
—— *Religion within the Limits of Reason Alone* (1793), trans. T. M. Greene and H. H. Hudson (New York: Harper and Bros., 1960).
—— *The Doctrine of Virtue: Part II of the Metaphysic of Morals* (1797), trans. introduction and notes Mary J. Gregor (Philadelphia: University of Pennsylvania Press, 1964).
—— *Kant's Political Writings*, ed. with an introduction and notes Hans Reiss, and trans. H. B. Nisbet (London: Cambridge University Press, 1970):
Idea for a Universal History with a Cosmopolitan Purpose (1784).
An Answer to the Question: 'What is Enlightenment?' (1784).
On the Common Saying: 'This may be True in Theory, but it does not apply in Practice' (1793).
Perpetual Peace: A Philosophical Sketch (1795).
The Metaphysics of Morals (1797).
The Contest of Faculties (1798).
MILL, JOHN STUART, *Collected Works of John Stuart Mill*, General Editor J. M. Robson (Toronto: University of Toronto Press, 1965–).
MILTON, JOHN, *The Poems of John Milton*, ed. John Carey and Alistair Fowler (London: Longmans, 1968).
The Monthly Review, or Literary Journal, enlarged (London: R. Griffiths, 1790–1825).

Ewald, J. L. 'Letters to Emma, concerning the Kantian Philosophy', translated from the German (Utrecht, 1794) (xiv (1794) 541–5).

Kant, Immanuel, 'To Perpetual Peace, a philosophical Project' (Koenigsberg, 1795), (xx (1796), 486–90).

Nitsch, F. A., 'A General and Introductory View of Professor Kant's Principles concerning Man, The World, and The Deity . . .' (Downes, 1796) (xxii (1797) 15–18).

Kant, Immanuel, 'Project for a perpetual Peace'. A Philosophical Essay. Translated from the German (Vernor and Hood, 1796) (xxii (1797) 114–5).

Willich, A. F. M., 'Elements of the Critical Philosophy: containing a concise Account of its Origin and Tendency; a View of all the Works published by its Founder, Professor Immanuel Kant; and a glossary of its Terms and Phrases' (Longman, 1798) (xxviii (1799) 62–9).

O'BRIEN, C. C. (ed.), *Reflections on the Revolution in France and on the Proceedings in Certain Societies in London Relative to that Event* (Harmondsworth: Penguin Books, 1969).

PAINE, THOMAS, *Rights of Man* (1791–2); repr., with an introduction Eric Foner and notes Henry Collins (Harmondsworth: Penguin Books, 1984).

The Parliamentary Debates from the year 1803 to the Present Time: Debates in the House of Commons (Hansard) (London, 1812).

PENN, WILLIAM, *Quakerism a New Nickname for Old Christianity, being an answer to a book, entitled, Quakerism No Christianity* ([London?], 1672).

—— *A Brief Account of the Rise and Progress of the People called Quakers* (London, 1694).

—— *Fruits of a Father's Love: being the Advice of William Penn to his Children, Relating to their Civil and Religious conduct, etc.* (London, F. Sowle 1726).

PHILLIPS, MARY, *Memoir of the Life of Richard Phillips, by his Daughter* (London, 1841).

Quarterly Review (London: John Murray, 1809–).

Meadley, G. H., '*Sermons on several Subjects by the late Rev. William Paley*' and *Memoirs of William Paley, D.D.*' (ii (August 1809) 75–88).

'Spanish Affairs' (ii (August 1809) 203–34).

Rose, George, '*Observations on the Historical Work of the late Right*

Honourable Charles James Fox' (London, 1809) (ii (November 1809) 243–55).

REISS, HANS (ed.), *Kant's Political Writings* (London: Cambridge University Press, 1970).

ROSCOE, HENRY, *The Life of William Roscoe* (2 vols.; London, 1833).

ROSCOE, WILLIAM, *Considerations on the Causes, Objects and Consequences of the Present War, and on the Expediency, or the Danger of Peace with France* (London: T. Cadell and W. Davies, 1808).

—— *Occasional Tracts relative to the War between Great Britain and France, written and published at different periods, from the year 1793* (London, 1810).

ROUSSEAU, JEAN JACQUES, *Du Contrat social* (1762), trans. G. D. H. Cole as *The Social Contract* (London: Everyman's Library, repr. 1955).

—— *Du Contrat social*, ed. C. E. Vaughan (Manchester: Manchester University Press, 1947).

—— *Émile* (1762), trans. Barbara Foxley, introduction P. D. Jimack (London: Everyman's Library, 1977).

SOUTHEY, ROBERT, *Letters from England. By Don Manuel Alvarez Espriella. Translated from the Spanish* (1807). Repr. and ed. J. Simmons (Gloucester: Alan Sutton, 1984).

WOOLMAN, JOHN, *A Journal of the Life, Gospel labours and Christian experiences of . . . John Woolman . . . To which are added his works, etc.* (Dublin, 1776).

WORDSWORTH, WILLIAM, *The Poetical Works of William Wordsworth* (5 vols.; Oxford: Clarendon Press, 1940–9).

—— *The Prelude, 1799, 1805, 1850*, ed. J. Wordsworth, M. H. Abrams, and S. Gill (New York: Norton Critical Series, 1979).

—— *The Borderers*, ed. Robert Osborn (Ithaca, NY: Cornell University Press, 1982).

—— *Poems, in Two Volumes*, ed. Jared Curtis (Ithaca, NY: Cornell University Press, 1983).

—— *The Prose of William Wordsworth*, ed. W. J. B. Owen and J. W. Smyser (3 vols.; Oxford: Clarendon Press, 1974).

Published Letters

The Correspondence of Edmund Burke, ed. T. W. Copeland (10 vols.; Cambridge: Cambridge University Press, 1958–70).

Collected Letters of Samuel Taylor Coleridge, ed. E. L. Griggs (6 vols.; London: Oxford University Press, 1956–71).

Letters, Conversations and Recollections of Samuel Taylor Coleridge, [ed. Thomas Allsop] (2 vols.; London: Edward Moxon, 1836).

Minnow among Tritons: Mrs S. T. Coleridge's Letters to Thomas Poole, 1799–1834 (London: Nonesuch Press, 1934).

Memoir and Letters of Sara Coleridge, ed. by her daughter [Edith Coleridge] (2 vols.; London: H.S. King, 1873).

De Quincey to Wordsworth: A Biography of a Relationship, ed. John E. Jordan (Berkeley and Los Angeles: University of California Press, 1962).

The Letters of Sara Hutchinson from 1800 to 1835, ed. Kathleen Coburn (London: Routledge and Kegan Paul, 1954).

The Letters of Charles and Mary Anne Lamb, ed. Edwin W. Marrs, Jun. (3 vols.; Ithaca, NY: Cornell University Press, 1975–8.)

Charles Lamb and the Lloyds, ed. E. V. Lucas (London: Smith, Elder, 1898).

Diary, Reminiscences and Correspondence of Henry Crabb Robinson, ed. Thomas Sadler (2 vols.; London and New York: Macmillan, 1872).

The Correspondence of Henry Crabb Robinson with the Wordsworth Circle (1808–1866), ed. Edith J. Morley (2 vols.; Oxford: Clarendon Press, 1927).

The Life and Correspondence of Robert Southey, ed. C. C. Southey (6 vols.; London: Longman, 1849–50).

Selections from the Letters of Robert Southey &c. &c. &c., ed. J. W. Warter (4 vols.; London: Longman, 1856).

New Letters of Robert Southey, ed. Kenneth Curry (2 vols.; New York and London: Columbia University Press, 1965).

Letters of William and Dorothy Wordsworth, ed. E. de Selincourt:
  The Early Years, 1787–1805, rev. Chester L. Shaver (Oxford: Clarendon Press, 1967);
  The Middle Years, 1806–11, rev. Mary Moorman and Alan G. Hill (Oxford: Clarendon Press, 1970);
  The Later Years, 1821–28, rev. Alan G. Hill (Oxford: Clarendon Press, 1978);
  1829–34, rev. Alan G. Hill (Oxford: Clarendon Press, 1979);
  1835–9, rev. Alan G. Hill (Oxford: Clarendon Press, 1982);
  The Letters of William and Dorothy Wordsworth: The Later Years (1821–

1850) ed. E. de Selincourt (Oxford: Clarendon Press, 1939).

The Letters of Mary Wordsworth 1800–1855, ed. Mary E. Burton (Oxford: Clarendon Press, 1958).

The Love Letters of William and Mary Wordsworth, ed. Beth Darlington (London: Chatto and Windus, 1982).

Letters from the Late Poets, Samuel Taylor Coleridge, William Wordsworth, Robert Southey, to Daniel Stuart, 1800–1838, ed. [Mary Stuart and E. H. Coleridge] (London: West, Newman, 1889).

Memorials of Coleorton, ed. William Knight (2 vols.; Edinburgh; D. Douglas, 1887).

Secondary Works

ABRAMS, M. H. 'Coleridge and the Romantic Vision of the World', *Coleridge's Variety: Bicentenary Studies*, ed. John Beer (London: Macmillan, 1974), 101–33.

ALLEN, WILLIAM (ed.), *The Philanthropist, or Repository for Hints and Suggestions Calculated to Promote the Happiness and Comfort of Men* (London, 1811–19).

ALTICK, R. D., *The English Common Reader, a Social History of the Mass Reading Public 1800–1900* (Chicago: University of Chicago Press, 1957).

ASHTON, ROSEMARY, *The German Idea: Four English writers and the Reception of German Thought 1800–1860* (Cambridge: Cambridge University Press, 1980).

ASPINALL, A., 'The Social Status of Journalists at the Beginning of the Nineteenth Century', *Review of English Studies*, 21 (1945), 216–32.

—— *Politics and the Press c.1780–1850* (London: Home and Van Thal, 1949).

BARBER, W. H., 'Voltaire and Quakerism: Enlightenment and the Inner Light', *Studies on Voltaire and the Eighteenth Century*, 24 (1963), 81–109.

BARTH, J. ROBERT (SJ), *Coleridge and Christian Doctrine* (Cambridge, Mass.: Harvard University Press, 1969).

BEELEY, HAROLD, 'The Political Thought of Coleridge', *Coleridge: Studies by Several Hands on the Hundredth Anniversary of his Death*, ed. Edmund Blunden and E. L. Griggs (London: Constable, 1934), 151–75.

BEER, JOHN, *Coleridge the Visionary* (London: Chatto and Windus, 1970).

—— (ed.), *Coleridge's Variety: Bicentenary Studies* (London: Macmillan, 1974).

—— *Coleridge's Poetic Intelligence* (London: Macmillan, 1977).

BERLIN, ISAIAH, *Against the Current, Essays in the History of Ideas* (Oxford: Oxford University Press, 1981).

BLUNDEN, EDMUND, *Leigh Hunt's 'Examiner' Examined* (London: Cobden-Sanderson, 1928).

—— and E. L. GRIGGS (eds.), *Coleridge: Studies by Several Hands on the Hundredth Anniversary of his Death* (London: Constable, 1934).

BOULGER, JAMES D., *Coleridge as Religious Thinker* (New Haven: Yale University Press, 1961).

BOULTON, JAMES, *The Language of Politics in the Age of Wilkes and Burke* (London: Routledge and Kegan Paul, 1963). .

BOURNE, H. R. FOX, *English Newspapers: Chapters in the History of Journalism* (2 vols.; London: Chatto and Windus, 1887).

BOYCE, ANNE OGDEN, *Records of a Quaker family: The Richardsons of Cleveland* (London, Samuel Harris, 1889).

BRAITHWAITE, WILLIAM C., *The Second Period of Quakerism*, 2nd edn. (Cambridge: Cambridge University Press, 1961).

BRETT, R. L. (ed.), *Writers and their Background: S. T. Coleridge* (London: G. Bell, 1971).

BRINTON, CRANE, *The Political Ideas of the English Romanticists* (London: Oxford University Press, 1926).

BRINTON, HOWARD, *Friends for 300 Years: Beliefs and Practice of the Society of Friends since George Fox started the Quaker Movement* (London: George Allen and Unwin, 1953).

BUCHDAHL, GERD, 'The Relation between "Understanding" and "Reason" in the Architectonic of Kant's Philosophy', *Proceedings of the Aristotelian Society*, 67 (1966–7) 209–26.

BUTLER, MARILYN, *Maria Edgeworth: A Literary Biography* (Oxford: Clarendon Press, 1972).

—— *Peacock Displayed: A Satirist in his Context* (London: Routledge and Kegan Paul, 1979).

—— *Romantics, Rebels and Reactionaries, English Literature and its Background 1760–1830* (Oxford: Oxford University Press, 1981).

—— 'Godwin, Burke and *Caleb Williams*', *Essays in Criticism*, 32 (1982), 237–57.

CALLEO, DAVID P., 'Coleridge on Napoleon', *Yale French Studies*, 26 (1961).

—— *Coleridge and the Idea of the Modern State* (New Haven: Yale University Press, 1966).

CAMPBELL, JAMES DYKE, 'Coleridge on Quaker Principles', *The Athenaeum*, 3438 (16 Sept. 1893) 385–6.

CARLYON, CLEMENT, *Early Years and Late Reflections* (4 vols.; London: Whittaker, 1843–58).

CARNALL, GEOFFREY, *Robert Southey and his Age, The Development of a Conservative Mind* (Oxford: Clarendon Press, 1960).

CASSIRER, ERNST, *Rousseau, Kant, Goethe: Two Essays*, trans. James Gutmann, Paul Oskar Kristeller, John Herman Randall, Jun. (Princeton: Princeton University Press, 1945).

—— *The Question of Jean-Jacques Rousseau*, trans. and ed., introduction and additional notes Peter Gay (Bloomington: Indiana University Press, 1963).

CHAMBERS, E. K., *Samuel Taylor Coleridge: A Biographical Study* (Oxford: Clarendon Press, 1938).

CHANDLER, JAMES K., *Wordsworth's Second Nature: A Study of the Poetry and Politics* (Chicago: University of Chicago Press, 1984).

CHRISTENSEN, JEROME, *Coleridge's Blessed Machine of Language* (Ithaca NY and London: Cornell University Press, 1981).

—— 'Once an Apostate always an Apostate', *Studies in Romanticism*, 21 (Fall 1982), 461–4.

COBBAN, ALFRED, *Edmund Burke and the Revolt against the Eighteenth Century: A Study of the Political and Social Thinking of Burke, Wordsworth, Coleridge and Southey* (London: George Allen and Unwin, 1929).

—— *Rousseau and the Modern State* (London: George Allen and Unwin, 1934).

—— (ed.), *The Debate on the French Revolution 1789–1800* (London: Nicholas Kaye, 1950).

—— *The Social Interpretation of the French Revolution* (Cambridge: Cambridge University Press, 1964).

COBURN, KATHLEEN, 'Poet into Public Servant', *Transactions of the Royal Society of Canada*, ser. 3, Vol. 54 (1960), 1–11.

—— 'Coleridge and Restraint', *University of Toronto Quarterly*, 38 (1968–9), 233–47.

COBURN, KATHLEEN, *The Self Conscious Imagination* (London: Oxford University Press, 1974).

—— *Experience into Thought: Perspectives in the Coleridge Notebooks* (Toronto: University of Toronto Press, 1979).

COLE, G. D. H., *The Life of William Cobbett*, 3rd edn. rev. (London: Home and Van Thal, 1947).

COLEMAN, DEIRDRE, 'A Horrid Tale in *The Friend*', *The Wordsworth Circle*, 12 (Autumn 1981), 262–9.

—— 'Coleridge and the Quakers', *The Wordsworth Circle*, 17 (Summer 1986), 134–42.

—— 'Jeffrey and Coleridge: Four Unpublished Letters', *The Wordsworth Circle*, 18 (Winter, 1987), 39–45.

COLMER, JOHN, 'An Unpublished Sermon by S. T. Coleridge', *Notes and Queries*, 203 (1958), 150–2.

—— *Coleridge, Critic of Society* (Oxford: Clarendon Press, 1959).

—— 'Coleridge and Politics', *Writers and their Background: S. T. Coleridge*, ed. R. L. Brett (London: G. Bell, 1971), 244–70.

—— 'Coleridge and the Life of Hope', *Studies in Romanticism*, 11 (1972), 332–41.

COOKE, MICHAEL G., *The Romantic Will* (New Haven and London: Yale University Press, 1976).

COOKSON, J. E., *The Friends of Peace: Anti-War Liberalism in England, 1793–1815* (Cambridge: Cambridge University Press, 1982).

CORRIGAN, TIMOTHY, *Coleridge, Language, and Criticism* (Athens, Ga: University of Georgia Press, 1982).

COTTLE, JOSEPH, *Early Recollections; Chiefly Relating to the Late Samuel Taylor Coleridge* (2 vols.; London: Longman, 1837).

—— *Reminiscences of Samuel Taylor Coleridge and Robert Southey* (1847), (repr. London: Lime Tree Bower Press, 1970).

CRANFIELD, G. A. *The Development of the Provincial Newspaper 1700–1760* (Oxford: Clarendon Press, 1962).

CRAWFORD, WALTER B. (ed.), *Reading Coleridge: Approaches and Applications* (Ithaca NY and London: Cornell University Press, 1979).

—— and E. S. LAUTERBACH (eds.), *Samuel Taylor Coleridge: An Annotated Bibliography of Criticism and Scholarship*, ii: 1900–1939 (Boston, Mass.: G. K. Hall, 1983).

CURRY, KENNETH, *Southey* (London and Boston: Routledge and Kegan Paul, 1975).

DEMARIA, ROBERT, 'The Ideal Reader: A Critical Fiction', *PMLA* 93 (1978), 463–74.

DEEN, LEONARD, W., 'Coleridge and the Radicalism of Religious Dissent', *Journal of English and Germanic Philology*, 61 (1962), 496–510.

EBBATSON, J. R., 'Coleridge's Mariner and the Rights of Man', *Studies in Romanticism*, 11 (Summer 1972), 171–206.

ELLENBURG, STEPHEN, *Rousseau's Political Philosophy: An Interpretation from Within* (Ithaca NY and London: Cornell University Press, 1976).

—— 'Rousseau and Kant: Principles of Political Right', *Rousseau After Two Hundred Years*, ed. R. A. Leigh (Cambridge: Cambridge University Press, 1982).

EMPSON, WILLIAM and DAVID PIRIE (eds.), *Coleridge's Verse: A Selection* (London: Faber and Faber, 1972).

ENDY, MELVIN B., *William Penn and Early Quakerism* (Princeton: Princeton University Press, 1973).

ERDMAN, DAVID V., 'Coleridge on Coleridge: The Context (and Text) of His Review of "Mr. Coleridge's Second Lay Sermon" ', *Studies in Romanticism*, 1 (Fall 1961), 47–64.

—— 'Coleridge as Editorial Writer', *Power and Consciousness*, ed. Conor Cruise O'Brien and W. D. Vanech (London: University of London Press, 1969), 183–201.

—— and Paul M. Zall, 'Coleridge and Jeffrey in Controversy', *Studies in Romanticism*, 14 (Winter 1975), 75–83.

EVEREST, KELVIN, *Coleridge's Secret Ministry: The Context of the Conversation Poems, 1795–1798* (Brighton: Harvester Press, 1979).

FEILING, KEITH GRAHAME, *The Second Tory Party 1714–1832* (London: Macmillan, 1938).

FISCHER, MICHAEL, 'Morality and History in Coleridge's Political Theory', *Studies in Romanticism*, 21 (Fall 1982), 457–60.

FOSTER, JOHN, 'Review of *The Friend*, *Eclectic Review*, 7 (1811), 912–31, repr. in *Coleridge: The Critical Heritage*, ed. J. R. de J. Jackson (London: Routledge and Kegan Paul, 1970), 92–110.

FOX, R. HINGSTON, *Dr. John Fothergill and his Friends: Chapters in Eighteenth Century Life* (London: Macmillan, 1919).

FREEMAN, MICHAEL, *Edmund Burke and the Critique of Political Radicalism* (Oxford: Basil Blackwell, 1980).

FRUMAN, NORMAN, *Coleridge, the Damaged Archangel* (London: George Allen and Unwin, 1972).

GALLIE, W. B., 'Kant's View of Reason in Politics', *Philosophy*, 54 (1979), 19–33.

GARDINER, PATRICK, 'Rousseau On Liberty', *Conceptions of Liberty in Political Philosophy*, ed. Zbigniew Pelczynski and John Gray (London: The Athlone Press, 1984), 83–99.

GRAHAM, WALTER, 'The Politics of the Greater Romantic Poets', *PMLA* 36 (1921), 60–78.

GRANT, JAMES, *The Newspaper Press: Its Origin, Progress and Present Position* (2 vols.; London: Tinsley Bros., 1871).

GRAVIL, R. *et al.* (eds.), *Coleridge's Imagination* (Cambridge: Cambridge University Press, 1985).

GREGOR, MARY J., *Laws of Freedom, A Study of Kant's Method of Applying the Categorical Imperative in the 'Metaphysik der Sitten'* (Oxford: Basil Blackwell, 1963).

GRIGGS, E. L., 'Samuel Taylor Coleridge at Malta', *Modern Philology*, 27 (1929), 201–17.

—— 'Robert Southey and the *Edinburgh Review*', *Modern Philology*, 30 (1932), 100–3.

—— *Thomas Clarkson: The Friend of Slaves* (London: Allen and Unwin, 1936).

—— '*The Friend*: 1809 and 1818 Editions', *Modern Philology*, 35 (1938), 369–73.

—— *Wordsworth and Coleridge: Studies in Honor of George McLean Harper*, ed. E. L. Griggs (Princeton: Princeton University Press, 1939).

—— *Coleridge Fille: A Biography of Sara Coleridge* (London: Oxford University Press, 1940).

—— 'Samuel Taylor Coleridge and Opium', *Huntington Library Quarterly*, 17 (1954), 357–78.

—— 'Coleridge as Revealed in his Letters', *Coleridge's Variety: Bicentenary Studies*, ed. John Beer (London: Macmillan, 1974), 31–53.

GRIMSLEY, RONALD, *The Philosophy of Rousseau* (London: Oxford University Press, 1973).

GROSS, JOHN, *The Rise and Fall of the Man of Letters: Aspects of English Literary Life since 1800* (London: Weidenfeld and Nicolson, 1969).

GUNNING, HENRY, *Reminiscences of the University, Town and Country of Cambridge from the year 1780* (2 vols.; London: George Ball, 1855).

HALEVY, ÉLIE, *A History of the English People in the Nineteenth Century*, i: *England in 1815* (London: Ernest Benn, 1924).

HAMILTON, PAUL, *Coleridge's Poetics* (Oxford: Basil Blackwell, 1983).

HAMPSHIRE, STUART (ed.), *Public and Private Morality* (Cambridge: Cambridge University Press, 1978).

HAMPSON, NORMAN, *Will and Circumstance: Montesquieu, Rousseau and the French Revolution* (London: Duckworth, 1983).

—— *A Bibliography of Samuel Taylor Coleridge* (Philadelphia: Printed for private circulation, 1903).

HANSON, LAWRENCE, *The Life of S. T. Coleridge: The Early Years* (London: George Allen and Unwin, 1938).

HARDING, ANTHONY JOHN, *Coleridge and the Idea of Love: Aspects of Relationship in Coleridge's Thought and Writing* (London: Cambridge University Press, 1974).

HAVEN, RICHARD, J. and M. ADAMS (eds.), *Samuel Taylor Coleridge: An Annotated Bibliography of Criticism and Scholarship*, i: 1793–1899 (Boston, Mass.: G. K. Hall, 1976).

HAYTER, ALETHEA, *Opium and the Romantic Imagination* (London: Faber and Faber, 1968).

—— *A Voyage in Vain: Coleridge's Journey to Malta in 1804* (London: Faber and Faber, 1973).

HILL, ALAN G., 'Wordsworth and the Two Faces of Machiavelli', *Review of English Studies*, 31 (1980), 285–304.

HILL, W. SPEED (ed.), *Studies in Richard Hooker* (Cleveland and London: Cape Western Reserve University Press, 1972).

HOBSBAWM, ERIC J., *The Age of Revolution: Europe 1789–1848* (London: Weidenfeld and Nicolson, 1962).

HOLMES, RICHARD, *Coleridge* (Oxford: Oxford University Press, 1982).

HOUSE, HUMPHRY, *Coleridge: The Clark Lectures 1951–52* (London: Rupert Hart-Davis, 1953).

HUNT, LEIGH, *The Autobiography of Leigh Hunt, with Reminiscences of Friends and Contemporaries*, ed. Roger Ingpen (London: Constable, 1903).

JACKSON, J. R. de J. (ed.), *Coleridge: The Critical Heritage* (London: Routledge and Kegan Paul, 1970).

JONES, RUFUS M., *The Later Periods of Quakerism* (2 vols.; London: Macmillan, 1921).

KEMP, JOHN, *The Philosophy of Kant* (London: Oxford University Press, 1968).

KEOHANE, NANNERL O., *Philosophy and the State in France: The Renaissance to the Enlightenment* (Princeton: Princeton University Press, 1980).

KIRK, RUSSELL, *The Conservative Mind, from Burke to Santayana* (London: Faber and Faber, 1954).

KORNER, S., 'Kant's Conception of Freedom', *Proceedings of the British Academy*, 53 (1967), 193–217.

LACEY, PAUL ALVIN, 'Samuel Taylor Coleridge's Political and Religious Development, 1795–1810', Ph.D. thesis (Harvard University, 1966).

LLOYD, HUMPHREY, *The Quaker Lloyds in the Industrial Revolution* (London: Hutchinson, 1975).

LOADES, ANN, 'No Consoling Vision: Coleridge's Discovery of Kant's "Authentic" Theodicy', *An Infinite Complexity: Essays in Romanticism*, ed. J. R. Watson (Edinburgh: Edinburgh University Press, 1983), 95–124.

LOCKRIDGE, LAURENCE S., *Coleridge the Moralist* (Ithaca NY and London: Cornell University Press, 1977).

—— 'Explaining Coleridge's Explanation: Toward a Practical Methodology for Coleridge Studies', *Reading Coleridge: Approaches and Application*, ed. Walter B. Crawford (Ithaca NY and London: Cornell University Press, 1979), 23–55.

LOGAN, Sister EUGENIA, 'Coleridge's Scheme of Pantisocracy and American Travel Accounts', *PMLA* 45 (1930), 1069–84.

LOVEJOY, ARTHUR O., 'Coleridge and Kant's Two Worlds', *Journal of English Literary History*, 7 (1940), 341–62.

—— *Essays in the History of Ideas* (Baltimore and London: Johns Hopkins Press, 1948).

MACCOBY, S., *English Radicalism 1786–1832 From Paine to Cobbett* (London: George Allen and Unwin, 1955).

MCFARLAND, THOMAS, *Coleridge and the Pantheist Tradition* (Oxford: Clarendon Press, 1969).

—— 'Coleridge's Anxiety', *Coleridge's Variety: Bicentenary Studies*, ed. John Beer (London: Macmillan, 1974), 134–65.

MACKESY, PIERS, *The War in the Mediterranean 1803–1810* (London: Longmans, Green, 1957).

MACKINNON, D. M., 'Coleridge and Kant', *Coleridge's Variety: Bicentenary Studies*, ed. John Beer (London: Macmillan, 1974), 183–203.

MACPHERSON, C. B., *Burke* (London: Oxford University Press, 1980).

MADDEN, LIONEL and DIANA DIXON, *The Nineteenth Century Periodical Press in Britain: A Bibliography of Modern Studies, 1901–1971* (New York: Garland, 1976).

MANNHEIM, KARL, *Essays on Sociology and Social Psychology*, ed. Paul Kecskemeti (London: Routledge and Kegan Paul, 1953).

—— *Essays on the Sociology of Culture*, ed. Ernest Mannheim and Paul Kecskemeti (London: Routledge and Kegan Paul, 1956).

MARR, G. S., *The Periodical Essayists of the Eighteenth Century* (London: J. Clarke, 1923).

MASTERS, ROGER D., *The Political Philosophy of Rousseau* (Princeton: Princeton University Press, 1968).

MEAD, GEORGE HERBERT, *Movements of Thought in the Nineteenth Century*, ed. Merritt H. Moore (Chicago: Chicago University Press, 1936).

METEYARD, ELIZA, *A Group of Englishmen (1795 to 1815), Being Records of the Younger Wedgwoods and their Friends* (London: Longman, 1871).

MILL, JOHN STUART, *Collected Works of John Stuart Mill*, ed. J. M. Robson, i– (Toronto: University of Toronto Press, 1965–).

MODIANO, RAIMONDA, 'Metaphysical Debate in Coleridge's Political Theory', *Studies in Romanticism*, 21 (Fall 1982), 465–74.

MOORMAN, MARY, *William Wordsworth: A Biography: The Early Years* (Oxford: Clarendon Press, 1957), *The Later Years* (Oxford: Clarendon Press, 1967).

MORLEY, EDITH J., *The Life and Times of Henry Crabb Robinson* (London: J. M. Dent, 1935).

MUNZ, PETER, *The Place of Hooker in the History of Thought* (London: Routledge and Kegan Paul, 1952).

O'BRIEN, C. C., and W. D. VANECH, *Power and Consciousness* (London: University of London Press, 1969).

ONG, WALTER J., 'The Writer's Audience is Always a Fiction', *PMLA* 90 (1975), 9–21.

ONG, WALTER J., 'Beyond Objectivity: The Reader–Writer Trans-action as an Altered State of Consciousness', *CEA Critic* 40 (1977), 6–13.

ORSINI, GIAN N. G., *Coleridge and German Idealism: A Study in the History of Philosophy with Unpublished Materials from Coleridge's Manuscripts* (Carbondale: Southern Illinois University Press, 1969).

OSBORN, ANNIE MARION, *Rousseau and Burke: A Study of the Idea of Liberty in Eighteenth Century Political Thought* (London: Oxford University Press, 1940).

PASCAL, BLAISE, *Pensées*, Trans. with an Introduction A. J. Krails-heimer (Harmondsworth: Penguin Classics, 1966).

PATON, H. J., *The Categorical Imperative: A Study in Kant's Moral Philosophy* (London: Hutchinson's University Library, 1946).

PELCZYNSKI, ZBIGNIEW and JOHN GRAY (eds.), *Conceptions of Liberty in Political Philosophy* (London: The Athlone Press, 1984).

PETERSON, SUSAN RAE, 'The Compatibility of Richard Price's Politics and his Ethics', *Journal of the History of Ideas*, 45/4 (1984), 537–47.

POTTER, STEPHEN (ed.), *Minnow among Tritons: Mrs S. T. Coleridge's Letters to Thomas Poole, 1799–1834* (London: Nonesuch Press, 1934).

PRICKETT, STEPHEN, *Coleridge and Wordsworth: The Poetry of Growth* (London: Cambridge University Press, 1970).

—— *Romanticism and Religion: The Tradition of Coleridge and Wordsworth in the Victorian Church* (Cambridge: Cambridge University Press, 1976).

RABINOWITZ, PETER J., 'Truth in Fiction: A Reexamination of Audiences', *Critical Inquiry*, 4 (1977), 121–41.

RAYSOR, T. M., 'Coleridge and "Asra" ', *Studies in Philology*, 26 (1929), 305–24.

READ, DONALD, *Press and People, 1790–1850: Opinion in Three English Cities* (London: Edward Arnold, 1961).

REARDON, BERNARD M. G., *From Coleridge to Gore: A Century of Religious Thought in Britain* (London: Longman, 1971).

REAY, BARRY, *The Quakers and the English Revolution* (London: Temple Smith, 1985).

REED, ARDEN, 'Coleridge, the Sot, and the Prostitute: A Reading of *The Friend*, Essay XIV', *Studies in Romanticism*, 19 (Spring 1980), 109–28.

REED, JOHN R., 'Inherited Characteristics: Romantic to Victorian Will', *Studies in Romanticism*, 17 (Summer 1978), 335–66.

REED, MARK L., *Wordsworth: the Chronology of the Middle Years 1800–1815* (Cambridge, Mass.: Harvard University Press, 1975).

RICHARDS, I. A., *Coleridge on Imagination* (London: Routledge and Kegan Paul, 1934).

—— 'Coleridge's Other Poems' and 'The Vulnerable Poet and *The Friend*', *Poetries: Their Media and Ends*, ed. Trevor Eaton (The Hague and Paris: Mouton, 1974).

ROBERTS, MICHAEL, *The Whig Party, 1807–1812* (London: Macmillan, 1939).

SAMBROOK, JAMES, *William Cobbett* (London: Routledge and Kegan Paul, 1973).

SANDFORD, Mrs HENRY, *Thomas Poole and His Friends* (2 vols.; London and New York: Macmillan, 1888).

SCHNEIDER, ELIZABETH, *Coleridge, Opium & 'Kubla Khan'* (Chicago: Chicago University Press, 1953).

SEWELL, ELIZABETH, 'Coleridge on Revolution', *Studies in Romanticism*, 11 (Fall 1972), 342–59.

SIMMONS, JACK, *Southey* (London: Collins, 1945).

STANLIS, PETER JAMES, *Edmund Burke and the Natural Law* (Ann Arbor: The University of Michigan Press, 1958).

STANSFIELD, DOROTHY, A., *Thomas Beddoes M. D. 1760–1808: Chemist, Physician, Democrat* (Holland: D. Reidel, 1984).

STEPHEN, LESLIE, and SIDNEY LEE (eds.), *Dictionary of National Biography*, 63 vols., (London: Smith, Elder 1885–90).

STORCH, R. F., 'The Politics of the Imagination', *Studies in Romanticism*, 21 (Fall 1982), 448–56.

STORR, V. F., *The Development of English Theology in the Nineteenth Century, 1800–1860* (London: Longman, 1913).

STUART, DANIEL, 'Anecdotes of the Poet Coleridge', *The Gentleman's Magazine* NS ix (May 1838), 485–92.

SULTANA, DONALD, *Samuel Taylor Coleridge in Malta and Italy* (Oxford: Basil Blackwell, 1969).

SUTER, J.-F., 'Burke, Hegel and the French Revolution', *Hegel's Political Philosophy*, ed. Z. A. Pelczynski (Cambridge: Cambridge University Press, 1971).

TAYLOR, CHARLES, 'Kant's Theory of Freedom', *Conceptions of*

Liberty in Political Philosophy, ed. Zbigniew Pelczynski and John Gray (London: The Athlone Press, 1984), 100–22.

TERRETT, DULANY, 'Coleridge's Politics 1789–1810', Ph.D. thesis (Evanston, Ill.: Northwestern University, 1941).

THOMAS, D. O., 'Richard Price and Edmund Burke', *Philosophy*, 34 (October 1959), 308–22.

—— *The Honest Mind: The Thought and Work of Richard Price* (Oxford: Clarendon Press, 1977).

THOMPSON, E. P., *The Making of the English Working Class* (London: Victor Gollancz, 1965).

—— 'Disenchantment or Default? A Lay Sermon', *Power and Consciousness*, ed. Conor Cruise O'Brien and W. D. Vanech (London: University of London Press, 1969), 149–81.

THOMPSON, W. D. J. CARGILL, 'The Philosopher of the "Politic Society": Richard Hooker as a Political Thinker', *Studies in Richard Hooker*, ed. W. Speed Hill (Cleveland and London: Cape Western Reserve University Press, 1972), 3–76.

THORNE, R. G. (ed.), *The House of Commons 1790–1820* (5 vols.; London: Secker and Warburg, 1986).

TOMPKINS, JANE P. (ed.), *Reader-Response Criticism: from Formalism to Post-Structuralism* (Baltimore and London: Johns Hopkins University Press, 1980).

VALENTINE, ALAN, *The British Establishment, 1760–1784: An Eighteenth-Century Biographical Dictionary* (Norman: University of Oklahoma Press, 1970).

VANN, RICHARD T., *The Social Development of English Quakerism: 1655–1755* (Cambridge, Mass.: Harvard University Press, 1969).

VEITCH, GEORGE STEAD, *The Genesis of Parliamentary Reform* (London: Constable, 1913).

VEREKER, CHARLES, *Eighteenth-Century Optimism: A Study of the Interrelations of Moral and Social Theory in English and French Thought between 1689 and 1789* (Liverpool: Liverpool University Press, 1967).

WATTS, MICHAEL R., *From the Reformation to the French Revolution*, vol. i of *The Dissenters* (Oxford: Clarendon Press, 1978).

WELLEK, RENÉ, *Immanuel Kant in England 1793–1838* (Princeton: Princeton University Press, 1931).

WHALLEY, GEORGE, *Coleridge and Sara Hutchinson and the Asra Poems* (London: Routledge and Kegan Paul, 1955).

—— 'Coleridge Unlabyrinthed', *University of Toronto Quarterly*, 32 (1962–63), 325–45.

—— ' "Late Autumn's Amaranth": Coleridge's Late Poems', *Transactions of the Royal Society of Canada*, ser. 4, vol. 2 (1964), 159–79.

—— 'On Reading Coleridge', *Writers and their Background: S. T. Coleridge*, ed. R. L. Brett (London: G. Bell, 1971), 1–44.

—— 'Coleridge's Poetic Sensibility', *Coleridge's Variety, Bicentenary Studies*, ed. John Beer (London: Macmillan, 1974), 1–30.

WHITE, R. J. (ed.), *The Political Thought of Samuel Taylor Coleridge* (London: Jonathan Cape, 1938).

—— (ed.), *The Conservative Tradition* (London: Adam and Charles Black, 1950).

WICKWAR, WILLIAM H., *The Struggle for the Freedom of the Press, 1819–1832* (London: George Allen and Unwin, 1928).

WILLEY, BASIL, *The Eighteenth Century Background: Studies on the idea of nature in the thought of the period* (London: Chatto and Windus, 1940).

—— *Nineteenth Century Studies, Coleridge to Matthew Arnold* (London: Chatto and Windus, 1949).

—— *The English Moralists* (London: Chatto and Windus, 1964).

—— 'Coleridge and Religion', *Writers and their Background: S. T. Coleridge*, ed. R. L. Brett (London: G. Bell, 1971), 221–43.

—— *Samuel Taylor Coleridge* (London: Chatto and Windus, 1972).

WILLIAMS, HOWARD, *Kant's Political Philosophy* (Oxford: Basil Blackwell, 1983).

WILLIAMS, RAYMOND, *Culture and Society, 1780–1950* (London: Chatto and Windus, 1967).

—— *Cobbett* (London: Oxford University Press, 1983).

WILLIAMS, T. C., *The Concept of the Categorical Imperative* (Oxford: Clarendon Press, 1968).

WOLFF, ROBERT PAUL, *The Autonomy of Reason: A Commentary on Kant's Groundwork of the Metaphysic of Morals* (New York: Harper and Row, 1973).

WOLIN, SHELDON S., 'Richard Hooker and English Conservatism', *Western Political Quarterly*, 6 (1953), 28–47.

WOODRING, CARL R., *Politics in the Poetry of Coleridge* (Madison: The University of Wisconsin Press, 1961).

WOODRING, CARL R., *Politics in English Romantic Poetry* (Cambridge, Mass.: Harvard University Press, 1970).

WOOLF, VIRGINIA, 'The Man at the Gate' and 'Sara Coleridge', *Collected Essays*, iii (London: The Hogarth Press, 1967), 217–21, 222–6.

Index